Pathway to Hell

Camp Parole Annapulis Md. Jan, 11th 18,68

Dear Friend

Laroy Lyman

Well I guess you will be surprised when you receive this I suppose you think I am verry fortunate in escapeing death I am thankfull to be thus spared to write to you our Regt lost a great many killed & wounded I know not how many. 16 wer taken prisoners when wer not wounded probubly as many wounded, Co K Prisoners Sergt Robt Bell, Corporal L B Ryder & self arived in Libby Prison without a scratch Sergt Charls Able of Co I was wounded in Shoulder & Wm Campbell of McSmethport wounded in Elbow severely I left them in Libby Prison the 9th but they will arive here tomorrow we 500 come down in the Steam Ship N.Y. some of the Men wer Sea sick last night I am well & hope this will find you all good my love to all I will write you soon again & full act of my experience while a prisoner about 300 prisoners wer captured when I was taken write soon your &

Yours Friend

Address
Angelo Crapsey
Co I 1st Rifle Regt Buck Tails
P.R.V.C.
Camp Parole Annapolis, Md.

1. Holograph of letter from Angelo M. Crapsey to Laroy Lyman, January 11, 1863.

Pathway to Hell

A Tragedy of the American Civil War

Dennis W. Brandt

Lehigh
University
Press

Bethlehem: Lehigh University Press

Associated University Presses
2010 Eastpark Boulevard
Cranbury, NJ 08512

Library of Congress Cataloging-in-Publication Data

Brandt, Dennis W., 1946–
    Pathway to hell : a tragedy of the American Civil War / Dennis W. Brandt.
       p. cm.
    Includes bibliographical references and index.
    ISBN 978-0-9801496-2-3 (alk. paper)
    1. United States—History—Civil War, 1861–1865—Psychological aspects—Case studies. 2. United States—History—Civil War, 1861–1865—Health aspects—Case studies. 3. Crapsey, Angelo M., 1842–1864. 4. Crapsey, Angelo M., 1842–1864— Mental health. 5. Crapsey, Angelo M., 1842–1864—Death and burial. 6. Soldiers— Pennsylvania—Biography. 7. Veterans—Pennsylvania—Biography. 8. Veterans— Mental health—United States—Case studies. 9. Post-traumatic stress disorder— United States—Case studies. 10. Suicide—United States—Case studies. I. Title.
    E468.9.B695   2008
    973.7'448092—dc22
    [B]

2008014194

To my grandchildren, Hunter and Sierra.
May you read my book when you grow up
and remember your Pap-Pap who loves you.

Contents

Foreword

THE RECORDS OF THE CIVIL WAR ARE COPIOUS WITH STORIES OF VETER-
ans who were typical of their kind. Rare indeed—perhaps even non-
existent until now—are detailed accounts of soldiers who survived
the war's horrors physically but not mentally.

Adding to the impact of Angelo M. Crapsey's tragic story is that it
is remarkably well documented, much of it told in the unfortunate
soldier's own words. Though far from being a scholar, Angelo was an
emotive writer and a prolific one. The young soldier's letters, actually, have a value beyond their character revelations. They provide a
down-to-earth picture of what the Civil War was like, both in its battlefield violence and in its everyday events. This feature, in itself, gives
the book an excellent reason for existing.

Dennis W. Brandt, however, has gone far beyond offering us simply another collection of Civil War letters. He has made *Pathway to
Hell* a unique psychological study.

Richard Wheeler

Preface

As RICHARD WHEELER OBSERVES IN THE FOREWORD, HISTORIES OF THE American Civil War abound with tales of physical horrors. Countless works describe bodies ripped open by artillery rounds, lines of men falling in hailstorms of musketry, and beleaguered surgeons casually tossing the latest amputated limb onto a mounting pile of human remains. Few, however, have dealt with the psychological horrors of the Civil War. This book throws a pebble into that unfilled hole by relating the tragic but fascinating story of one soldier's personal hell.

Our star-crossed hero was Angelo Crapsey, a bright and brave young man who left for war afire with patriotism but who returned home a completely different person. His story is not an analysis of complex battles. There will be no deep examination of generals' orders or revelation of politicians' maneuverings. This is a tale of one soldier, one town, and one regiment that paid dearly for its fame with blood. The young man's story is also one of his father, of a friend and mentor, and of the "enthusiastic" religion that drove their lives.

The story is as relevant today as it was during the Civil War. Weapons may have leaped forward in accuracy and killing power, and America's enemies today are more vicious than Lee and Grant could have imagined, but fear and the morality of killing have not changed for soldiers from Western civilizations. Young Americans are as of this writing returning from tours of duty in the Middle East with emotions they did not take with them. The knowledge gleaned from recent wars enables us to better understand what happened to the men who endured the same terrors nearly a century and a half ago.

This book recounts some dramatic behavior, but it is likely that most war veterans rarely, if ever, display overt symptoms. My father-in-law provides a prime example of how war can keep its hooks in a man in ways imperceptible even to his family. S. Sgt. George Francis Finet, mortar section leader, Company L, Twenty-third Infantry, landed at Omaha Beach June 7, 1944, and less than a year later had

11

earned five battle citations and a bronze star. He should have earned a Purple Heart but refused to report a leg wound because, he said with exaggeration, "Men were getting Purple Hearts for cutting themselves shaving." I was married to his daughter for many years before she learned the source of that scar on her father's calf.

Once home, George did not turn to alcohol or drugs to escape memories and never became violent. He worked twelve hours a day running the family service station and raised eight children with a hand that was firm but never cruel. Always he was intensely patriotic and proud of his military service. After years of marching in Memorial Day parades, an expanded waistline closeted his army uniform into a permanent state of parade-rest. Eventually, the ravages of advanced age and ill health ordered his body to stand down, too. He rarely spoke of the war except with old army buddies, and they spent most of their time together laughing over the good times. Only near the end of his life did George begin to relate some of his more gruesome war experiences. Even then, he just hinted at how bad they really had been.

But in the years following his return home, sleep routinely transported him back to war. His subconscious did not need to create nightmares with contrived monsters, just flashbacks to a real-life image more macabre than the best horror writer could conceive. Each night his mind returned to the Normandy hedgerows to gaze upon a wounded soldier with the lower half of his face shot away. The soldier's eyes followed George's every step, pleading eyes that had to act in place of the mouth he no longer had. His wife Betty eventually questioned George's nocturnal restlessness and frightful moaning. After he revealed the dream's horrific content, the nightmare fled and restful sleep again became possible. Then, shortly before his death nearly sixty years later, he watched the motion picture *Saving Private Ryan*. The nightmares returned in full force.

Some readers may be inclined to close the cover at this point and move on to lighter fare. I urge them to continue reading. This book is neither a dalliance into horror writing nor a technical treatise geared to enlighten mental health professionals. I am a historian and approach the subject strictly from that point of view. I am also a storyteller determined to reach an audience that ranges beyond Civil War scholars and serious "buffs." I assure all readers that there is much to learn here. The story, believe it or not, even has its lighter moments.

The penultimate chapter attempts a psychohistorical analysis, which may send shivers through some historians. Many in the discipline deem retro-psychology pointless and misleading because it is necessarily based on anecdotal evidence. While understanding my colleagues' trepidations, I contend that it would be foolish not to study the psychological impact of previous wars. Reason dictates there were as many psycho-tensions at Antietam and Gettysburg as at Omaha Beach, the Chosin Reservoir, or Ke Sahn. Soldiers certainly feared death as much at Cross Keys and South Mountain as their descendents do now in Baghdad and the mountains of Afghanistan.

When it adds to the flow, Angelo takes over the narrative, drawing on the forty-seven letters and one diary I was able to uncover. Sadly, Angelo references other letters and diaries that have never surfaced or perhaps ended their existence in family stoves. I debated paraphrasing his accounts in lieu of quoting them. But he was there. I was not. Few Civil War soldiers expressed themselves as succinctly or described battles in such vivid detail. That made the decision for me. I had to give it to the reader straight from the participant's mouth. At times, his contemporaries will describe our hero in ways he never understood about himself.

Editing of Civil War documents is a controversial issue among historians. Purists insist that period missives must remain in their "native" state. While that chalks up one on the side of historical accuracy, it often makes reading Civil War era correspondence a challenge for those inexperienced with the writing styles of the day. Angelo's descriptions of his surroundings and experiences in battle rank among the best ever written, but he was typically incautious of proper writing techniques. Given that paper was not always available and expensive if it was, most soldiers' letters used every inch of space. That meant avoiding indentation and paragraphs—assuming they even knew about such literary techniques—and writing run-on sentences. Many a Civil War letter cries out for the clarification that a few periods would add. They also capitalized words seemingly at random, which further confuses modern readers.

Spelling was another of Angelo's shortcomings, although he was better in this regard than many. "Been" he spelled "bine," the pronoun "we" invariably became the adjective "wee," he always spelled "very" with two "Rs" (common then), and "always" always contained two "Ls." Words such as "pay" and "day" he spelled with an "ey," and he never added the final "E" to "were." All this provides a dreary and challenging effort for inexperienced readers. I wanted to avoid that.

I decided that editing original documents was vital as long as I never compromised the writers' intentions or drained the significance that scholarship understandably demands. With but a few exceptions, I left all original words intact but edited to:

- Correct spelling errors
- Insert words in brackets that are clearly missing when their absence could confuse the reader (usual practice even by purist standards)
- Insert punctuation where necessary to improve reading clarity
- Change case according to modern rules
- Install paragraphs where it aids readability
- Remove any text that does not directly advance the story or understanding of the characters

With the exception of the standard use of brackets for word insertion and ellipses (. . .) for omissions, there is no indication when editing has occurred.

May you enjoy getting to know Angelo Crapsey. You will be saddened by his tale.

Acknowledgments

MY DEEPLY FELT THANKS TO ALL THOSE WHO ASSISTED IN THE CREATION of this work: Krista Lyman of Roulette, Pennsylvania, who permitted me to use and reproduce her great-great-grandfather Laroy's letters, diaries, and photographs as well as thirty-one of Angelo Crapsey's extant letters; Kenneth Graves, who gave me both his time and the eight Angelo letters his father found in the attic of the New York house he bought in 1942; Robert Currin, curator of the Potter County Historical Society, who assisted in Potter County history and always provided encouragement. Bob runs a nicely organized historical society on a budget too small to buy shoestrings, but he is no loafer; Keri S. Ullman, MSW, clinical social worker, who offered professional consultation on Angelo's mental condition; Dr. Beth Arburn Davis, SID, good friend, erstwhile journalist, and now a psychologist who offered her technical expertise; Dr. Thomas Lowry, esteemed psychiatrist and historical researcher and author, who honored me with his article; Richard Wheeler, successful historian, author, and wounded veteran of Iwo Jima. I thank him for his foreword and more so for his brave service; David Crowely, Cuba town historian, who lent invaluable support putting me on the trail of Kenneth Graves; Michael Musick, celebrated researcher at the National Archives in Washington, who led me, as he has countless others, in the right direction for tidbits of knowledge I would not have known existed. It is a great loss for the world of history that he has since retired from his position at the National Archives; Pastor John Pearson of Boyertown, Pennsylvania, Lutheran historian, who set me on the track to find data on a young John Crapsey and the religious movement in New York State during the nineteenth century; Ellsworth Swift of Cuba, New York, for a variety of data on the town of Cuba; Lyle Slingerland, who supplied background of his ancestor, Seneca B. Pomeroy; Judy Offen for her e-mail heads-up on her ancestor's wedding performed by John Crapsey; the Robbins family: Bertha and Lloyd Robbins, Robert Robbins, and

15

Miriam Robbins Midkiff, who live all across the country but who combined to give me solid data on their ancestor Charles Robbins; Ronn Palm, proprietor of Civil War Images, 229 Baltimore Street, Gettysburg, Pennsylvania, for graciously allowing me to pick from his huge personal photographic collection; Michael Kirchmeier for introducing me to John Crapsey descendant Raymond Handy and Mr. Handy for allowing me to use his photo of John Crapsey; Paula S. and James W. Warren of St. Paul, Minnesota, nationally known genealogists whose research saved me a large amount of time and money. They are responsible both for uncovering the early history of John Crapsey and putting me in contact with living Crapsey descendents; Dan's Creative Portraiture of Coudersport, Pennsylvania, for supplying live photography and creating a database of old photographs; Susan Austin, whom I have met only by mail (e-mail and snail) and who provided data about the Banfield family and, therefore, Angelo's activities in Cuba, New York; and friend and former colleague David Aurand, a gun enthusiast who supplied his historical knowledge of firearms. He is frequently the butt of my jokes, but unfortunately he returns the favor with excess enthusiasm and more than a smattering of sophistication.

Abbreviations

Abbreviation	Source
CMSR	Compiled Military Service Records, RG-94, National Archives and Records Administration
GNMP	Gettysburg National Military Park
HCWRTC	Harrisburg Civil War Roundtable Collection, U.S. Army Military History Institute, Carlisle, Pa.
KGC	Kenneth Graves Collection
KLC	Krista Lyman Collection
NARA	National Archives and Records Administration
O.R.	*War of the Rebellion: A Compilation of the Official Records of the Union and Confederate Armies* (always references series 1 unless otherwise stated)
O.R. Atlas	*Atlas to Accompany the Official Records of the Union and Confederate Armies*
Pension	Department of the Interior, Pension Records of [soldier] [company] [regiment], National Archives and Records Administration

Pathway to Hell

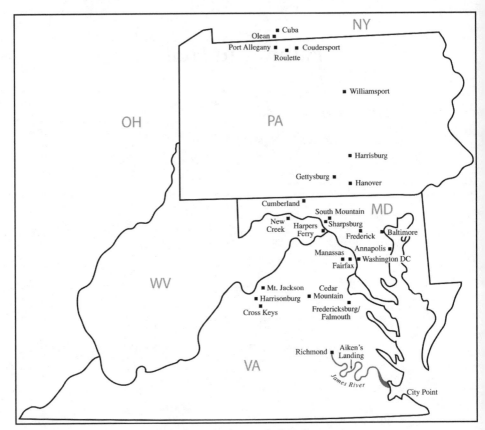

2. Angelo M. Crapsey's travels before, during, and after the war.

Prologue: And So It Concludes

The actual tragedies of life bear no relation to one's preconceived ideas.

—Jean Cocteau

THE DOG DAYS PRESSED HARD ON THE MOUNTAINS OF POTTER COUNTY that fourth day of August in the year our Lord 1864. Residents accustomed to northern Pennsylvania winters yearned to stretch out beneath the canopy of the surrounding white pine forest and escape a scorching sun. Necessity, though, was a harsh overseer that sent the good folks of Roulette into their fields every year at this time to gather the hay that guaranteed their livestock's winter survival. Across the narrow valley that embraced the village, an army of husky arms flailed away, separating belly-high grasses from their earthly bonds.[1]

One lucky crew slew its last blade, shouldered their tools, and headed for the boss's house, anticipating the cool water that would soon be cascading down parched throats and draining heat from sun-baked faces. As they walked, they discussed how to spend the rest of the day. Working was not one of the choices. Their decision came unanimously and lifted their spirits. By the time they reached the house, they were laughing and swapping the insults that men share with an implied wink and deliberately use to set women's tongues to clucking.

Thankful Lyman had the tongue doing the clucking. Precious little amused the woman of the Lyman household. Being Laroy's wife was a unique experience guaranteed to grind any woman's sense of humor to a nubbin. As usual, Laroy was off seeing to another of his countless business affairs instead of being here to direct his workers. Duty came first, and she rushed her eldest daughter to the cellar to

---

1. Diaries of Laroy Lyman, 1854–86, Krista Lyman Collection (hereafter KLC).

draw water for refreshment. Only then did she scold the men for making merry on a workday. Other tasks required attention, she reminded them. Laroy would soon enough let them know about it if he were here.[2] The men laughed. They had decided to spend the rest of the day hunting. If Laroy were here, he would already have rifle in hand and his hounds running free. Thankful knew they were right and surrendered to the work that made her days so tedious. Meanwhile, the house reverberated with the joy of men anticipating an afternoon of self-indulgence.[3]

Laughter died the instant Angelo Crapsey entered the room and announced he was going on the hunt. The men emphatically told him that could not happen. Angelo demanded to know why. Hadn't he always been part of their hunting parties? Hadn't he always been the one Laroy most trusted to set out his dogs? They couldn't leave behind the best shot in town.[4]

Angelo's claim of marksmanship was no idle boast, which was why no one wanted to see him in possession of a firearm.[5] Truth was, they would be glad if he just went away and never came back. Yes, once he had been a friend, and, yes, it was terrible how war had transformed him. But who could tell what he might do next? The Lymans' patched-together window offered plain evidence of his latest escapade. The men filed out of the house and soon were loping across the fields behind a pack of baying hounds, leaving Thankful to cope with her houseguest as best she could.[6]

Angelo saved her the trouble and left the room. Thankful assumed he was going off to sulk again—not that he required a rebuff as harsh as today's for wallowing in self-pity.[7] Dutifully she turned back to the chores. Suddenly, there he stood again, staring

---

2. Diaries of Laroy Lyman; Diaries of Thankful Lyman. Thankful's attitude is a paraphrase of viewpoints and events documented in both diaries that describe their unrelenting prowork and antimerriment attitudes, especially in Thankful's case. The Lymans long ago cemented the cellar well closed.

3. Department of the Interior, Pension of Angelo M. Crapsey, deposition of John Crapsey, Nov. 7, 1892; deposition of Isaac Sears, Apr. 2, 1891; affidavit of John V. Weimer, Apr. 2, 1891; deposition of Stephen P. Reynolds, May 5, 1893.

4. Pension of Angelo M. Crapsey, depositions of Isaac Sears, Apr. 23, 1885, and William S. Brine, May 5, 1893. Brine described Angelo as "a crack shot." Both Sears and Brine were present at this event. Laroy's hunting hounds were among his most prized possessions.

5. Pension of Angelo M. Crapsey, deposition of Seneca B. Pomeroy, May 13, 1893.

6. Pension of Angelo M. Crapsey, depositions of Isaac Sears, Apr. 2, 1891, John V. Weimer, Mar. 11, 1891, and Thankful Lyman, undated; Diaries of Laroy Lyman.

7. Pension of Angelo M. Crapsey, deposition of Seneca B. Pomeroy, May 13, 1893. This behavior will be detailed later in the story.

at her with that "wild, haggard look."[8] She needed an extra second to see the rifle in his hands. Laroy had hidden the gunroom key but obviously not well enough. Her mind scrambled for clever words to make him relinquish the rifle. All the while he remained frozen, staring, unresponsive. When at last he moved, he raced past her and out the door. The men in the hunting party would have to deal with him after all.[9]

The baying of the dogs led Angelo to the hunting party. The men saw him approaching and hastily debated what to do. Overpowering him would not be difficult, but that might get someone shot first or goad Angelo into a later act of retribution. Isaac Sears, Laroy's longtime employee and Angelo's friend in better days, came up with a plan. A group hunt's plum position was waiting in a blind while the others flushed game your way. Ike offered the job to Angelo and pointed out a shady "watching place" along the Allegheny River. Angelo raced off to await the parade of trophies that soon would be racing past him.[10]

Any animal racing past Angelo that day would do so on its own volition. The men went off in a different direction, leaving Angelo to ponder an ever-lengthening solitude.[11]

The sun was slipping behind the mountains by the time the hunters returned to the Lyman house and discovered that Angelo had yet to return.[12] Ike Sears, conscience perhaps pricking him for instigating the group's deceit, went out to search. He called Angelo's name, but the only responses came from farm animals and birds peeping twilight songs. Ike had not spent much time in school, but he was wise enough to sense that something was wrong. He went to the spot by the river where he had told Angelo to wait.[13] What he found would remain forever fresh in his memory.

> [I] found him lying on the ground on his back. His gun was between his legs, breech end at his feet, the muzzle on his breast. A stick forked at the

---

8. Pension of Angelo M. Crapsey, depositions of Viola Peck Robbins, date unknown, and Alice Crapsey McBain, Nov. 7, 1892.

9. Pension of Angelo M. Crapsey, depositions of Thankful Lyman, undated, and Sybil Lyman Burdick, Nov. 20, 1892.

10. Pension of Angelo M. Crapsey, affidavit of John V. Weimer, Apr. 2, 1891, and deposition of Isaac Sears, Apr. 23, 1885.

11. Pension of Angelo M. Crapsey, affidavit of John V. Weimer, Apr. 2, 1891, and deposition of Seneca B. Pomeroy, May 13, 1893.

12. Pension of Angelo M. Crapsey, deposition of Seneca B. Pomeroy, May 13, 1893; Diaries of Laroy Lyman.

13. Pension of Angelo M. Crapsey, deposition of Isaac Sears, Apr. 23, 1885; Pension of Isaac Sears, Co. I, 76th Pa. Sears was drafted six weeks after the incident.

lower end was in his hand. It was plain enough that he had pulled the gun off with the forked stick as the fork was against the trigger when I found him.[14]

Ike retrieved the others. In the waning light they could barely make out the drying pool of blood that fanned out from the remains of Angelo's head. Those with the stomach to look saw a once handsome face despoiled by a mask of gore and gunpowder. One man tried to take the rifle from Angelo's hands and was stunned that he had to pry his fingers from the barrel. The men carried the body to the Lyman house and laid it in the parlor. Thankful and her children were horrified at the sight of Angelo's mangled face, a wound Laroy Lyman described coldly: "He had shot the ball into the left eye & stove his brains all in." Horrible, yes, but not surprising.[15]

The county convened a coroner's inquest and assigned several men from the hunting party to serve, Ike Sears among them. The case was an open-and-shut suicide, so they closed the books without spending much time on it. The men from the hunting party would have been only human had they tried to convince themselves that Angelo was better off and how none of it had been their fault. Guilt may have gnawed at them, but they had to have been relieved that it was over at last.[16]

Gloom hung over the Lyman home on August 6. Laroy ordered Angelo's rough-hewn casket positioned before the huge fireplace before which the two of them had shared many private moments. Grieving friends and family jammed the house to remember a young man who had once been so full of energy and promise. They would miss him—as he once was, not the monster war had created and tossed back into their midst. In the years ahead, Thankful Lyman and her daughters often would express thanks that they had all escaped injury by his hand.[17]

One person, though, never arrived at the funeral, a man whose absence undoubtedly had the women shaking their heads and men

14. Pension of Angelo M. Crapsey, deposition of Isaac Sears, Apr. 2, 1891.
15. Pension of Angelo M. Crapsey, depositions of Stephen P. Reynolds, Feb. 3, 1885, Sybil Lyman Burdick, Nov. 25, 1892, and Seneca B. Pomeroy, May 13, 1893; Diaries of Laroy Lyman. Pomeroy recalled Angelo leaning against a tree, but everyone else remembered him lying flat on the ground. Angelo's stiff fingers were obviously a sign of rigor mortis.
16. Pension of Angelo M. Crapsey, depositions of Stephen P. Reynolds, Feb. 3, 1885, and Seneca B. Pomeroy, May 13, 1893.
17. Diaries of Laroy Lyman; Pension of Angelo M. Crapsey, depositions of Thankful Lyman, Nov. 30, 1883, and Sybil Lyman Burdick, Nov. 25, 1892.

using words they dared utter only in stag company. Angelo's father was not there. But, then, nothing "Crazy Crapsey" did surprised anyone. Some of those present opined as to how Angelo's death surely must have been God's vengeance on that false prophet father of his. They just made certain not to say it within Laroy Lyman's earshot.[18]

Later that day, a humble cortege lumbered the short distance to the Lyman graveyard where they buried Angelo a few dozen yards from the Allegheny River. When it was over, Laroy made a diary entry in his usual straightforward manner: "We took Angelo to the grave & buried him to await until Jesus comes. We had plenty of help to bury him."[19]

༺❀༻

Only Providence knows what went through Angelo Crapsey's tortured mind the instant before he pushed the trigger. We do know much of what happened to him before that awful day and why his life ended so tragically. This is his story, a true one, as best it can be understood separated from events by such a vast distance of time. The Civil War forced 620,000 men to make the ultimate sacrifice, or so the official statistics state. Angelo and many like him do not count among the dead, yet they are as much casualties as those who died in battle or succumbed to disease in a squalid army hospital.

Angelo entered the service of his country as a young man eager to serve the cause of the Union. Instead, war set him on a journey down the pathway to hell and offered no return passage.

---

18. Diaries of Laroy Lyman. I will expand on the story of John Crapsey in subsequent chapters.
19. Ibid.

1
Influences

Who shall set a limit to the influence of a human being?
—Ralph Waldo Emerson

ROULETTE'S RED SCHOOLHOUSE ASSUMED ROLES BEYOND THE EDUCA-
tion of the town's children. Sometimes it served as a church. Other
times, it provided a convenient site for community meetings. There
was to be a meeting there the night of April 9, 1861.

Two of the attendees arrived together. Laroy Lyman was one of
them, a man so huge he had to duck and turn sideways to pass
through many a doorway. Had the word "macho" been in the popular lexicon then, it certainly would have applied to him.[1] The other
was Rev. John Crapsey, a small, almost delicate man, with soft hands
that long ago had disassociated themselves from physical labor. A
stranger might assume these polar opposites would not bother to
exchange casual nods when passing on the street, much less embrace
a deep friendship. If they were companions, surely Laroy dominated
the relationship. Appearances were deceiving.

Almost ten years earlier, Rev. John Crapsey had walked into Roulette assuming it was just another town hungering for the Word as
only he could deliver it. The village had heard stories about this
preacher and opened its schoolhouse door to find out firsthand. In
one memorable night, John Crapsey grew into his own brand of
giant, and Laroy Lyman became his principle disciple. But for others
in Roulette, a few experiences with the Crapsey style of religion made
them hunger for something more than the reverend's religious counsel. They wanted his blood.[2]

---

1. Robert R. Lyman Sr., *History of Roulet, Pa. and the Life of Burrel Lyman,* 38–39; Diaries of
Laroy Lyman. Laroy once spent a week chasing down a bear and drew a detailed map of the
excursion. Angelo Crapsey was on that hunt.

2. Lyman, *History of Roulet;* U.S. Census, 1860. The town's original name was Roulet, but
"Roulette" has long been in use. It is pronounced either "Rau-let" or "Raw-let," accenting "let."

There were those present at one Crapsey service in 1852 who swore they experienced visions of a shuddering earth opening its graves. Others were certain they saw the dead either consumed by conflagration or elevated into paradise. Reverend Crapsey claimed he shouted Christ's last words in Aramaic and then leaped into the center of the room to exhort his flock to a fury even he had not imagined possible. Laroy had leaped to his feet and shouted, "I must repent!" To his last day on earth, the big man insisted that the Holy Spirit then and there punched him smack in the ribs. Through it all, "the beautifulest music" sprang from heaven and "lights . . . and streaks of fire" danced about him. Eventually everyone sprang to his feet, and many spoke in unfamiliar languages.[3]

At least that was how John Crapsey and Laroy Lyman recalled the experience. Others also must have seen it that way, too, because Roulette overnight developed a core group of mesmerized "Crapsey-ites."[4] Reverend Crapsey held more services on the school's second floor while school was in session. His excited congregations set the building to shaking so much that pupils could not write their lessons. Before long, rumor said the schoolhouse shook even when no one was there (without explaining how they knew that if no one was there). A few nervous sorts tried to explain the weird events using their meager knowledge of physical laws. Had they been world-class scientists it would have made no difference to Crapsey and his followers, who believed only the presence of God explained all events.

Much had passed in the decade between those events and Angelo Crapsey's arrival at the schoolhouse that April evening in 1861. Life was still full upon this virile lad whom many said approached each day with "a lively and cheerful" disposition. He was handsome, too, with dark hair and captivating blue eyes that motivated at least one young lady to obtain his photograph and pine over the possibilities.[5] While love played a role in inviting his father and Laroy for this talk, it was not love for the opposite sex but love of country.

Angelo announced he was going to enlist in the army. With the election of Abraham Lincoln, the Deep South states deemed the

---

3. A. P. Miller, *A Modern Pentecost: An Account of the Marvelous Ministry and Mediumship of the Rev. John Crapsey*, 1–2, 31–33; Laroy Lyman to Mr. A. Henshaw, Aug. 27, 1853, KLC; Lyman, *History of Roulet*, 38–43. See also Fodor Encyclopedia of Psychic Science Web site, http://www.spiritwritings.com/fodorr.html.

4. The "-ite" suffix was common then for followers of a particular faith led by an individual. The followers of William Miller, founder of the Seventh Day Adventist movement, were "Millerites." Those who followed Alexander Campbell were "Campbellites."

social divide so towering they felt compelled to rip themselves from the United States. For months, the tension in Charleston Harbor had been building toward an inevitable confrontation. Three days before the cannons roared at Fort Sumter, Angelo knew he had to take part in restoring the Union. A few days more and a hundred thousand other young Northerners would be giving similar notice to friends and relatives, but they did not have to make their announcements to John Crapsey and Laroy Lyman.[6]

Angelo's fervent pro-Union stance put him at odds with his two mentors. Their opposition came not from political sentiment but the strong pacifist philosophy their religious convictions demanded, a tenet they both preached with mesmerizing force. But Angelo's feisty nature never allowed him to back down from any challenge. He had become his own force and one of a select few who dared debate Laroy. If he could argue with Laroy, he could argue with anyone.

Angelo needed courage to speak his mind in Roulette, a village that had voted itself into becoming Potter County's political odd duck. In the 1856 presidential election, the village had voted solidly Democratic while the rest of the county gave first-ever Republican candidate, John C. Frémont, a landslide majority. In 1860, Abraham Lincoln crushed his opposition countywide but won by only four votes in Roulette. Four years later, the village again went contrary to the rest of the county when it overwhelmingly rejected Lincoln and embraced the immediate peace platform of the Democratic Party. To many in Roulette, the Union was not worth a war.[7]

Bitter feelings surely resulted from Angelo's political jousts because political debates often generated bitter feelings during those turbulent times. After nearly a year's experience in the army, Angelo offered a hint at those adversarial relationships when he wrote Laroy, "I suppose many has been the time the Secesh of Potter and McKean have hoped they would hear of the death of Angelo. Tell them I am as true to the Union as ever and will fight for its protection as long as I can breathe."[8] Upon his return home, those bouts would come back to haunt him at a time when he was busy enough haunting himself.

5. Willie Lyman to Laroy, July 6, 1864, KLC; U.S. Census, 1860, Michigan, Lenawee County, Cambridge Township. Willie Lyman was Laroy's cousin. Prior to Angelo's and Laroy's visit in 1864, he wrote that a young lady named "Wealthy" had seen Angelo's photo and was eager to have one in her album.

6. Diaries of Laroy Lyman.

7. *Potter County Journal*, Nov. 18, 1856, Nov. 16, 1860, and Nov. 9, 1864.

8. Angelo to Laroy, Mar. 1, 1862, KLC.

A month after enlisting, Angelo wrote Laroy a letter from camp in Harrisburg that reinforced some of what he said that April evening. "You may think it seems strange for me to leave my work when I was getting such wages. Strange it was but I love the old flag dearly."[9] Not even four months of grueling military life dampened his political ardor, as he expressed in another letter to Laroy from camp near Darnestown, Maryland.

Well, Laroy, I will say a little of the peace party of Potter and McKean [counties]. Their motto is very seductive. Every person wishes peace. What can they do to secure peace? Can they suppress the rebellion against the U.S. states, lay down their arms, come again and partake again of the glorious fruits of the Union? No, that is not what the peace party wants or can they persuade the South to lay down their arms and give up the forts and army and navy that the South has taken.[10] That can't be done. Peace with them means secession and disunion, and it is unaccountable how any man professing common honesty can join a party that they know means exactly opposite to what they profess and propose what they cannot accomplish if they wished it. But they mean disunion and if they accomplished it, then the Union will be dissolved never to be formed again and civil laws destroyed and the liberty of our people blasted forever.[11]

Angelo called Southern sympathizers "worse than the Rebels of the South" and closed another letter with his simple solution for dealing with them: "Tell the traitors they need shooting and then raise a company of home guards and shoot them if they don't behave."[12]

Unionists in the Potter-McKean/southern New York area had reason for concern. A week before the assault on Fort Sumter, a Potter County man, calling himself "Chairman of the Committee and Board of Managers" of an unnamed organization, wrote to Confederate president Jefferson Davis pleading for money to raise a Southern army in the region. He boasted that he had "lodges formed all through the States of Pennsylvania and New York" and had "10,000 men enlisted for the Confederate States." All he needed was $11,347 to make this army miraculously appear from nowhere. Now, if Presi-

---

9. Ibid. May 22, 1861.

10. Immediately after secession—and in some cases before—the seceded states seized Federal forts, arsenals, and naval yards, and any men stationed there.

11. Angelo to Laroy, Sept. 15, 1861, KLC.

12. Angelo to Laroy, Mar. 1, 1862, and postscript, date uncertain but probably from his letter of May 23, 1861, KLC.

dent Davis would be so kind as to mail the cash—in gold, of course, because "Southern money . . . will not pass here."[13]

However committed Angelo may have been to his Union ideals, it had to hurt that Laroy and his father lacked enthusiasm for his decision to fight. It was their country being pulled apart, yet they would not take arms to save it. But as Angelo's mentors had always acted independently, so now must he seek his own counsel. He was a man, if only in the overconfident yearning for independence that blooms within nineteen-year-olds. We cannot be certain those differences of opinion later affected his mental state, but it must be kept in mind as a factor that led to that disastrous day in August 1864.

To know Angelo Crapsey, you must first know more about his two principle male influences.

JOHN CRAPSEY

If any bells pealed in Hinsdale, New York, on January 1, 1842, they celebrated the New Year and not the humble nuptials of John Crapsey Jr. and widow Mercy Rhuama Frantz, née Barnum. Bachelor Crapsey needed a woman to take care of his worldly needs. Widow Frantz had inherited her late husband's farm and needed a man's strong arms to provide for her and her three daughters. John may not have been the romantic ideal—there is doubt about his arm strength—but he did possess two key marital qualities: he was willing, and he was there. Economic necessity may have motivated the Crapsey union more than passion, but nature has a way of overcoming emotional blandness. Sometime around the vernal equinox of 1842, the couple slipped into bed and conceived their only child.[14]

Angelo M. Crapsey squeezed his way into the world December 9, 1842. John's written recollections give no reason to believe that his

---

13. *War of the Rebellion: A Compilation of the Official Records of the Union and Confederate Armie* (hereafter *O.R.*), ser. 4, 1:210–11, Charles W. C. Macomac of Brindleville (Oswayo), Potter County to Jefferson Davis, Apr. 7, 1861. The name was probably a pseudonym. No such name exists in Potter County censuses 1850–70. This offer was not unique. See *O.R.*, ser. 4, 1:216, Thomas Yeatman to Jefferson Davis, April 10, 1861. Yeatman offered two companies of Connecticut men to the South.

14. Pension of Angelo M. Crapsey, affidavits of Richmond Barnum, July 6, 1885, and Ann Marian Taylor, Mar. 11, 1891; Miller, *Modern Pentecost*, 23; *St. Paul Pioneer Press*, Sept. 19, 1903, obituary of John Crapsey; U.S. Census, 1850, New York, Cattaraugus County. Mercy "Mary" Rhuama Barnum was born September 10, 1812. The dates of her marriage to, and death of, Elias Frantz are unknown. Her daughters were Catherine (ca. 1833), Anna Maria (ca. 1835), and Ann Orilla (ca. 1838).

son did not sprint through his first nine years of life with the energy of a colt. Three stepsisters surely doted on their baby half brother while John hurried his son's nose into the Bible to stress the glories of reading and the fear of God Almighty. The details from this period of Angelo's life are obscure, but we can guess that being a Crapsey was probably not boring. How could it be when the religious enthusiasm of the family head put him on a path to being deemed "crazy?"[15]

John Crapsey's dramatic view of religion found root in a life that had dealt him a harsh hand before he was old enough to realize it. They lowered his mother into a grave two weeks after his birth, and his father soon handed him to others to raise, a common form of nineteenth-century day care that sometimes turned into a permanent living arrangement. At the age of nine, John's life worsened when his father placed him into indentured servitude to toil under a master who never hesitated to use the back of his hand as a motivational tool.[16]

With the onset of adolescence's hormonal stirrings, John tied his pathetic belongings into a sack and escaped into the darkness and the freedom the New York countryside willingly offered. There was a price for sovereignty. Filling an empty belly was a constant struggle, and often a blanket of stars provided his only covering at night. Odd jobs sustained life until at last he found work with a butcher who guided his employees with a soft hand and tossed in regular meals and a warm place to sleep as a bonus. For the first time, John found comfort in a boss's voice, a voice that espoused the beauty of education. John heeded his mentor's advice well and eventually found himself inside a humble Albany schoolhouse teaching children the intricacies of mathematics and the hodgepodge that passes for English spelling rules.[17]

But school teaching was not to be John Crapsey's lifework. Religion was avalanching through New York State then, God served up by itinerant preachers who fired congregations so hot the area gained a reputation as the "Burned Over District."[18] Lay preacher William Miller had predicted the precise moment in 1843 when Christ would return

---

15. Pension of Angelo M. Crapsey, deposition of John Crapsey, Dec. 6, 1884.

16. Miller, *Modern Pentecost,* 20.

17. Ibid., 21; U.S. Census, 1820, New York, Duchess and Rensselaer counties. John Crapsey's malevolent boss was Henry Ames from Hyde Park, Duchess County. His benevolent manager was Aaron Drum, a butcher living in Rensselaer County.

18. Whitney R. Cross, *The Burned-Over District: The Social and Intellectual History of Enthusiastic Religion in Western New York, 1800–1850.*

to earth to save the holy and purge the wicked with fire. Many believed him and continued to believe even after the predicted night of Armageddon passed by uneventfully. John dived headlong into that theological wave and soon was studying religion at the seminary in Poultney, Vermont. Afterward, he joined the Albany Lutheran Synod. A shy preacher at first, John's restraint gradually melted until he could deliver a sermon that grabbed listeners and refused to let go.[19]

In 1840, he assumed the pulpit of a church in East Hinsdale, New York. There was no actual pulpit because there was no actual church, just a congregation of ten parishioners who met wherever they could find space. John "shook the bushes" in search of converts, holding revivals with enough praise-the-Lords and hallelujahs to glut the most barren soul. Many folks found his intensity difficult to accept, but his congregation still quadrupled within four years. When the Albany Synod decided to drop John ostensibly for failure to attend meetings, his flock pleaded to keep him as their pastor. Albany saw things differently, so John Crapsey skirted the issue in the manner that would become his nature. Citing an unexplained "affliction of his family," he ended affiliation with the Albany Synod and assisted in the creation of a reformed synod that eventually formalized his minister's credentials. His followers apparently did not mind that their pastor essentially had ordained himself.[20]

The year after Angelo's birth, John crusaded the length of the Erie Canal preaching why the nation must free the black man from bondage, an attitude no doubt amplified by his experience in indentured servitude. With him went a stack of antislavery propaganda leaflets that he pressed into every palm, willing or not. The town of Rochester, however, served up a disgruntled audience that became so riled by what they heard that they gave the reverend two choices: skedaddle with his leaflets or take them headfirst into the canal. John

19. Miller, *Modern Pentecost.* John Crapsey studied at Lay Conference Academy, now Green Mountain College, from November 1837 to July 1838. Sylvester Bliss, *Memoirs of William Miller: Generally Known as a Lecturer on the Prophecies, and the Second Coming of Christ.* William Miller, founder of Adventism, was raised just across the New York state line from Poultney and once lived and held public office in West Poultney.

20. *Journals of the Annual Meetings of the Franckean Evangelic Lutheran Synod; Proceedings of a Convention of Ministers and Delegates from Evangelical Lutheran Churches in the State of New York;* Miller, *Modern Pentecost,* 23; *St. Paul Pioneer Press,* Sept. 19, 1903. John Crapsey ended affiliation to the Albany Lutheran Synod in 1844 and was ordained February 8, 1849, by the Reformed Lutheran Synod. Stories are mixed as to whether John resigned or Albany dropped him. He says the former, but his statements in *A Modern Pentecost* are always questionable. The political and social tenets of the Lutheran faith then included abolition, temperance, and pacifism.

selected option one but carried it out in his inimitable fashion by running through town shouting the gospel of Negro freedom and flinging leaflets into every open door and window he passed.[21]

Life went as well as it could for a family headed by an absentee father controlled by emotion. Until 1852. That was a year of death when John Crapsey began to view life and faith even more uniquely than he had in the past. That was the year he perhaps slipped into emotional instability. There were good reasons for that to happen.

John and Mercy barely had time to celebrate their tenth anniversary when fever attacked one of their daughters. They rushed a doctor to her side, but those ministrations accomplished nothing. John turned to his Maker, spending days and nights laying hands on his stepdaughter and exhorting Him for a cure that never came.[22] John collapsed by his stepdaughter's grave and then spent two feverish weeks himself battling the disease. Fever lost this fight, and John "leaped" from bed shouting thanks to Jesus for his miracle cure. Mercy thought he was daft with the fever and told him to get back into bed before he had a relapse.[23]

Fatalistic visions sprang into John's mind. They were fever-induced, most likely, but he saw them as prophecies from a higher plain of existence. The visions revealed that other loved ones must suffer, and some would have to die. That was a forgone conclusion once fever took hold in a community, but John sought only mystical explanations. Proof of his newly discovered prescient abilities came when fever struck Mercy. Once more he lived by the bedside of a loved one. Once more he threw his soul into prayer and the laying on of hands. Once more, nights of anguished supplication failed. On March 3, Angelo and his two remaining stepsisters awoke motherless.[24]

Mercy was barely cold in the ground when the disease gripped Angelo. Additional verification of his visions, John assumed, more proof that God had granted him the precious gift of second sight. Again he prayed himself into exhaustion, this time over his son's pros-

---

21. Cross, *Burned-Over District;* Miller *Modern Pentecost; Journals of the Annual Meetings.* Typical of John Crapsey, he later claimed that Rochester's abolitionist movement sprang from this incident, ignoring the fact that an antislavery movement had already been established prior to his visit.

22. Miller, *Modern Pentecost,* 24. The stepdaughter was Anna Maria Frantz, who died January 8, 1852.

23. Ibid., 25. Mercy's comment is a paraphrase of what John Crapsey claimed his wife said.

24. Ibid. Pension of Angelo M. Crapsey, Statement of Jeremy M. and Joseph Raub, Apr. 11, 1889.

trate form. Like his father, Angelo was strong enough to defeat the disease. John later insisted his faith healing had been so powerful that Angelo sprang from bed ready to get on with life. Over the years, however, Angelo's miraculous cure varied in John's retelling from instantaneous to a more realistic two weeks.[25]

But at the time, Angelo's so-called miracle recovery convinced John that the Lord had blessed him not only with second sight, but with the power to heal, a conclusion that ignores the fact that two-thirds of his patients had died. These gifts, like the message of abolition, had to be given to the world—forced upon it, if necessary. He sent the children to live with neighbors, spent the next six months in preparation, and then hit the road armed with new pamphlets and a finely honed gift of gab.[26]

In the months that followed, John wandered from town to town "lecturing on religion" and offering his self-proclaimed healing powers to the infirm. As it would throughout most of his life, survival depended on the sales of tracts and handouts from benefactors who "gave him what they had a mind to." But if his mesmerizing sermons hypnotized some, others found his message disturbing, especially after some listeners began to shake uncontrollably during his services. Then, uncanny events began to occur that some swore were miracles created by the reverend's heaven-blessed hand. A canoe that had broken its line and was racing down the Allegheny River returned to shore when Reverend Crapsey ordered it. During his services, Bibles moved and doors opened and closed without human intervention. Was it God? Was it the devil? Was it the wind? Or was Crapsey a conjurer? News of his alleged powers spread, and each retelling stretched his reputation further from the truth.[27]

That was when John Crapsey encountered Roulette. The eerie events that occurred there in 1852 terrified many in the village, especially after several young people overnight tossed away lifelong beliefs to embrace the Crapsey brand of religion. Some who had initially accepted his ideals had second thoughts. A friend of Laroy Lyman's who had shaken by his side now blamed their uncontrolled behavior on a combination of "sicoligy and eletricity and clairvoyance." She

25. Miller, *Modern Pentecost*, 26; Pension of Angelo M. Crapsey, depositions of John Crapsey, Jan. 29, 1887, and Richmond Barnum, July 26, 1885.

26. Miller, *Modern Pentecost*, 26–27.

27. Pension of Angelo M. Crapsey, deposition of John Crapsey, Jan. 29, 1887; Miller, *Modern Pentecost*, 6, 7, 27–30; Lyman, *History of Roulet*, 39–42.

warned Laroy, "I hate Crapsey as you would a rattlesnake. I tell you he is worse than the devil himself." She pleaded with him not to "let Crapsey shake any more devils into you for he shakes ten in instead of one out." A Lyman relative called Crapsey's services "an abomination to a civilized community." Laroy's father and brother pleaded with him to forsake this fearsome preacher and return to the Baptist fold.[28]

Once Laroy made up his mind, nothing but the direct command of the Almighty could change it. To prove his resolve, he followed Reverend Crapsey into the Allegheny River for a full-immersion baptism and unhesitatingly did it in January. Laroy emerged from the river reciting the last chapter of Revelation and then began preaching in an unknown language. A miracle, Reverend Crapsey claimed. Speaking in tongues—glossolalia. From that moment, John and Laroy were spiritual and intellectual kindred.[29]

At least one other person not only did not object to John's reputation but embraced both it and him. On January 18, 1853, Angelo gained a stepmother and a new stepsister, Viola. Widow Lura Ann Peck, née Jackson, filled a void in John's life. Convenience and necessity may have founded his second marriage as much as his first, but Lura was ten years younger than her husband and perhaps added a little zing to his lonely life. The Crapseys produced four surviving offspring in ten years and took literally the " 'til death us do part" portion of their wedding vows.[30]

Marital bliss was short-lived. By the end of January, a committee from five towns, including Laroy's father and brother, confronted the preacher. They gave him three days "to clear out and let us see your face no more forever . . . This is the will of the people," they asserted. "Mark it!"[31] The only thing John marked was his critics as evil as the priests and Pharisees who had persecuted Jesus. So, seventy men

28. Catherine Weimer to Laroy Lyman, Feb. 21, 1853, KLC; Diaries of Laroy Lyman.

29. Diaries of Laroy Lyman; Miller, *Modern Pentecost*, 1–2, citing *The Spiritual Telegraph*, ca. June 1855. Laroy's diaries reveal his frequent reading of the Bible and that Revelation was his favorite section. Slurred speech is a symptom of hypothermia, which he surely suffered after taking a midwinter dip in a northern Pennsylvania stream. See Mayo Clinic Web site, www.mayo clinic.com/health/hypothermia/DS00333/DSECTION=2.

30. Miller, *Modern Pentecost*, 37; Pension of Angelo M. Crapsey, deposition of John Crapsey, Dec. 6, 1884. John and Lura's children were Alice (b. May 2, 1855), William Merrick "Willie" (b. Feb. 19, 1858), Hattie "Suky" (b. Dec. 20, 1860), and George Bayard (b. Mar. 22, 1863). Lura was born January 11, 1826. Nicknames courtesy of Miriam Robbins Midkiff.

31. The *Potter Union* supposedly published this quote, but no copies of that antebellum newspaper were found. The quote here is from Miller, *Modern Pentecost*, 15.

showed up with an arrest warrant to mark it for him. He refused to cooperate. The mob tossed him onto a wagon bed, leaving him bruised and stunned. Two law officers made certain the mob's next stop was the magistrate's office and not a tree with a conveniently large lower limb.[32]

Formal charges were predicated on his alleged harmful influence on one young man, but he swore under oath that he had suffered no damage from the reverend's hocus-pocus. The magistrate had little choice but to say, "Not guilty." The mob grew livid and expressed an urge to string Crapsey "between the heavens and earth." Self-control prevailed, and as a last resort they bribed him to leave town for good. Crapsey accepted the money and left, feeling "as though every earthly friend had deserted" him, a state of depression no doubt assuaged by the twenty-five-dollar bulge in his pocket.[33]

But Elder Crapsey, as Laroy called him, possessed a stiffer neck than anyone could have imagined. He returned to Roulette the following August for one more try at converting the ignorant. Instead of an attentive congregation, he found a scowling crowd waiting. Three times he tried to mount the rostrum, and three times men yanked him to the ground. Determined to speak even "if they tore the very flesh from . . . my bones," he began his sermon from ground level. Instantly, women began banging pots and pans, and opposition preachers shouted prayers. John tried to outholler his adversaries until his voice cracked and his face flamed. Fury rose within him. Laroy advised passive resistance, but John's self-control deserted him that night. He went home sporting a black eye, fortunate that was the totality of his injuries.[34]

If John Crapsey could not preach, life had no foundation. He moved his family into a farm in Tioga County a stone's throw from both the Potter County and New York state lines. A neighbor could never remember seeing him lift a finger to work it, recalling Angelo as being "the mainstay of the family" who did "all kind of work" around the farm. John settled for occasional preaching to small groups and "peddling books sometimes." Indolence remained ingrained. Throughout his life, his net worth never exceeded a few hundred dollars.[35]

---

32. Miller, *Modern Pentecost,* 37.

33. Lyman, *History of Roulet;* Laroy Lyman to A. Henshaw, Aug. 27, 1853, KLC. The so-called victim was sixteen-year-old Jonathan Card, Laroy and Thankful Lyman's nephew.

34. Diaries of Laroy Lyman; Miller, *Modern Pentecost.* This event took place Aug. 14, 1853.

35. Pension of Angelo M. Crapsey, affidavit of Charles and Viola Robbins, Nov. 15, 1882, deposition of Charles E. Phipps, Jan. 29, 1887, and statement of E. R. Waite, Nov. 8, 1892; U.S.

John abandoned efforts to turn Roulette's wayward sheep into an obedient flock, but he did return to visit the Lymans and hold private services in their home. Folks did not object as long as he stayed indoors and did not bother anyone else. Short of murder, they could do little else. He was a guest of the Lymans, and it was best not to get on Laroy's blacklist.[36]

Angelo's first visit to the Lymans was a turning point in his life. That day, a boy met a man the likes of whom he had never known before and never would again. Angelo soon had a friend. More importantly, he had found a teacher and idol who would change the direction of his life.

That redirection may have led to his doom.

ANGELO AND LAROY

Laroy Lyman may have advocated nonviolence against God's thinking species, but that philosophy did not extend to the animal kingdom. By his own critter body counts, he played a considerable role in eradicating the wolf from Pennsylvania's indigenous species and threatened to do the same to the white-tailed deer. While never more at home than in the forest tracking game, he wore more business hats than he had hooks to hang them on, exemplifying "business diversification" long before anyone thought up the term. With his fearful size, piercing eyes, and plainspoken demeanor, those who dared question him inevitably suffered doubts of how sincere his pacifism was. Neither did he find physical violence inherently abhorrent. He once witnessed a local antislavery man thump a proslaver into unconsciousness and thought he had witnessed a grand event.[37]

Arguing his minority points of view is what most excited him. Debates drew him as moth to flame but put the flame in mortal danger. "Swearing, stealing, lying, cheating, drinking, talking vein talk,

---

Census, 1850, New York, Cattaraugus County, and 1860, Pennsylvania, McKean County. The Crapsey farm was located in Brookfield, a post office in northwest Tioga County bordering Potter County and one mile south of the New York state line.

36. Diaries of Laroy Lyman.

37. Ibid. The attacker was Giles Bleasdale Overton, who would captain the Potter County Rifles and later Co. H, 14th U.S. Inf. O.R. Howard Thomson and William H. Rauch, *History of the "Bucktails", Kane Rifle Regiment of the Pennsylvania Reserve Corps* wrongly states Overton's first name as "George," duplicating an error in a Harrisburg newspaper. A man named Dent was on the short end of the beating.

boasting and fornication, and all manner of evil doing" were on his list of wrongs he had to see righted. Being right was everything to Laroy, even if others' feelings suffered in reaching that goal. After he had angered an acquaintance by making a particularly insensitive remark, for example, he sloughed it off by writing in his diary, "If I tell the truth, what if a man is mad?" The only opinions that mattered to Laroy Lyman were Laroy Lyman's.[38]

Angelo gave away eight inches and many pounds to Laroy, but he was one of the rare individuals cheeky enough to buck the big man, bravery no doubt buffered by his father's relationship with Laroy. By 1857, Angelo was getting many opportunities to test his mettle against the Lyman legend. The Crapsey family had moved to Liberty (modern-day Port Allegany), nine miles west of Roulette. That was not close enough for Angelo, who was already spending a large part of his time in Roulette working for Laroy. Nudged by an unsubtle hint from John Crapsey, Laroy had agreed to buy the minister a small farm if Angelo lived in Roulette full-time. Laroy spent money freely on what he believed, and he believed in Reverend Crapsey. Laroy also got himself a cheap farmhand. Or so he thought.[39]

The bargain pleased Angelo. Left behind was an indigent father who had made many enemies. Ahead lay life under the tutelage of a successful businessman whose hunting skills had earned him admiration as a latter-day Orion. No matter how ornery Laroy behaved or unpopular his views, no one ever considered running the great L.L. out of town. Lyman roots wound too deeply within Roulette's soil for mere controversy to pluck them out. After all, a Lyman had founded the village. Besides, no one wanted to test the giant man's devotion to pacifism.[40]

---

38. Diaries of Laroy Lyman. On November 7, 1854, Laroy told a friend that his fancy carriage "could be had" the day he died. Laroy was astounded that the friend considered the remark tasteless. His diaries contain many similar encounters. Convinced that Saturday was Sabbath, Laroy offered one thousand dollars to anyone who could use the Bible to prove otherwise. He never paid.

39. Pension of Angelo M. Crapsey, affidavit of John Crapsey, Dec. 19, 1889, and deposition of Joseph Josia Robbins, Jan. 18, 1893; John Crapsey to Laroy Lyman, June 4, 1855, KLC; Diaries of Laroy Lyman. Angelo began working for Laroy on November 9, 1857. The town of Port Allegany was not yet incorporated. The exact date of the Crapsey's move is unknown. Lyman, *History of Roulet*. The Crapsey home was near Canoe Place, a spot along the Allegheny River that had long been a terminus for wilderness travelers and a name familiar to modern-day residents of "Port."

40. Lyman, *History of Roulet;* Diaries of Laroy Lyman. Laroy's brother Harris was even larger than Laroy, reportedly standing six feet, six inches in height. The author, who is six feet, one inch and, at the time, too much over two hundred pounds, experienced Laroy's size when he

On November 9, 1857, Angelo moved into the Lyman household. He went straight to work but turned out not to be the cheap farm-hand Laroy had thought. After proving his worth, the lad stunned Laroy with an outrageous salary demand of fifteen dollars a month. On another occasion, he kept Laroy at the kitchen table past 2:00 AM demanding his back wages until even the obstinate Laroy wore down and paid up. Angelo had learned the skill of business negotiation faster than Laroy might have preferred.[41]

Laroy had long organized community hunting parties, and from the day of his arrival Angelo was part of them all. The output from just one of these ventures covered the Lyman farm with the carcasses of more than fourteen hundred critters of all shapes, sizes, and methods of locomotion.[42] Angelo brought down his first deer on one of those hunts, but he still had much to learn. A week after that first deer kill, he again was on the track and dreaming of a second harvest. The excited boy retrieved Laroy to show him the trail he had found and pleaded for them to set off in search of the quarry. Laroy explained that if Angelo wanted to follow those animal tracks he was welcome, but the rabbit that left them did not have antlers.[43]

Angelo soon learned from Laroy how to differentiate deer tracks from rabbit tracks and much more that would guide him through life. He asked countless questions about hunting and surviving in the wilderness, and Laroy was eager to share. Laroy's older children were girls, and his only son was then too young to hunt. Here was a young man both tough enough to stand up to Laroy and eager to learn at the feet of the master. No one reveled more in being the master than Laroy Lyman.[44] The lad's shooting skills soon so rivaled his teacher's that Laroy began bragging in his diary whenever he defeated Angelo in a shooting match. Together they ran stride for stride on days-long hunts over the mountains. On their return, Angelo entered the Lyman home as a virtual family member. Laroy's diaries mention Angelo's name more than any other nonfamily member in the four years before the Civil War. When Laroy's father

---

tried on a pair of his buckskin pants, and they fit with room to spare. In one way, the aging Laroy was ahead of his time: he dyed his hair.

41. Diaries of Laroy Lyman.

42. Ibid. It was Laroy's practice to create an itemized list of every creature killed on these hunts.

43. Ibid. This event took place Nov. 30, 1856.

44. Ibid. Laroy filled diaries with examples of his inflated ego, although he would have argued that he was right, not egotistical.

died in 1858, he gave Angelo the honor of selecting the casket and laying out the body.[45]

There was a catch, though. If Angelo wanted to learn from Laroy, he also had to receive a formal education. Being well read was the key to Laroy's financial success and religious authority, a lesson not lost on Angelo. He finished his schooling in Roulette at the age of seventeen, unusual anywhere for a lad from his economic background, but especially so in a mountainous region where illiteracy was commonplace. Both Laroy and John Crapsey were proud of their writing skills, and Angelo surpassed them in many ways. The two even enrolled in an evening writing class at the schoolhouse. Later, after war had left its unmerciful stamp on his mind, Angelo would cling to writing as his mental grip became too slippery for personal interaction.[46]

Angelo had endured nearly two decades of religion under the tutelage of his father and again with Laroy. Logically, he should have developed similar religious passion, but again he proved his independence. Laroy's sister, Prudence Lyman Boyington, said that she did "not think religion . . . troubled [Angelo] very much." Lura Crapsey never considered her stepson to be "of a religious turn of mind," and John ruefully agreed with his wife.[47] Angelo managed an amazing degree of autonomy that seemed to have kept him above the controversy his father and Laroy had generated while extracting those characteristics from his mentors that suited his personality. From both men, he borrowed passion. From Laroy, he learned reason and ambition. But he would use those traits to develop patriotic, not religious, ideals.

And those traits eventually would kill him.

---

45. Ibid.

46. Ibid. Angelo to Laroy, Jan. 4, 1862, KLC. Angelo hinted at devilish behavior in school when he wrote, "How I wish that I was a schooler. Wouldn't I have a little fun!" U.S. Census, 1880, Minnesota, Cottonwood County, Southbrook Township, 67. Education meant something to the John Crapsey family, too. In 1880, his seventeen-year-old son George was listed as "in school." The tuition for Angelo and Laroy's reading class was one dollar, which Laroy paid.

47. Pension of Angelo M. Crapsey, depositions of Prudence Lyman Boyington, Nov. 22, 1892, and John and Lura Crapsey, Nov. 7, 1892.

2
Growing Up

The childhood shows the man, as morning shows the day.
—John Milton

JOHN CRAPSEY MAY HAVE GAINED A FARM BY SENDING ANGELO TO LIVE with Laroy, but his son's departure dropped the farmwork onto the reverend's unwilling shoulders. John did the only thing he considered possible under the circumstances: he hired someone to do the work for him. The laborer of choice was neighbor and Angelo's old schoolmate, Charles H. Robbins. Charlie was destined to share the experience of war with Angelo and witness a key event in his psychological demise. Before that, he would have to experience working for John Crapsey.[1]

Charlie's motives for taking the job naturally included earning money, but he had to know that the Second Coming might precede his first payday at the Crapsey farm. What Charlie yearned for most was independence from a father whose religious practices were more hell-bent than heaven-sent. Joseph Josia Robbins frequently held religious sessions with a Methodist minister. A whiskey bottle, the contents of which gradually diminished throughout the evening, provided the evening's spirits. Josia insisted his family be well read, but the Bible was the only book he permitted in the house. Those other books might contain devilish ideas such as the earth being round. The Bible spoke of the four corners of the earth, and everyone knows that round things can't have corners.[2]

---

1. Pension of Angelo M. Crapsey, deposition of Charles H. Robbins, Jan. 18, 1893.

2. Newspaper interview with Charles H. Robbins, date and newspaper name not preserved but probably from Newaygo County, Michigan, courtesy of Lloyd Robbins. Charles H. Robbins was born Apr. 19, 1844. Joseph Josia Robbins was born in Oswego County, New York, Dec. 4, 1820, and died in Hesperia, Michigan, July 27, 1905.

At the age of thirteen, Charlie escaped from home and headed to the Erie Canal to work as a cabin boy. The five-dollar monthly salary was welcome enough, but tips from gamblers turned it into a windfall. On his return, he offered his father one hundred dollars if he would grant his blessing for him to live elsewhere. That was when he started working for John Crapsey.[3]

Angelo may have shared with Charlie the experience of a zealously religious father, but he left no outward sign that he had moved from home in anger. Wartime correspondence displays no disaffection for his father. Only later would harsh feelings burst into the open. Even then, there is the question of whether the outbursts were truly aimed at his father or an imaginary enemy conjured by his feverish mind.[4]

However emotional the background of Angelo Crapsey may have been, much of it must have been right. Friends and relatives said he "was well thought of and he could be relied upon in all he said or did" and that he was a "kind-hearted boy" with good personal habits. Even gruff Josia Robbins thought that Angelo was "truthful, . . . very steady in his ways, [and] clear-headed." No one could recall him ever drinking liquor. Laroy expressed chagrin whenever Angelo dressed up to "go a gadding," but having fun was never Laroy's strong suit.[5] During Angelo's army career, comrades with every reason to envy him and hate his father would elect him corporal. While retaining cordiality with peers, he would sometimes march at his colonel's side and write letters while seated in his captain's tent.[6]

On the other hand, folks sometimes had to measure Angelo's temper with a short ruler. On one occasion, he accidentally ran into a fence gate. Seconds later the gate lay some yards from the fence, and the gate's hardware ended up even farther away. On another occasion, an uncooperative oxen team had him shouting a streak of blue words and throwing every article within reach, including several items securely fastened prior to the tantrum. Laroy had to grab the reins to prevent a mini-stampede.[7]

---

3. Ibid. If young Charlie could not tolerate his father, the older version did. When Josia died, he had been living with his son for many years.

4. Angelo to John Crapsey, May 8, 1862, Pension of Angelo M. Crapsey; Diaries of Laroy Lyman. Laroy occasionally gave John Crapsey money. On one occasion, it was one hundred dollars, which made Elder Crapsey "jump for joy." Neither was John Crapsey above asking Laroy for money, but seldom did he do anything to earn it.

5. Pension of Angelo M. Crapsey, depositions of Charles H. Robbins, Jan. 18, 1893, Prudence Lyman Boyington, Nov. 22, 1892, and John Crapsey, undated; Diaries of Laroy Lyman.

6. Angelo to Laroy, Oct. 11, 1861, and June 14, 1862, KLC.

7. Pension of Angelo M. Crapsey, depositions of Seneca Pomeroy, May 13, 1893, and Isaac

Like his modern-day counterpart, the teenager had a fascination with speed and enjoyed racing in Laroy's bobsled throughout snowy northern Pennsylvania winters. While on assignment to draw maple sap, he exceeded the specified Lyman speed limit and damaged the sled. When Laroy demanded he repair it, Angelo flew into a snit familiar to parents of teenage boys since time began. Laroy made it clear that either he repair the bobsled or he was fired. Angelo pondered the two options and chose a third: he quit. A few days later, Laroy met Angelo in the general store and again confronted him over the issue. Angelo launched into a temper tantrum and stormed away. By May, he had repaired the sled, Laroy had forgiven him, and the incident became a humorous memory he would recall in an army letter.[8]

It is not surprising that Angelo could have ripped a fence apart. While at maturity he stood only five feet, six inches tall, he packed 155 pounds of muscle on that small frame even after five months of punishing army life.[9] Charlie Robbins "thought him as strong and well as any of the young men of any acquaintance" and "never knew of his being sick or injured." Others described Angelo as "a rugged, healthy man, vigorous, mentally and physically sound." For certain, he was robust enough to rip a fence gate off its hinges with his bare hands.[10]

Angelo was mentally tough, too, for he had learned from his two adult influences not to fear criticism, including the freely offered criticism by those two adult influences. A different generation had molded him, one that had come to maturity during turbulent political times. His life experiences had shaped a consummate patriot as strong in his convictions about the sanctity of the Union as his father and Laroy were about religion and pacifism.

By opposite examples, John and Laroy also taught Angelo that businessmen earn a lot more money than itinerant preachers. When Edwin L. Drake changed the world forever by digging the first successful oil well, Angelo took work as a borer and listed "oil worker" as

---

Sears, Nov. 22, 1892. Sears called Angelo "smart acting." Diaries of Laroy Lyman. The fence gate incident took place the day before Laroy's father died.

8. Diaries of Laroy Lyman. Laroy was part owner of the store in which the second encounter took place. Potter County is still known for its maple syrup, which the author highly recommends.

9. Angelo to Laroy, Aug. 20, 1861, KLC. The author's compilation of nearly eleven thousand Civil War soldiers, mostly from south-central Pennsylvania, reveals an average height of five feet, seven inches, which, with an equal number of five-foot, eight-inch men, also represents median height. There was a higher percentage of men shorter than median height than taller.

10. Pension of Angelo M. Crapsey, depositions of Charles and Viola Robbins, Nov. 15, 1882, and Joseph J. Robbins, Apr. 2, 1891; Angelo to Laroy, Aug. 20, 1861, KLC.

his occupation when he enlisted. Laroy also had taught him that being the boss topped being a laborer. Angelo studied the craft of drilling, made notes on every operational detail, and before long had saved enough money to buy into a new well near Cuba, New York, a town well acquainted with John Crapsey and his ministry.[11] In spite of possessing work-hewn hands and having a father with a notorious reputation, some of the town's prominent citizens befriended Angelo, among them Frank Burbank Sibley, a "quiet and unassuming" boy on his way to putting his name among the town's most prominent citizens. The two would correspond during the war, and Angelo would reveal some of his most personal thoughts and feelings to Sibley.[12]

Those and other social intimacies with members of the middle class gave Angelo the facility to deal with people from varying backgrounds. But it was a double-edged sword. His own words, written well before his slide into insanity, reveal strong doubt that he would ever receive the kind of advanced education that Frank Sibley took for granted. How could a humble oil borer, the son of a crazy, wandering preacher, climb such tall social obstacles? In spite of his above-average skill at writing, ten of Angelo's letters close with apologies for bad writing and/or spelling. As war took its toll, that insecurity would become a deep and self-destructive depression.[13]

But in 1860, life was good. Angelo was having fun on the road selling what Lyman family lore says was a special gun-cleaning liquid.[14] He hawked one hundred dollars' worth at Angelica, New York, alone. John Crapsey accompanied his son and no doubt used the sales events to pitch his religion and beg his son for a few dollars from the receipts. A devilish Angelo shows up in one of his letters from there, the lad with a dry wit and teasing wink. Today we would call him a smart-ass.

---

11. Angelo to Laroy, July 23, 1860, KLC. Angelo claimed the well was 143 feet deep and produced twelve barrels a day. Pension of Thomas Learn, Co. K, 85th New York, affidavits of Margaret Karn and John C. Learn. Rev. John Crapsey officiated at Learn's wedding in Cuba on Dec. 28, 1844. *History of Allegany County, N.Y.* At the time, the Genesee Valley Canal passed through Cuba and gave rise to a boat-building industry there.

12. U.S. Census, 1860, New York, Allegany County, 742; John Minard, *Civic History and Illustrated Progress of Cuba, NY,* 1910; Alfred University, University Archives, Special Collections, private e-mail to the author, Aug. 8, 2006. Frank Burbank Sibley was born in Cuba, New York, Feb. 24, 1845. He later attended Alfred University and became supervisor of Cuba. It was said of him, "Once given, his word was never broken."

13. Angelo to Frank Sibley, Feb. 7, 1863, KGC.

14. The assumption of the gun-cleaning liquid comes from a note included with a letter presumably written by either Laroy's son, Milo, or grandson, Robert.

I am ready to start in the morning for I went to Olean[, New York,] today and got some more liquid and bottles. I have got 10 lbs of the liquid and 160 bottles and eleven dollars in my pocket. I have had apples, pears, peaches, and plums to eat and you can get enough fruit at Olean but not very cheap. I have had lots of fun last week. I was up at Cuba a fixing some liquid and a fellow came to see me and he got some acid in his eye. You reckon he howled? So do I think so. He thought I [was] making plating. He found it too. Plating in good earnest.[15]

Life was a wide, open road. Angelo had the raw material to triumph, and he wanted that prosperity to happen close to home. On October 20, 1860, he purchased land near Roulette with money borrowed from Laroy.[16] Time would surely have tempered the rough edges. Pennsylvania's greatest hunter might have molded a raw boy into one of Pennsylvania's greatest businessmen.

If only the South hadn't fired on Fort Sumter.

15. Angelo to Laroy, Sept. 3, 1860, KLC.

16. Diaries of Laroy Lyman; *Potter County Journal,* various issues; Victor L. Beebe, *History of Potter County Pennsylvania.* Angelo purchased land from John S. Mann, Coudersport attorney and antebellum editor of the *Potter County Journal.* No formal record of this land transfer was found in the Pennsylvania Archives.

3

Pennsylvania Calls

War is an ugly thing, but not the ugliest of things: the decayed and degraded state of moral and patriotic feeling which thinks nothing worth a war, is worse.

—John Stuart Mill

THE SMOKE OF BATTLE HARDLY HAD DISSIPATED OVER CHARLESTON Harbor before Northern men began flocking to army recruiting centers. The officers they encountered usually were not professional soldiers but local luminaries as long on patriotism, money, and political connections as they were short on military skill. Those were the days of the citizen-soldier, and no level of martial naïveté was too insignificant to prevent well-heeled greenhorns from leading their lesser-heeled counterparts into battle.

Thomas Leiper Kane provides a classic example. The native Philadelphian was short in stature and prone to illness, but he had an itch for adventure he just had to scratch. At seventeen, he traveled overseas to Paris to further his education and there fell in with a group of radicals hell-bent on public protest. When he returned to the United States, he helped slaves escape bondage and traveled west to befriend the Mormons, acts that many of his contemporaries considered reason enough to suffer imprisonment in this life and eternal damnation in the next.[1]

Thomas Kane's father was among that group. When he thought that his son had objected too vehemently to one of Congress's many

---

1. Ezra J. Warner, *Generals in Blue: Lives of the Union Commanders*, 256–57; Pension of Thomas L. Kane; Bulletin of the Thomas L. Kane Memorial Chapel, Kane, Pa. Today it is difficult to imagine how hated the Mormons were during the nineteenth century. Even after their escape to Utah, they ran afoul of the U.S. Army. In 1858, Kane helped negotiate a peace between Brigham Young and the army. Though he was not a Mormon, the church honors him with a statue in Salt Lake City and a memorial chapel in Kane, Pennsylvania. *O.R.*, 5:493, Report of Gen. J. E. B. Stuart, Dec. 20, 1861. Stuart called Thomas Kane "Colonel Kane of Utah notoriety."

attempts to mediate the slavery question, Judge John K. Kane ordered a cell door slammed in Thomas's face. That event surely made life at home tense, so Thomas headed to the family's landholdings in the wilds of McKean County. There he took work planning a new railroad and later married a progressive woman destined for a medical career. While he was at it, he helped found a town that still bears his last name.[2]

By the time President Lincoln issued a call for seventy-five thousand volunteers to suppress the rebellion, Thomas Kane was already actively engaged and ensconced in Smethport, seat of McKean County, twenty miles from Roulette. Headquarters were in Laroy Lyman's favorite hotel, the Bennett House.[3] Kane was only interested in recruiting a glamour regiment. That meant cavalry, but the governor had so many of those requests that he denied Kane permission. Thus, he fell back on his second choice: a rifle regiment of marksmen. He lived in an area that had plenty of those. He and several handpicked associates traveled throughout four counties spreading the gospel according to Uncle Sam. Everywhere they tacked up posters that shouted a need for marksmen willing to spare three months in the service of their country. Only those who could handle a rifle need apply.[4]

The sales pitch worked. Rough-and-tumble lumbermen, oil borers and farmers, boys clean-shaven and men with grizzled faces arrived in Smethport to coalesce into a company they called the McKean Rifles. A few eager fellows from New York crossed the state line to put their marks on the enlistment sheet, too. Some of the recruits understood Kane's poster only after someone read it to them but compensated with a rugged constitution and the ability to shoot a rifle with deadly accuracy. Whatever their appearance and wherever they called home, all of them worked hard to survive a land so rugged that folks called it the Wildcat District.[5]

No one exemplified that image better than James Landrigan, a gangly lumberman with features that shouted his Nordic roots. He was a bit older than most of his comrades, and the vision in his right eye had been failing since an accident three years before, but no one

2. Warner, *Generals in Blue*, 256–57. The town is Kane, McKean County, Pennsylvania.

3. Diaries of Laroy Lyman. Smethport (pronounced as if spelled "Smithport") is county seat of McKean County, adjacent western county to Potter. Laroy Lyman often slept at the Bennett House during business trips. It burned down in 1882.

4. Thomson and Rauch, *History of the "Bucktails,"* copy of the original handbill in face-page 8.

5. Based on my reading of nearly a hundred pensions of Co. I men, it is apparent that illiteracy was not as common among the mountain boys as might be assumed.

doubted his prowess.[6] Jim Landrigan was as unlikely a candidate to create a legend as ever lived. But there, on the main street of Smethport, Pennsylvania, he did just that. The story is so familiar that it has achieved legendary status, but it deserves one more mention because Angelo would soon make it an important part of his life.

Landrigan eyed a recently harvested buck hanging in front of a butcher shop and decided that he had to own its oversized tail. No use bothering with legalities. A quick whip of his knife, and the tail was his. He soon pinned it to his hat. The moment Thomas Kane saw Landrigan's headgear, he knew he had found the perfect symbol for his rifle regiment. In that part of Pennsylvania, the white-tailed deer was, and still is, a life-form second in importance only to humanity.[7] Harvesting one meant food, warmth, decoration, and the attainment of manhood. Kane ordered all of his men into the woods and to return wearing a bucktail in their hat. No one had to tell north woodsmen how to do that, and soon every recruit's hat sported a remnant of white-tailed deer. It seemed unimportant if some of the tails had previously flicked at the back end of does or if they were not really the species' hind appendage.[8]

Jim Landrigan's whimsical crime created an icon that would shortly turn into a sideline career for Angelo. Few recall his hand in maintaining the image, but history will always remember the outcome. This outfit from Pennsylvania's north woods had planted a seed that would germinate into one of the most famous regiments in the Civil War. They would fight under a symbol destined to become so beloved that other units would copy it and the enemy would hold as a badge of honor whenever they captured one. The world would forever know Thomas Kane's marksmen as "The Bucktails."

The swearing-in ceremony took place in front of the Bennett House in an atmosphere a Smethport newspaper described as "very

---

6. Pension of James Landrigan, Co. I, 1st Pa. Rifles; Personal Sketches, Grand Army of the Republic Memorial Book, McKean Post No. 347, McKean County Historical Society. Born in 1834 in Wyoming, New York, James Landrigan survived the war to complain that everyone misspelled his name and then spelled it two different ways in his pension correspondence. He claimed injury to his right eye when a ball struck him. Thomas Kane's son, a doctor, blamed the vision loss on a cataract. While described as "remarkably strong," at six-foot, one hundred sixty pounds Landrigan was six inches taller but only five pounds heavier than Angelo.

7. See Pennsylvania Department of Conservation and Natural Resources, www.dcnr.state.pa.us/forestry/deer/index.aspx

8. Thomson and Rauch, *History of the Bucktails*, 11, alleges that some men cut strips from Landrigan's deer to make pseudotails. Other sources of this famous story are from the colorful version in Glover, *Bucktailed Wildcats*, and snippets from Bates, *History of Pennsylvania Volunteers*. Forty-second Regt. ("Bucktails"), P.V., Order Book of Co. K, 1863–64, F. D. Beary, "Battle Flag History," MG 234, Pennsylvania State Archives.

affecting." Charlie Robbins claimed to have been there although his name is absent from a roster published in a Smethport newspaper. Wherever he chose to enlist, he was no doubt making the final break from his father's control. Recruits were supposed to be at least eighteen years of age, but that event lay more than a year into Charlie's future. Parental permission would have bypassed the problem, but he was probably disinclined to ask his father for favors. He skirted the age issue using the same method employed by thousands of other boys eager for military service. He lied.[9]

Potter County's clarion call blared forth on April 19. After sending the Smethport unit off to Harrisburg and assisting with recruiting efforts in Shippen (modern-day Emporium), Thomas Kane arrived in Coudersport to "rousing cheers." By 9:00 AM the next day, seventy men of the Potter County Rifles prepared to follow their Smethport brethren. If Kane ever brought up the subject of bucktails in Coudersport, the newspaper did not report it.[10]

Where Angelo enlisted is uncertain. His name is absent from a roster published in the Coudersport newspaper. Service records list his place of enlistment as "McKean County" and Thomas Kane as his enlisting officer. That may have meant a face-to-face encounter or only that records routinely listed Kane as recruiter. Descriptive lists that could provide an answer are noticeably missing from both the National and Pennsylvania Archives. In 1893, Charlie Robbins claimed he had enlisted in Smethport with Angelo, but the absence of both their names in the newspapers' list of recruits makes that questionable. John Crapsey remembered that his son had enlisted in Liberty and recalled that Angelo "took his wages to pay his expenses on his way to Williamsport to join his regiment."[11] That may indicate that he traveled to Harrisburg on his own and caught up with the Smethport group either midway or in Harrisburg. Angelo's own words written to Laroy after he arrived in Harrisburg seem to verify that: "I got there a week ahead of the boys."[12]

However they got there, Harrisburg overnight had become temporary home to thousands of would-be soldiers, an influx of human-

9. *McKean Miner,* Apr. 30, 1861; Adjutant General's Office, Volunteer Organizations, Civil War Muster Rolls and Papers, 13th Inf. Pa. Reserves, Box 4248, National Archives and Records Administration, Washington, D.C.

10. *Potter County Journal,* May 1, 1861. Coudersport was then, and still is, the seat of Potter County.

11. Pension of Angelo M. Crapsey, depositions of John Crapsey, Jan. 29, 1887, and Charles H. Robbins, Jan. 18, 1893.

12. CMSR of Angelo M. Crapsey, discharge certificate; Pension of Angelo M. Crapsey, affidavit of John Crapsey, Apr. 7, 1888; Angelo to Laroy, May 22, 1861, KLC.

ity that dumped a huge problem into Gov. Andrew Gregg Curtin's lap. Only five days after President Lincoln's call for troops, Camp Curtin had become home to twenty-nine companies of soldiers, and more were arriving every day. A Harrisburg newspaper tried to keep a running tabulation of incoming units, but the job soon became so overwhelming they gave up. With Pennsylvania quickly exceeding its quota of recruits, Curtin wired Thomas Kane not to bring more than two companies to Harrisburg. Kane was not with his men when they received the telegram, so they ignored the order and kept coming.[13]

On May 2, the Bucktails detrained in the midst of the confusion and added to the commotion with the Repass Brass Band, which had hitched a ride at Williamsport.[14] A newspaper hailed "THE ARRIVAL OF BACKWOODS SOLDIERS" and was impressed that "nearly every man had his own rifle and . . . looked as if they were familiar with its use." Considering that military ordnance was still a rare sight in the city, it is understandable that they found the rifles impressive. Those bucktails made a splash, too.[15]

Harrisburg's initial enthusiasm for war faded as streets filled with eager men and boys, many of whom were away from home for the first time and acting it. Before the night of May 5 ended, two of the Bucktails were sobering up behind bars and a third nearly died after his head made strong and intimate contact with a policeman's nightstick. Some of the Bucktails took exception to the policeman's brutality and threatened to riot, especially after citizens doused some of them with water from an upstairs hotel window. Only the coincidental arrival of an armed battalion from Camp Curtin prevented disaster. Angelo's involvement in the near melee is unknown, but it would

---

13. Executive Correspondence, Jan. 1, 1860–Feb. 27, 1862, RG 26, Department of State, Secretary of the Commonwealth, Pennsylvania State Archives; Thomson and Rouch, *History of the Bucktails,* 15–16; *Patriot and Union,* Apr. 22 and 26, 1861; *Cameron Citizen,* May 17, 1861. When state authorities refused to cover the cost of train fare, L. A. Mackey of Lock Haven spent $480 of his money to buy the Bucktails' tickets.

14. The Repass (Repasz) Band was well known in its day and served during the war with the 11th and 29th Pennsylvania Infantry Regiments and the 8th Pennsylvania Cavalry. It still exists today. See Repass Family Home Page at www.repass.net/repass/bandhistory.asp

15. *Patriot and Union,* May 3, 1861; Thomson and Rauch, *History of the Bucktails,* claims the Bucktails arrived on May 4, but newspapers disprove that. Kane's men were not the first company of the future Bucktail Regiment to arrive. The Tioga Rifles had easier access to the railroad and had arrived quietly two days earlier. *O.R.,* 51/1:351, Fitz-John Porter to Lorenzo Thomas, May 1, 1861. Porter, assigned by Washington to coordinate with the state in organizing the volunteer regiments, reported an "almost total absence at Harrisburg of arms, ammunition, and all ordnance and quartermaster's equipment and commissary stores."

have been out of character for him to participate in such violence, particularly with liquor as the catalyst.[16]

Governor Curtin devised a solution to his military overpopulation, but it was going to cost the state three million dollars: a special "reserve" corps that would require men to commit for three years or the end of the war. Three weeks of haggling with the legislature got him his wish. If the federal government accepted his corps, fine. If the war ended first, better yet. Meanwhile, Curtin had a way to keep thousands of men occupied and hopefully out of trouble, not to mention building a good-sized private army to defend Pennsylvania.[17]

The Potter County boys arrived in Harrisburg just as the state's quota for three-month regiments had filled. They sought to join three-year regiments then forming, but openings were limited and politics favored men from western counties. They were not happy about being the odd men out. Many became so disgusted they went home, and by mid-June less than thirty remained. Governor Curtin personally told the rest they could obtain an honorable discharge and go home without disgrace.[18]

But the boys from Potter did suffer disgrace. Angelo was so scornful of them that he made critical remarks in three consecutive letters to Laroy, words he would have to eat two years later.

> There are a lot of Potter boys who run away and a lot of them got upset for they are not as well satisfied with the fare . . . There has been 100 or more of the Potter and McKean boys have gone home. I don't disgrace my parents by deserting or turning back in such times as these are . . . I shall go for 3 years [and] not return like a coward as some of the men do."[19]

Angelo's criticism was unfair. Politics and numbers were to blame, not cowardice, and many of the Potter County boys who returned home enlisted with other regiments—at least fourteen with the 1st

---

16. *Patriot and Union,* Apr. 27 and May 6, 1861; *Pennsylvania Daily Telegraph,* May 7, 1861. The policeman's victim was E. S. Aylesworth of the Cameron Rifles. Both Harrisburg newspapers supplied detailed accounts of the near debacle but from differing points of view, but both used only Aylesworth's last name. His initials are on a handwritten muster roll of the Cameron Rifles, courtesy of Ronn Palm, Civil War Images, Gettysburg, Pennsylvania. The 1860 census lists no Aylesworth family in the Shippen (Emporium) area but one in Coudersport: sixteen-year-old Elmer. Some of the Bucktails pressed charges against the policeman, John Newman, who was arrested and released on a three-hundred-dollar bond.

17. *O.R.* 3/1:256, E. M. Biddle to Simon Cameron, June 5, 1861.

18. *Potter County Journal,* June 13, 1861. The article's author was S. S. Greeman (possibly Sylvester S. Greenman), one of those who returned home. See also *Cameron Citizen,* June 21, 1861.

19. Angelo to Laroy, excerpted from letters of May 23 and 30, and June 1, 1861, KLC.

Pennsylvania Light Artillery alone. Later, they had to be miffed when they heard that a company from Chester County had joined Thomas Kane's Bucktail Regiment. How could an easterner be a Bucktail?[20]

On May 15, 1861, Andrew Curtin's Pennsylvania Reserve Volunteer Corps moved from theory into reality. Before summer's end, the Bucktails would join twelve other infantry regiments and one each of cavalry and light artillery to form Pennsylvania's unique Reserve Corps. Since the Bucktails were the first rifle regiment formed in the state, they adopted the name "First Pennsylvania Rifles." The state added "13th Pennsylvania Reserves" so as not to confuse them with the 1st Pennsylvania Reserve Infantry Regiment. After federal muster, Washington had "42nd Pennsylvania" waiting in the wings. The regiment's officers insisted on "Kane Rifle Regiment" even though Kane refused the colonel's insignia they elected him to wear and settled for the lieutenant colonel's position.[21]

Time would prove "Reserves" to be a misleading title for Curtin's special corps. Fate would not permit these boys to sit in the rear and watch others fight, and those sharpshooting Bucktails would usually be in the front. As one member later put it, "They can't have a fight but our boys are in it."[22] To say his statement was dead-on is not mere wordplay, as a grim statistic proves. The Reserve Corps began with a head count of 15,856 volunteers. On September 27, 1862, ten days after the battle of Antietam, a general reported little more than 5,000 men responding to roll calls. The general predicted the corps' fighting capacity would be "useless" in a few more battles "unless its ranks are promptly filled."[23]

By that time, Angelo Crapsey would be struggling with his own sense of utility.

---

20. CMSRs of all men of Battery E, 1st Pa. Light Artillery (43rd Pa.); *Potter County Journal,* May 1, 1861.

21. Third Annual Reunion—Regimental Association of the Bucktail or First Rifle Regt. P.R.V.C., 1890; MG 7, folder 0278, Pennsylvania State Archives. An event at a Bucktail reunion twenty-two years after the war shows how some veterans felt about being in the Reserves Corps. A motion to fund a monument to the corps proved controversial when William Rauch objected "on the grounds that the Bucktails having acted as an independent capacity during the war" should have their own monument. Rauch's motion was defeated 36 to 17.

22. Letter of Pvt. William Presely, Co. B, Dec. 23, 1862, Harrisburg Civil War Round Table Collection, U.S. Army Military History Institute, Carlisle, Pa.

23. Truman Seymour to Andrew G. Curtin, Sept. 27, 1862, Pennsylvania Archives, RG-19, Box 54; Executive Correspondence, Andrew G. Curtin to Abraham Lincoln, Sept. 30, 1862, Col. H. G. Sickels to Andrew G. Curtin, Dec. 26, 1862, and George D. Ruggles to A. G. Curtin, Jan. 12, 1863, Commonwealth of Pennsylvania, RG-26, Department of State, Pennsylvania Historical and Museum Commission, Boxes 61 and 63; *O.R.,* 21:878, Maj. Gen. John F. Reynolds to Headquarters, First Army Corps, Jan. 10, 1863.

4

When It Was Still Called Glory

The paths of glory lead but to the grave.
—Thomas Gray

Now THAT HE WAS IN HARRISBURG, ANGELO FOCUSED ON THE VENTURE before him and showed that he had no naïveté about the life-altering decision he had made. "Camp life is not home," he wrote Laroy. "I knew it before I started. Soldiers life is hard but I should be [able] to take care of myself."[1] He decided to break clean from civilian life by signing over his Cuba oil well share to his business partner and offering his land to Laroy should he not return. Like most soldiers, he was homesick, and his heart sank when mail call concluded without hearing his name. Still, he remained resolute, as he explained to Laroy.

> I am far away and in the army and fighting for the Stars and Stripes. I look with eager eyes every time the mail comes in to see a letter from some friend in Roulette. I look in vain. I think you must of written to me before this time . . . I wish I could see you one hour. I would like to talk with you. I shall not come back with out an honorable discharge. There is 700 Southern rebels within 26 miles of Chambersburg. They are 85 miles from here. They will get all they want. Let them come.[2]

Angelo professed a cavalier attitude toward battle, as did many lads at that early time of the war. Truth was, while he had seen and caused the violent death of many an animal, he never had witnessed a man torn open by a bullet. He would soon gain firsthand knowledge of that gruesome event. It would not happen in battle but at the hands of a comrade in the supposed safety of their Harrisburg camp.

George B. Mattison and H. S. Miller were tent mates, both Potter County men, and neither destined to serve with the Bucktails. It would

---

1. Angelo to Laroy, May 22 and 30, 1861, KLC.
2. Ibid., May 22, 1861.

have been better if at least one of them had gone home. While oiling his rifle, Miller attempted to remove the lock and discovered the hard way that it held a live round. George Mattison learned an even harder lesson when the bullet tore through his skull. The round exited Mattison and just missed striking Seneca Minard's head. Mattison thus earned a dubious distinction as Potter County's first war victim. His wife and children were little comforted that the regiment buried the man of the house with full military honors. They would discover that since he had not yet mustered into federal service, Washington would not grant them a pension.[3]

Rifle fire was not the only instrument of death that Angelo witnessed. As soon as all those men got together in one place, disease ran wild, especially among country boys who lacked immunity from childhood diseases commonplace to city dwellers. Angelo was most concerned with contracting ague, a generic name then applied to various diseases accompanied by high fever and severe chills. Measles was another common assailant. Charlie Robbins, not yet mustered into service, was one of many one who succumbed to its assault. Surgeons quarantined him for a time before sending him home to recover. The regiment would not see him again until August.[4]

While the Reserve Corps trained to become a cohesive unit, tension swelled in western Virginia. Southern troops had seized the arsenal town of Harpers Ferry and threatened other sections of "Loyal Virginia," the future West Virginia.[5] Washington had no force immediately available to send there, but Pennsylvania did. Two regiments of Andrew Curtin's home-brewed war machine stood primed and ready—at least as ready as novice regiments could be after such a short existence. The Bucktails was one of them.

Once in the field, dreams of glory flattened under the weight of terrible food, dirty water, nights sleeping on wet ground, and grueling marches over rugged, mountainous terrain. When they set up a camp on the Pennsylvania-Maryland border, conditions were so

---

3. Ibid; *Potter County Journal*, May 1, 1861. Thomson and Rauch, *History of the Bucktails*, the *Pennsylvania Daily Telegraph*, *McKean Miner*, and *Cameron Citizen* all recounted the tragic event differently. Miller was from Oswayo, Potter County. Mattison's rifle was doubtless his own and probably a percussion model. Perhaps the hammer snapped shut and even without a cap caused a spark that ignited the charge in the barrel. I have not spoken to anyone with knowledge of Civil War weaponry who understands how this scenario could have occurred as Mattison described.

4. Angelo to Laroy, May 30, 1861, KLC; CMSR and Pension of Charles H. Robbins, Co. I, 1st Pa. Rifles.

5. *O.R.*, 2:689, 717, 726–27.

swampy and potable water so scarce that they changed its name from Camp Mason and Dixon to "Camp Misery and Despair."[6] Death also went along on their first jaunt, but it was not in the form of bullets, as Angelo related to Laroy:

> Just now my ear caught the sound of death march. As I looked out of my tent I saw a company with the remains of one of their comrades which was poisoned at Hyattstown[, Maryland] by a traitor. He has suffered much. It was thought he would recover but he has gone the way that all must go sooner or later. They buried him with military honors in a little grave so that his friends can take him up.[7]

When Angelo next experienced tragedy, the victim would be one of his friends from Cuba, New York. He told Frank Sibley about it.

> Frank, you may think it is rather strange that I don't write to you. I will tell you the reason. It was that Hascall was very sick and I wanted to see if he did not get better before I wrote to you. I can safely say he is gaining but it is very slow for he has been very low, so low that I was afraid he would not live. I have just been talking with him. He says he sends his respects to you and the rest of his friends. He says he wishes you to tell his folks not to be scared for he thinks he will be well in a week or two. He wishes they would write. It seems they do not.[8]

On October 29, 1861, Sgt. Benjamin Franklin Hascall died from the effects of typhoid fever.[9]

Death continued to haunt the Bucktails. The next victim was not a friend of Angelo's, but the man would suffer a violent and portentous death. Knowing as we do of Angelo's ultimate fate, his description of how the man died is especially chilling.

> A sergeant of Company F committed suicide. He had been unwell for a few days and seemed to be a little shattered. He took his rifle and loaded

---

6. Thomson and Rauch, *History of the Bucktails*, 44; *National Tribune*, Dec. 10, 1881. Federal muster was required when a state force crossed a state line, but the Bucktails did not do that. That would cause problems come first payday and even later when they applied for pensions because their first date of service was in doubt.

7. Angelo to Laroy, Aug. 31, 1861, KLC.

8. Angelo to Frank Sibley, Oct. 8, 1861, KGC.

9. Pension of Benjamin F. Hascall, Co. I, 1st Pa. Rifles. Hascall was the product of a broken home and the sole support for his mother and two siblings. Before the war, the family became impoverished and had to live with a relative in Cuba, which is where Angelo and Frank came to know him. Benjamin's middle name courtesy of Doris Wheeler, descendant of Benjamin's sister.

it when there was no one about and put the muzzle into his mouth and tucked the gun off with his toes. I heared the gun when he shot himself for their quarters are near ours.[10]

"Unwell" came nowhere near to describing the condition of Sgt. William H. Rehrig. Ranting and delirious from the elevated temperature that typhoid fever often inflicts on its victims, he offered a frightening preview of Angelo's demise three years later. Most unnerving from Angelo's perspective is his depiction of Rehrig as "shattered," the very word people would later apply to him. A comrade blamed the regimental surgeon for not sending Rehrig to the hospital, but the doctor countered that he did not because the hospital was already overcrowded.[11]

In spite of disease, discomfort, and the death of comrades, Angelo claimed to be enjoying himself. Rugged country could hardly bother a Laroy Lyman protégé. This excursion to western Virginia was no different than his experiences at home, except that Laroy was not along, and this game had two legs and could shoot back. Pride shined in a letter to his father in which he described how he and three others had gone forward as scouts during which he had used the wilderness skills that Laroy had taught him. Angelo visited Cumberland, Maryland, on a run to pick up the mail and was impressed by a regiment of Indiana soldiers wearing Zouave uniforms. On the other hand, reality reminded him that they had to be concerned with "4 thousand Rebels within 20 miles of us."[12]

Angelo may have been enjoying himself, but Laroy's continuing silent pen hurt. He had his photograph taken and sent a copy to Laroy along with a subtle prod that he hoped might engender a letter. "I hope you will get it and keep it to remember the little hunter who used to roam by your side over the mountains of the Allegheny."[13]

On July 21, 1861, the direction of the war changed abruptly. The war's first great battle had taken place near a Virginia rail junction called Manassas, not far from a meandering stream named Bull Run. Confederate forces had routed the Union troops, and orders sent the Bucktails scampering back to Harrisburg for reassignment. The trip

---

10. Angelo to Laroy, Oct. 4, 1861, KLC.
11. Ibid.; Pension of William H. Rehrig, Co. F, 1st Pa. Rifles. Rehrig took his life on Oct. 1, 1861, after a two-week illness. The army speculated on murder but could find no cause to sustain an investigation. Rehrig left behind a wife and many children.
12. Angelo to John Crapsey, July 10, 1861, KLC.
13. Angelo to Laroy, Aug. 3, 1861, KLC.

proved exhausting because officers would not allow them off the filthy cattle cars that triple-functioned as sleeping quarters, dining room, and privy. It was also a fruitless trip because new orders sent them right back to the western Virginia region.[14]

There was good news for Angelo, though. A letter arrived from Roulette. He tore into it and found a miniature photograph of Laroy accompanied by a piece of bone intended to be a lucky charm. Angelo snatched paper and pencil to reply.

> It [is] with pleasure that I am to answer your kind return letter which I received the 16th, the one you sent by Mr. Haffey.[15] I was much pleased to receive your miniature and that lucky bone you sent me. Laroy, I would not of received any picture that would of pleased me as much to see as yours for it reminded me of old times when we used to hunt so much, and it seems just to me as if I shall hunt one fall more with you. I hope so . . . Laroy, I will keep that picture and that lucky bone, and when I fall they fall with me. I suppose you have received my likeness. If not it is at father's and you must get it.[16]

Angelo also notified Laroy that forty-five recruits had arrived in camp, among them a recovered Charlie Robbins. The new men shouted Angelo out of a sound sleep, and they all celebrated the reunion. "I tell you, Laroy," he wrote, "I received them with a cordial welcome . . . They are all well but I know some of them can't stand it for it is a hard life . . . I stand it first rate."[17]

Angelo continued to laugh off days of marching and sleeping in the rain because, he told Laroy, western Virginia was "some of the pretti-

---

14. *Tioga County Agitator,* Aug. 7, 1861, "Col. Crocket" to the *Agitator,* letter dated July 31, 1861. When returning to Harrisburg, the regiment had to camp outside the city. The returning three-month soldiers were rioting because they had received discharges but no pay. Somehow, the Bucktails have taken the blame for this violence, which was impossible since they were far from Harrisburg at the time it began. On October 22, 1997, Harrisburg mayor Stephen Reed issued a proclamation giving a Bucktail reenactment group permission to return to the city, a symbolic reversal of a ban allegedly issued in 1861 by then mayor William Kepner. No documentation was found to support this ban. In 1998, the author phoned Mayor Reed's office and was referred to the office of state legislator Stephen Readshaw as the source of the story. Representative Readshaw's assistant named her source as two prominent historians at the Gettysburg National Military Park, but both denied saying any such thing.

15. CMSR and Pension of John Haffey, Co. I, 1st Pa. Rifles Sgt. John K. Haffey was a resident of Bradford, McKean County. Irish by birth and a minister by profession, he was frequently detached for recruiting service and quartermaster functions. Anyone traveling between home and the regiment would inevitably carry correspondence in both directions. Haffey would be discharged on February 24, 1863, for "chronic hepatitis and large varix" (swollen vessel of the leg).

16. Angelo to Laroy, Aug. 20, 1861, KLC.

17. Ibid.

est land that I ever saw" and reminded him "of the wild woods of Potter." Days, though, did not pass like those at home. They included the
mundane duties of drill, guard duty, and policing the campground.
For a time, the Bucktails guarded mutineers from the 19th New York
Infantry, men Angelo thought should be sentenced "to serve the rest
of their enlistment upon the dry and barren Tortugas at the Florida
reefs."[18]

There was enough free time for Angelo to establish a business. Jim
Landrigan may have started the Bucktail image and Thomas Kane
taken credit for the idea, but Angelo turned it into a marketing oper-
ation. He had the ideal wholesaler to supply him. He wrote Laroy urg-
ing him to get in on the deal.

> This is the Bucktail Regiment and the boys have not all good buck tails
> and our colonel wears them and the regiment will have them. Let them
> cost what they will. I want you to get 50 or 100 if you can and send them
> to me by express. Let it cost what it will. If you have not the money to
> express them with, send them & I will pay it when they arrive. I will pay
> you for them by the piece at your own price. Be sure and get them imme-
> diately and forward them to me. Write soon.[19]

Angelo had plenty of time to hawk bucktails after the Reserve Corps
settled into winter camp near what is now CIA headquarters at Lang-
ley, Virginia.[20] Fighting, as it would each winter of the war, went on
hiatus. Weather permitting, adversaries still felt each other out, prob-
ing for an opening and harassing each other. Angelo took a step closer
to learning the harsh realities of war on one of those patrols when he
witnessed his first violent death in conflict. He sent a letter to Laroy
describing it, a letter he wrote while seated in the captain's tent.

> Oct 20th, 5 companies of our regiment under command of Col. Kane
> went down in the direction of Fairfax[, Virginia] to the Loudon & Hamp-
> shire Railroad 5 miles from our last camp. [Our] men turned at that place.

---

18. Angelo to Laroy, Aug. 20 and 31, 1861, KLC; Thomson and Rauch, *History of the Bucktails,* 63. The 19th New York Infantry assumed they had enlisted for three months only to learn
that a clause in their enlistment gave Washington the right to keep them for two years. At bay-
onet point, they were given a chance to acquiesce, but 203 of them refused (Angelo claimed
209). The prison at the Dry Tortugas off the Florida coast was often called America's Devil's
Island and later would be the place of incarceration for Dr. Samuel Mudd of Lincoln assassi-
nation infamy.

19. Angelo to Laroy, Oct. 4, 1861, KLC.

20. The camp was named Camp Pierpont after Francis Harrison Pierpont, the governor of
"Loyal Virginia."

There was about 50 Rebel cavalry which were on picket. They were guarding the railroad. A part of Company H was immediately deployed as skirmishers. About [?] men in all deployed part on one side of the road & part of on the other side. The remaining 4 companies halted in a ravine waiting for bigger licks. I could see the whole skirmish, I mean see our men shoot when our men commenced the fire. The Rebels were within about 40 rods of us.[21] Our men kept up the fire until the rebels got into the woods about one half mile distant. Four of the Rebels fell from their horses but were put on again & got away. Probably they died the 5th. One at the distance of a half mile fell to rise no more. The ball passed through his head. He belonged to the Louisiana Tigers.[22] His comrades tried to get him but our men fired at them and they left him.

We returned to camp by the way of the Frying Pan Road, passing Hunters Mills. At that point there was about 20 Rebels. They asked, who comes there? Col. Kane shook his hat at them & they saw the bucktails upon it and fled like wild men. Skirmishers were thrown out but no enemy were found. We passed on about 7 miles. It was then dark, and our pickets of our camp fired upon us, a whole volley upon us, but no one was hurt.[23]

Monotony broke for the Reserve Corps on October 28 when their commanding general scheduled a review. When Angelo wrote Laroy about it, he was proud enough to burst his shirt.

Yesterday there was a grand review of [Maj. Gen. George Alexander] McCall's Division . . . It was a splendid scene. There was 15 regiments in all. They formed in line by close column by division . . . The line was as long as from your house down to Fishing Creek or as near as I could judge.[24] It would of been a line 5 times as long if they were formed in two ranks or line of battle. Where do you suppose the Bucktail Regiment was? Well, I can tell you it was next to the cavalry on the right wing. Isn't that fine for us? Don't that look like our taking the lead? Well, I guess they are able. This line was formed upon low ground near our camp & to the right about ½ mile. There is quite an eminence of land which gives a fine view of us by the spectators which were gathered up there, some from Wash-

---

21. One rod equals 5.5 yards.

22. The Louisiana Tigers was one of the most famous Confederate infantry regiments. Recruited off the docks of New Orleans, they were fierce fighters and reputedly almost as dangerous to comrades and Southern womanhood as they were to their Northern adversaries. They saw some of the worst fighting of the war and suffered enormous casualties.

23. Angelo to Laroy, Oct. 22, 1861, KLC; *O.R.,* 5:288, Report of Maj. Amiel W. Whipple, Oct. 22, 1861. Whipple proved that he was zoologically challenged when he confused the two regiments and called the Bucktails the "Tiger Tail Rangers."

24. Fishing Creek flows into the Allegheny River just west of Roulette slightly less than a mile from the Lyman house.

ington but no distinguished officers. There was a great many spectators looking & one of our boys heared them say the Bucktails do the best.[25]

He was just as proud of the fact that "bucktails are selling at $1 apiece."[26]
While the Pennsylvania Reserves' review impressed Angelo, Gen. George B. McClellan's November 20 demonstration at Bailey's Crossroads boggled his mind. For three hours, the entire Army of the Potomac marched past a long line of government officials and 25,000 curious spectators who braved a major traffic jam to reach the reviewing area.[27] Naturally, Laroy soon received a detailed accounting of it.

I suppose you have heard of the great review at Bailey's Crossroads of 70,000 troops. There was 90 regts of infantry & 20 batteries of artillery numbering 100 guns in all & 9 regiments of cavalry. It was the greatest ever on this continent. General McClellan & President Lincoln & Secretary [of War Simon] Cameron & [Secretary of State William Henry] Seward & several princes & staff took position at the right wing upon a little eminence overlooking the whole army & then passed along the lines & then took his former position . . . There the bugle was sounded & then the divisions marched past the general & president. McCall's Division was the division on the right and the Bucktails were the first to pass inspection & and you may guess Angelo took a good squint at the general & Rail Splitter [Lincoln] & the ladies but kept the position of a soldier. Our regiment done good marching & the *N.Y. Herald* gave us credit . . . Returned to camp about dark. Our march was 16 miles that day & I saw the rebel earth works at Munson Hill & many wonders. Oh yes, I forgot to say that the cannon roared like thunder when the salute of 20 batteries were fired.[28]

His monthly pay was one thing that did not please him.

Laroy, you wanted to know what office I hold. I am corporal. I get $13 per month. The last act of Congress raised the pay of privates to corporal's

---

25. Angelo to Laroy, Oct. 30, 1861, KLC.
26. Ibid., Oct. 22, 1861.
27. Bailey's Crossroads, aka Bailey's Corners and Ball's Crossroads, is located in Virginia eight miles southwest of Washington at the intersection of modern-day routes 7 and 244, then called the Alexandria-Leesburg and Columbia turnpikes, respectively. The *New York Herald,* Nov. 21, 1861, wrote, "For hours vehicles innumerable, of every description, were piled indiscriminately, waiting their turn to get into the line."
28. Angelo to Laroy, Nov. 24, 1861, KLC; *New York Herald,* Nov. 21, 1861, described the Bucktail Regiment as one "particularly admired for the steadiness and regularity of its movements and the solder-like bearing of the men."

pay which was $13 per month but did not raise the pay of non-commissioned officers. I think it was not right for a corporal has more to do than a private. The pay has always been $2 per month more for corporals & it ought to be so still. But I feel as if I could fill any place where men are needed to persecute [*sic*] the war against those Rebels who are trying to overthrow this government.

Angelo procured some leave time to tour Washington and wrote Laroy about it with the joyous attitude of an impoverished child set loose in a toy store. The letter again demonstrates Angelo's devilish sense of humor, however politically incorrect it may be in modern times.

Well my trip to Washington. I got some of my teeth filled with a little gold for Uncle Sam's hard crackers made them hurt, as the Darkey said when he stepped upon a coal of fire. I saw the White House & the Capital. Well I guess it is as large as your corncrib. I say it is quite a house, that's so. I went into the Rotunda & saw many fine pictures, say the embarkation of the Pilgrims & the discovery of the Mississippi River & many fine paintings. Just pass along into the next room & see the statues & see the Yankee chopping down a tree & many figures that were very fine & the statue of [George] Washington & [Andrew] Jackson & [William Henry] Harrison &c, &c, &c.[29]

Next is the Patent Office. This building is a very large one & everything [in] it that you can think of in the shape of the machinery & Washington's sword & buckskin belt & his uniform & tent & camp equipage. There is not a captain in the army that has as poor [a] uniform & sword belt as Washington & I saw a musket that was presented to James Buchanan by the Emperor of Moravia & it was stuck full of little stones called diamonds. It was a flintlock & a whole stocked concern about as long as a shooting match, say 7 feet in length. I saw the Declaration of Independence written by [Thomas] Jefferson & J[ohn] Q[uincy] Adams [*sic*] and many things too numerous to mention.[30]

Yesterday this company was on guard until 12 o'clock today . . . I will tell you of a drunken Irishman who had to be tied hand & foot & gagged to keep him still & so he had a pair of no. 10 boots on & his feet was very small & when I looked after the Irishman, I found his boots tied together

---

29. Angelo to Laroy, Nov. 24, 1861, KLC.

30. Angelo compared President Buchanan's rifle with a contest rifle that had a long barrel, that is, the "shooting match" gun. "Whole stocked" means that the weapon was wooden to the muzzle. Angelo's knowledge of history was shaky, though. John Quincy Adams was just shy of his ninth birthday when his father, John Adams, assisted Thomas Jefferson in writing the Declaration of Independence.

all right but he had eloped barefooted. Fortunately a guard halted him. I rearrested him & took and tied him again & not far from the place where he was tied. Jimmy, a companion of his, happened to be in the same fire. Pat called to Jimmy saying, "Are ye going to be after staying here all night? Say, Pat, call the corporal of the guard No. 3. We'll be after making them some trouble . . ." It would of made you laugh like split if you could of heared the fun.[31]

In the time between the two reviews, Northern troops suffered a humiliating defeat near Leesburg, Virginia, on a precipitous cliff overlooking the Potomac River. While the battle was nowhere near the scope of Bull Run, it was shocking due to the death of an officer who was Abraham Lincoln's friend. The Bucktails were not involved, but the incident unnerved Angelo.

I suppose you have the whole act of the battle at Balls Bluff. I think it was a bad move for there was no troops to support Col. [Edward Dickinson] Baker in that terrible battle. There we were within 10 miles of the scene of action & could hear the cannons send forth their terrible notes of death. We still lay as you might say, slumbering, while our fellow comrades were being slaughtered by great superiority of numbers. If we had of moved on to Leesburg we could of formed a junction with [Gen. Nathaniel] Banks & it would have saved that battle, but that day was not to be a day of general battle or it would of been done. I hear that the rebels are falling back from Fairfax.[32]

Angelo closed one of the longest letters he ever wrote with: "This may be the last letter & it is a short one. Write one as short. Send them bucktails double quick."[33] To another letter, he added a postscript for Thankful Lyman, who had sent him a few encouraging words. As he had in previous letters and would again, he feels the need to justify his decision to enlist.

---

31. As this story shows, Civil War ethnic humor was not limited to blacks. The Irish were especially susceptible to stereotyping, as were Germans, particularly those who were recent immigrants.

32. Angelo to Laroy, Oct. 30, 1861, KLC. Angelo either used the wrong date in the letter heading, forgot what day it was, or wrote the letter after midnight on the 30th because he considered the 28th to be "yesterday." *O.R.*, 5:32–33, Report of Maj. Gen. George B. McClellan, Aug. 4, 1863. Ball's Bluff cost 921 Union casualties, mostly captured. That casualty figure would create little stir later in the war, but in that phase it stunned the North. Bruce Catton relates the tale of Ball's Bluff in his inimitable fashion in *Mr. Lincoln's Army*. The South did not have "great superiority of numbers." See also Warner, *Generals in Blue*, 480–81.

33. Angelo to Laroy, Oct. 30, 1861, KLC.

Thankful, I was very happy to receive a line from you & hope this letter will be received by you as from one that is ever true to his word & one that is unaccommodated by tables to write upon or the comfortable fireplace & such necessaries which camp life does not afford. I am in a little tent 7 feet square with 4 comrades who are busily engaged in writing. Every now & then I get a thump against my elbow and therefore if you can read this, you will do well. You may think it quite strange my enlisting when I did. I did not enlist because others were enlisting but I thought it was my duty & I am still of the same opinion & am not sorry in the least.[34]

Angelo's early days in the military demonstrate that army life apparently agreed with him, however distasteful it was to almost everyone else. Ironically, pacifist Laroy Lyman had inadvertently turned Angelo into the consummate soldier. But death was becoming familiar even without his firing a shot at the enemy or they shooting at him. He had already witnessed men die by accident, poison, suicide, disease, and skirmishing. So far, he had experienced nothing that would likely send a healthy young man onto a pathway to hell.

That was about to change.

---

34. Iibd., Nov. 24, 1861.

5

Fight!

In a battle all you need to make you fight is a little hot blood and
the knowledge that it's more dangerous to lose than to win.
—George Bernard Shaw

BRIG. GEN. JAMES EWELL BROWN STUART'S FORCE MOVED CAUTIOUSLY
toward Dranesville, Virginia. "Jeb" Stuart had not yet reached his
zenith of fame. He would ride the crest of that wave a few months
later after his cavalry pulled off a daring ride around a befuddled
Union army. On December 20, 1861, he was still a competent but relatively unknown (to the North) Confederate cavalry commander
charged with protecting a wagon train on a foraging expedition. Four
regiments of infantry and a battery of artillery supported Stuart's gro-
cery-shopping mission. His men were edgy. Rumors abounded that
the Yankees had fired artillery rounds at carriages transporting inno-
cent women. Such tales, whether true or not, surely stirred Stuart's
cavaliers to revenge.[1]

Yankee general Edward Otho Cresap Ord was about to give Stuart's
men the opportunity to vent their rage. Ord had caught wind of the
Rebel movement and ordered troops forward to meet them. The
Bucktails were not under his direct command, but they had impressed
the general enough that he requested them for his lead regiment.
The boys left the camp they called "Bucktail City" about 6:00 AM.[2]
Reaching the vicinity of Dranesville, they took position on "the first
high ground north of the turnpike fork" and saw their first Confed-

---

1. *O.R.*, 5:490–93, Report of Brig. Gen. J. E. B. Stuart, Dec. 23, 1861; 1:999, D. H. Hill to Gen.
G. T. Beauregard, Dec. 16, 1861. The village of Dranesville, Virginia, lies northwest of Washington on the Leesburg Pike, today's Route 7.
2. *O.R.*, 5:477–80, Report of Brig. Gen. E. O. C. Ord, Dec. 21, 1861; 5:489–90, George A.
McCall to Capt. H. J. Biddle, Dec. 19, 1861; Warner, *Generals in Blue*, 349–50. Edward Otho Cresap Ord was a career officer who had participated in the capture of John Brown at Harpers
Ferry two years before. In May 1862, he earned major general's stars.

erate battle flag unfurl. Nearby, a brick house stood atop a tactically desirable piece of higher ground. The Bucktails "double-quick[ed] with spirit" and beat the Rebels there, forming into line of battle amid sporadic rifle fire. They did not have long to wait before a blast from Southern cannon sent them headlong into their first battle.[3]

Angelo's blood raced as he saw the Rebel force coming toward him. "See the sons of bitches!" he shouted to a comrade. He even admitted his profane outburst in a letter to his father, adding, "I felt as if I just want to shoot at them." He got his wish and afterward told his parents all about it.

Not more than 3 minutes elapsed before slam bang went the cannon. I could see into the muzzle of it. The fire rolled out of it with a tremendous howl. The shell passed over our heads saying "Secesh" and struck in a field just beyond and burst. We then took cover behind the house and by lying down they could not hit us for the ground was a little higher. Just in front of us 20 men of this company was put into the house. It took all of the 2nd platoon. My place in the company is at the left of the first platoon . . . We marched forward when within 20 rods of the rebels we halted and lie down then arose and fired and loaded at will.

After the battle had raged for an hour and one man lie just to the left dead and many getting wounded, we fell back about 3 rods. The rebels then thought they had won the day and charged to take our battery. During that time many crept out to their old position. I rose and saw them within 15 rods coming. I took aim at one and fired, then fell down to load, and when I arose they were going into the woods pell mell. One more shot left my gun. They had received a galling fire from us. The artillery was pouring canister & grape into them and balls. Not a few them were fired.[4]

Angelo supplied Laroy with even more detail and spiced his letter with metaphors, calling Confederate cannons "bulldogs" and Union artillery "brass bands." He also garnished his letter with puns.

Well, Laroy, the bullets flew like hail & those big bull dogs barked & howled as if they were bound to bite some of us & they threw lots of little shot called grape & canister & killed 2 of the Bucktails. The cannon balls came whirring through the air & smashing down everything that was in range except a tree about 3 feet in diameter & that got a hole popped into it as large as your head & went more than half way through it. Them tor-

3. *O.R.*, 5:481–82, Report of Thomas L. Kane, Dec. 21, 1861.
4. Angelo to John Crapsey, Feb. 25, 1862, Jean Frances Follett and Family Papers, 1862–1989, Minnesota Historical Society, St. Paul, Minn.

mented shells! Col. Kane said he did not think that they were oyster shells. Well about this time our brass band consisting of two 12's & two 24 pounders begun to send forth their notes of thunder & this regiment moved forward but kept a little out of range of the Rebels' artillery for they were shooting at our battery but they did not do any damage.[5]

We marched upon a little knoll within 15 or 20 rods of the Rebels & they were in thick pine brush & when they made ready to show we all fell down & their balls passed over us & then we would rise & fire & lie down to load. It was load at will & some would fire when they were lying down. Others would rise & pop away. One poor fellow about 3 rods to my left was just about to fire when he fell to rise no more.

I fired 10 times in all & many times rose up to get a shot & could not see any one & then would get down for I did not want to waste my ammunition for no one knew how bad we would need them charges before the battle was over. Well, the bullets came pretty close to me. It was ping ping, whiz whiz & one of them struck the man behind me. It passed very close to me & many more too. It wounded him in the top of his shoulder slightly.

The battle lasted an hour or more, I guess 1 ½ hours. The 6th to 9th [Pennsylvania Reserve] Regiments were to the right of this Regt & took active part in the latter part of the battle. 8 Companies of this regt slowed the fire of nearly 3 regts, but they were down in a little valley & we were on a little higher ground. If they fired a little too high the balls went over us & if they fired too low the balls would strike the ground & glance over. Ours would hit some one if we fired high or low & our Artillery killed a great number. They tried to take our battery but they met a heavy fire & retreated, or what could run. We followed them about 1 ½ miles passing over their dead & wounded. It was a terrible sight. The small pine was so thick that we could hardly get through it. It is scrub pine or Norway pine. We did not have any overcoats or rations for the night & the general thought it best to return to camp . . .

Well, Laroy, I wish that I could see you & tell you a little about it. 20 of our men were in a brick house, so the Rebels fired into it with rifled cannon. The boys that were in the house are from Potato Creek & about Smethport & Lieutenant [Bruce B.] Rice.[6] There was a little house about

---

5. Robert K. Krick, *Lee's Colonels,* 109. The Rebel artillery unit shooting at Angelo was commanded by Capt. Allen Sherrod Cutts, a planter from Americus, Georgia. *O.R.,* 5:477–80, Dec. 21, 1861, Report of Brig. Gen. E. O. C. Ord. Cutts's Union counterpart that day was Capt. Hezekiah Easton, whose men bounded onto the field so enthusiastically that they ran past their designated area and overturned one of their cannons. Easton's battery righted itself and made up for its poor start.

6. Robbins interview. Charlie Robbins was in this platoon and claimed that his great uncle owned the house. Potato Creek is a community near Smethport, McKean County, Pennsylvania. Bruce B. Rice, a twenty-four-year-old resident of Eldred, McKean County, received a mortal wound at the battle of Cross Keys June 8, 1862, and died six days later.

150 yards from our cannon & the Rebels took possession of it & our battery put 14 cannon ball through it & the Rebels left it double quick. The Rebels say their loss is 400 killed, wounded & missing. Well it was quite a battle. The papers are full of yarns about the fight & lots of the reports are false.[7]

After a month of reflection, he had some second thoughts that he shared with his father.

I did not feel very sad to see the rebels lie dead. I felt bad when I heared the wounded groan and ask for water. It looked the worst to see the poor horses some with their legs shot off. It looked very cruel. Well it was quite a battle. The rebels must of lost 500 killed and wounded. It seems very strange there was no more killed on our side.[8]

Angelo grossly overestimated Confederate casualties, but the carnage surely seemed worse than it was to a soldier experiencing his first combat.[9] He wrote more about the aftermath of the battle of Dranesville in a letter to Frank Sibley.

You wanted me to tell you if I saw any arms & equipment that the Rebels threw away when they fled. I did & plenty of it. Rifles & muskets plenty of them & knapsacks and blankets by the hundreds . . . They dragged their guns off by hand for their horses were all killed or nearly all. They left 4 caissons filled with ammunition. 3 of them our men brought away & the other was blown up by a shell striking it. I did not get any trophies for I was looking for the game instead of the spirits . . . There was a general time a plundering, after we drove them from the field, by the other regiments & the artillerymen & when I returned to the battlefield everything of account had been taken such as revolvers & Southern money or scrip & officers trappings, swords &c. The haversacks were filled with nice biscuits that the citizens had furnished them with. Well, it was quite a sight to behold & as sure as you [?] they would get just where I wanted to shoot. Wasn't that too bad?[10]

7. Angelo to Laroy, Jan. 4, 1862, KLC; *O.R.*, 5:488–90, Report of Capt. Hezekiah Easton, Dec. 21, 1861.

8. Angelo to John Crapsey, Feb. 25, 1862, Jean Frances Follett and Family Papers.

9. *O.R.*, 5:490–94, Report of Brig. Gen. J. E. B. Stuart, Dec. 23, 1861; 5:473–76, George A. McCall to George B. McClellan, Dec. 22, 1861; 5:477–80, Report of Brig. Gen. E. O. C. Ord, Dec. 21, 1861; 5:489, Return of casualties for Union forces at Dranesville. Stuart reported 43 killed (27 left on the field), 143 wounded, and 8 missing or captured. He assumed "the enemy's loss was over 50 killed." Gen. Ord reported 7 Union dead and 60 wounded. Of the enemy, Ord wrote, "Their dead left on the field is variously estimated from 50 to 75." The Bucktails reported 3 men killed as well as 2 officers and 24 men wounded.

10. Angelo to Frank Sibley, Jan. 10, 1862, KGC.

3. Angelo's map of Dranesville with map references highlighted by the author. KLC.[12]

Angelo omitted one detail about the destroyed caisson and the three dead Southern artillerymen he had witnessed. He correctly noted that the three artillerists had died when their ammunition chest exploded. What he failed to mention was that the corpses gave him his first whiff of broiled human flesh. Even that may not have been his most horrific experience. The explosion had blown the heads off all three men.[11]

A Confederate general called the affair at Dranesville[12] "quite a serious check," and that was just fine with the North. After the debacles at Bull Run and Ball's Bluff, they needed any victory to kick Yankee spirits up a notch. Angelo's morale seemed high. He had entered into his first battle while "enjoying the best of health," and escaped with body intact. From the upbeat tone of his letters, his mind appeared to be in the same positive condition.

His use of profanity in the letter to his parents is intriguing, not because he had uttered it on the battlefield, but that he told his parents exactly what he had said and seemed to have done so offhandedly. Most Civil War soldiers would have omitted the profanity or spelled the expression "sons of b———s" and let the reader fill in the missing letters, especially if they had been writing to their parents and more especially if his father was a minister.[13] In letters to Laroy, on the other hand, he avoided any expression his mentor might have construed as in bad taste. He even felt obliged to apologize for a harmless remark such as the following.

It would of done men [a] heap of good if the Rebel traitor, [Brig. Gen. John Buchanan] Floyd, had of been taken.[14] I would like to have him in a cage to exhibit in the North. I think one would have to tie a knot in his tail as they do little pigs to keep them in the pen. What do you think about it? I don't know but you will think I am a little vulgar to say tail. Well, you know who is writing.[15]

---

11. *O.R.,* 5:479, Report of Gen. Edward O. C. Ord, Dec. 21, 1861.

12. *Atlas to Accompany the Official Records of the Union and Confederate Armies* (hereafter *O.R. Atlas*), plate 13. The official military map demonstrates that Angelo's rendering is accurate. To compare them, rotate Angelo's map ninety degrees counterclockwise. The hand with a pointing index finger was then commonly used in newspapers.

13. Angelo to John Crapsey, Feb. 25, 1862, Jean Frances Follett and Family Papers.

14. Ezra J. Warner, *Generals in Gray,* 89–90. Virginian John Buchanan Floyd was secretary of war in the James Buchanan administration and stood accused of transferring arms to the South during the months preceding the war, the source of Angelo's disparaging opinion. Floyd served as a Confederate brigadier general at the battle of Fort Donelson in January 1862, but authorities removed him from command for allegedly abandoning his post.

15. Angelo to Laroy, Mar. 1, 1862, KLC; Diaries of Laroy Lyman contain frequent condemnation of anyone using profane language.

Winter was upon them, and that put fighting on pause until the robins returned. In the meantime, the Bucktails had to deal with a different kind of fighting: politics. In spite of his army commitment, Colonel Biddle had won election to Congress the previous October and decided that a rented home in Washington beat a free tent in the field. At least one unnamed Bucktail took Biddle to task for "cast[ing] them off" and "stab[bing] them in the back."[16] That put the colonelcy open for election, and this time the entire regiment would be voting. It was a terrible way to choose officers, and the system would soon end in the federal army, but it was what they had then. Thomas Kane was the obvious choice. They had elected him back in May. Although he had turned down the honor then, he now sought the position. He had distinguished himself with his bravery at Dranesville. After a bullet tore into his upper jaw and lodged there, he bandaged it and kept fighting until the pain got the best of him. He then turned command over to Capt. Hugh W. McNeil.[17]

Kane also had gained enemies within the regiment, with Hugh McNeil number one on the list. Gen. Seth Williams may have lauded Kane's performance at Dranesville, but McNeil described it as "both drunk and crazy," ignoring the possibility that Kane's painful facial wound and the resulting shock to the brain may have affected his behavior.[18] McNeil, though, was not the first person to accuse Kane of impetuousness. Some had criticized him during the regiment's risky campaign behind enemy lines the previous summer. McNeil's motives may have stemmed from personal ambition, as subsequent events suggest.[19]

Others thought that Capt. Charles Frederick Taylor of the Chester County company might make a better captain. Fred Taylor, however, hated the "miserable system of electing officers" and supported Kane

---

16. *Gettysburg Star and Banner,* Dec. 19, 1861.

17. *O.R.,* 5:1008, Maj. Gen. Gustavus Woodson Smith to Brig. Gen. Daniel Harvey Hill, Dec. 26, 1861; 5:477, General Orders No. 63, Army of the Potomac, Dec. 28, 1861; Pension of Thomas L. Kane. Kane claimed he suffered a lifetime of "repeated abscesses in the upper jaw and from neuralgia," as well as double vision.

18. *O.R.,* 5:476, General Orders No. 63, Army of the Potomac, Dec. 28, 1861; Hugh McNeil Collection, 1855–1916, MG-87, Pennsylvania State Archives.

19. Fred Taylor to his sister, Dec. 6, 1861, "Colonel of the Bucktails: Civil War Letters of Charles Frederick Taylor," *Pennsylvania Magazine of History and Biography,* vol. 97, 333–61.

even while admitting that the Bucktails' founder would probably lose.[20]
Lose Kane did, by 223 votes, an outcome that disgusted Angelo.

> I think that Kane ought to of had the office & I voted for him & so did the
> McKean Co. [men]. It was just like an election for president. The ones
> that lied the most & drank the most whiskey elected their man. It was abus-
> ing Kane very much & it is likely he will resign in a few days.[21]

Angelo further proved his admiration for Kane by sending home a
photograph of his lieutenant colonel and asking his father to keep it
safe. He had mostly sarcasm for Hugh McNeil. "Our new colonel has
taken command," he told Frank Sibley. "There has been no battalion
drills since he has taken command and it is hard to tell how he will
make it go. I guess he will pass with an answer." Angelo had at least
one reason to applaud his new colonel. Among McNeil's first acts was
an attempt to stem the flow of liquor into camp. What the other Bucktails thought about prohibition is a story for another day.[22]

Angelo's good health slipped for the first time, and the captain
released him from picket duty for several days. He was fortunate to
bunk in a log cabin, but life in a campsite where "the mud was half
knee deep" could hardly offer cheer to the infirm.[23] He lamented to
Laroy that Christmas had been "a dull time" and dreamed of having
"a good piece of venison to roast," especially since he was certain
Laroy had "killed about 25 deer." He added, "If I live through this
war, it is quite likely that you & I will have a good hunt & shoot at."[24]
A month beyond his first battle, he revealed to Laroy the first sign of
the wear and tear of army life.

> How changed things are from last year. As my mind turns back to the past
> enjoyments it seems like a dream. Who would of imagined that at this time
> there would of been such an army raised in the United States to put down
> the Rebels that have sought to overthrow this government. I hope the time
> will soon come when the rebellion will be crushed & the Union restored
> again. Goodbye my friend, Laroy.[25]

---

20. Ibid.
21. Angelo to Laroy, Jan. 24, 1862, KLC.
22. Angelo to Frank Sibley, Feb. 7, 1862, KGC; Muster Rolls, 13th Pa. Reserves. Two letters
imply that headquarters had taken special notice of the liquor problem.
23. Angelo to Laroy, Jan. 24, 1862, KLC; Angelo to his father, Feb. 2, 1862, Pension of Angelo
M. Crapsey.
24. Angelo to Laroy, Jan. 4, 1862, KLC.
25. Ibid., Jan. 24, 1862.

Winter camp gave Angelo time to stay abreast of the war and all its political machinations. One of the North's greatest fears was that England would come to the aid of the Confederacy. That seemed more likely after a Federal warship stopped a British vessel in open waters and removed two Confederate officials en route to England.[26] Britain protested and threatened military reprisal. Angelo showed remarkable insight when he told Laroy about it. He also included an unsubtle plea for Laroy to get involved.

> Friend, it [is] hard to say how long it will be before this war will end, for England is bound to pick a quarrel & if she does, it will be a long time before it will be settled & I think this nation will be ruined in a minute. All I have to say until then [is] pitch in and let every boy & man from the ages of 15 to 65 turn out rifle in hand & bound to kill them English sons of traitors or scoundrels. It is quite likely that our fleet would have to leave the Southern ports, all of them, except those sunk at Charleston[, South Carolina]. The English Lion may roar all it pleases but they can't raise the blockade of that port. Bully for that. I think that our troops will have to make a strike soon or the Southern Confederacy will be acknowledged & then there will be more trouble. I think that if [our] troops would gain a good victory that they will not be acknowledged.[27]

While his patriotism remained as strong as ever, a small sense of dread began sneaking into his letters, and he still felt it imperative to justify his enlistment.

> I suppose you thought it quite strange for me to go to war. Well, I lost considerable by going when I did, but I am here and think I made up my loss at Dranesville. 500 dollars would not of done me more good than it did me to get a few pops at them. I don't know as my courage is so very good but that is the time it will try one's grit. Many was the time I saw things that will be remembered until death. I am anxious to meet them again. It may put an end to me. Time will tell. I suppose many has been the time the Secesh of Potter and McKean have hoped they would hear of the death of Angelo. Tell them I am as true to the Union as ever and will fight for its protection as long as I can breathe here on deck . . . We conquer, gallant Captain, or die.[28]

---

26. The American warship was the *San Jacinto,* captained by Charles Wilkes. The English ship was the *Trent,* an unarmed vessel. The two Confederate diplomats were James Murray Mason and John Slidell. Hence, history remembers the event as both "The Trent Affair" and the "Mason and Slidell Affair." The capture was popular with the North, but Lincoln had no choice but to release the two men and apologize to Britain.

27. Angelo to Laroy, Jan. 4, 1862, KLC.

28. Ibid., Mar. 1, 1862.

Sick or not, the feisty Angelo remained alive and well, as he made clear to Frank Sibley.

I have not been out of my cabin scarcely any this week for last Sunday evening one of my comrades & I got into a scuffle and I threw him on the stove. I fell on top but my hand was under him upon the stove & very quick I did extract it, and as I did it peeled the skin from my hand & burned it terribly. The back of my hand is a perfect raw sore, and I do not go on guard or drill. I think if there was any chance to get a pop at the Rebels I would be on hand. It being my left hand it does not keep me from writing. I am glad for that.[29]

The first and one of the few of Angelo's extant comments on the slavery issue came in response to Frank Sibley's search for a school project topic. Angelo's suggestion predated Abraham Lincoln's final Emancipation Proclamation by nearly a year.[30]

Well, you wanted me to tell you who to take for subject. Take Gen. James Lane for your biography & your oration. Would it not be policy to abolish slavery before peace shall be made with the South? It has been so called a sacred institution but the time has come when it is no more a divine institution. Well, you may think I am very much taken up with the idea of freeing the slaves. I think it is time for that curse to be removed from the nation.[31]

Angelo's choice of James Lane for Frank's theme seems more a stab at Roulette's peace advocates than any genuine feeling for an enslaved race. Given that Potter County only had fifteen black residents in 1860 (three of whom were five or younger), seldom had he encountered a person of the black race and probably never conversed with an educated one.[32] Racial issues were something Potter County residents read about in the newspaper, and that included James Lane. The provocative Kansas senator had earned fame or infamy (depending on one's point of view) in antebellum Kansas leading forces in which blacks fought alongside whites. However progressive his social thinking may seem, his behavior in battle was closer

29. Angelo to Frank Sibley, Feb. 7, 1862, KGC.

30. Diaries of Laroy Lyman; U.S. Census, 1860, Pennsylvania, Potter County. There were no black residents in Coudersport, the surrounding township of Eulalia, or Roulette. Frank Sibley's letter to Angelo was not found, but the conversation is implied by Angelo's response.

31. Angelo to Frank Sibley, Feb. 7, 1862, KGC.

32. Population of the United States Compiled from the Original Returns of the Eighth Census, part 9, 410–11.

to barbaric than heroic, although his opponents behaved no better. Fairly nicknamed "The Grim Chieftain," he played no small role in coining the expression "Bleeding Kansas." Rebel guerrilla leader William Clarke Quantrill so hated Lane that he promised to burn him at the stake if the chance ever presented itself.[33]

There is a bitter irony to Angelo's topic selection. James Lane would commit suicide shortly after war's end, providing more evidence that violence can undo men no matter how stolid toward death or dedicated to ideals they may be.

And Angelo was about to experience yet another bout with death.

---

33. Dudley Taylor Cornish, *The Sable Arm: Negro Troops in the Union Army, 1861–1865*. James Lane and Confederate general James Henry Lane are two different men.

6
Down in the Valley

In violence we forget who we are.
—Mary McCarthy

As the winter of 1861–62 neared its conclusion, the two armies awakened and lumbered into motion. While Gen. George McClellan positioned more than one hundred thousand men for an attack on Richmond, the Bucktails spent most of April touring Virginia via rail and shoe leather, neither of which offered express service. Diarrhea snagged Angelo as it did virtually every soldier, but he kept his spirits high as anyone could while enduring that miserable disease. After all, a mighty army was coiling to strike at the Confederate capital. By early May, he was confident that the Confederacy would "soon go up the spout."[1]

Every Yankee's spirits should have been soaring as spring drew near. A general named Grant had scored victories and seized territory in Tennessee, much of the North Carolina coastline was under federal control, and the Stars and Stripes again fluttered over New Orleans. But after a promising start, the Virginia theater became a different story. General McClellan's movement toward Richmond more resembled a crawl than a march. Meanwhile, Stonewall Jackson was out in the Shenandoah Valley proving that he should never have been nicknamed for an immobile object. Befuddled Yankees swore that Jackson's army vanished and reappeared like an army of ghosts. Abraham Lincoln peeled off some of George McClellan's troops and sent them to the Valley to stop Jackson.[2,3]

---

1. Angelo to his father, May 8 and 9, 1862, Pension of Angelo M. Crapsey.
2. James I. Robertson Jr., *Stonewall Jackson: The Man, the Soldier, the Legend*, chap. 15, "Victory in the Valley." McClellan never forgave Lincoln for draining off his forces.
3. Ibid. In Shenandoah Valley terms, "lower" translates to north and "upper" to south, relative to the northern flow of the Shenandoah River. Stonewall Jackson suffered one defeat at Kernstown and initiated court-martial proceedings against one of his generals because of it.

Brig. Gen. George Dashiell Bayard, twenty-six-year-old West Pointer and veteran of the Plains Indian wars, commanded some of those Federal troops. He had two cavalry regiments and eight pieces of artillery at his disposal but needed infantry support. Whatever foot soldiers joined his "Flying Brigade" had better shoot straight and maintain a fierce pace on the march. That was a working definition of the Bucktails. Bayard did not need the whole regiment, however, but that was fortunate. The Bucktails were on the verge of splitting in twain anyway.[4]

Thomas Kane did not resign after losing the election for colonel to Hugh McNeil, but the discord between them led to a schism within the regiment. When McNeil went home to duel with a case of typhoid fever, Kane took the opportunity to train his four loyal companies in special battle tactics in which the men spread out, ducked when fired at, and hid behind something to reload. That seems like common sense today, but it violated nineteenth-century shoulder-to-shoulder maneuvers. The tactics impressed General McClellan enough for him to assign Kane's four companies to George Bayard's special force. For the remainder of the summer, the split Bucktail regiment fought in separate parts of Virginia.[5]

Bucktails in the van, Bayard's Flying Brigade marched into the Shenandoah Valley more than an hour ahead of the main army. Horses allegedly fell from exhaustion, but Kane's Bucktails kept marching, albeit with heavy straggling. Angelo bragged to Laroy how he had been "the third foot soldier to occupy Woodstock" and that he had entered the town with Colonel Kane at his side. All their efforts would be for naught, however. In the end, Stonewall Jackson would add more victories to his growing fame. Some of the Bucktails would have to die giving it to him.[6]

꿍꿍꿍

Confederate infantry brimmed with confidence as it nestled into a woods outside Harrisonburg, Virginia. They were fresh from routing a force of Yankee cavalry and were awaiting the next bunch of

---

4. Warner, *Generals in Blue*, 256–57.

5. Wallace Brewer to his parents, June 30, 1862, in William W. Means, *Corporal Brewer: A Bucktail Survivor*, 215–16. Kane's four "pet" companies were C, G, H, and I.

6. Angelo to Laroy, June 14, 1862, KLC, *Pennsylvania Magazine*. Capt. Fred Taylor asserted that half of the men fell from exhaustion.

"deluded victims of Northern fanaticism and misrule," as their commander called his Northern foe. They did not have long to wait. Coming straight toward them were 120 unsuspecting Bucktails advancing "in regular order across the field and hollow."[7] Orders said to hold fire until the Yankees came "within 50 steps." The Southerners followed orders precisely. When the order to fire came, their first volley struck the Bucktails with frightful accuracy.[8]

Angelo survived to tell Laroy all about it.

Col. Kane was sent out with 120 Bucktails & the 1st Pa Cavalry to look for the Rebels & we were out of town about 3 miles [when] the Rebels fired upon us for they were in ambush. We took cover behind the trees & went at them Indian fashion. We whipped the 58th Virginia Regiment & then the 1st Maryland came in so we picked them off like pigeons. General [Turner] Ashby, the notorious rebel, rode in & rallied his men for a charge & he was shot through the heart & his horse was killed.[9] The Rebels charged on us & we had to run, run for our lives for they had flanked us & were like to capture us & we had to run through an open field & we had showers of bullets sent after us. The Rebels were within 5 rods of me when I climbed the fence. Col. Kane was wounded in the leg and was taken prisoner. Our loss killed was 16, 44 wounded & Capt [Charles Frederick] Taylor taken prisoner. Total killed, wounded & missing 52 out of 120.[10]

Angelo escaped unharmed, but Charlie Robbins was less fortunate. A bullet ripped into his upper left arm and broke bone. That usually meant an amputation, but somehow the surgeons did not apply that radical procedure. Still, Charlie would never again be able to raise his arm above shoulder height.[11]

George Bayard said the Bucktails "fought splendidly" and gave them a grander compliment when he reported that his force was "utterly used up . . . except the Buck-tails." Survivors took deep breaths

---

7. Thomson and Rauch, *History of the Bucktails*, 153, claims there were 105 Bucktails on the charge.

8. *O.R.*, 12/1:795–96, Report of Brig. Gen. Isaac R. Trimble, undated. Trimble coined the "deluded victims" expression.

9. *O.R.*, 12/1:712, Report of Lt. Gen. Thomas J. Jackson, Apr. 14, 1863. Brig. Gen. Turner Ashby was Jackson's impetuous cavalry commander, having won his star only two weeks before this encounter. Jackson said Ashby had "personal heroism and prompt resource" but once relieved him because of his men's bad discipline. See Robertson, *Stonewall Jackson*, 866n, for a theory that Ashby's men shot him. The Bucktails would disagree.

10. Angelo to Laroy, June 14, 1862, KLC (emphasis in original). *O.R.*, 12/1:712, Report of Lt. Gen. Thomas J. Jackson, Apr. 14, 1863, confirms Angelo's story.

11. Pension of Charles H. Robbins.

and looked skyward to offer thanks. A 43 percent casualty rate will sober the haughtiest of men.[12]

If Harrisonburg did nothing else, it proved that the Bucktails had become certifiably famous. When Col. Bradley T. Johnson's Confederate force crested a hill at the beginning of their charge, Johnson said that the Bucktails' first volley "was one of the most effective and well-directed fires I ever witnessed during the war."[13] Johnson's men captured a bucktail and proudly mounted it on his regiment's color staff. Thirty-six years later, Johnson was shocked to learn that his men had significantly outnumbered the Bucktails that day. At the time, he thought the odds about even.[14]

How ironic that Laroy, the pacifist, and Angelo, the consummate fighting Yankee, may have combined forces to supply an object that bolstered the esprit de corps of a Confederate regiment.

Unlike Dranesville, there was little time to reflect on the fight at Harrisonburg. Stonewall Jackson was moving, and where he went, so went the Union army. At least it tried. When Jackson felt ready, he allowed the armies to meet. The battle of Cross Keys, located midway between Port Republic and Harrisonburg, began in a ghastly way for the Bucktails. Confederate artillery opened as the Federals emerged from a woods. A shell struck one of the lead men, "blowing him to fragments."[15]

Afterward, from camp in Mount Jackson, Virginia, Angelo told Laroy the rest.

> The battle lasted 6 hours. The Rebels drove our left wing 1 mile & our right wing drove them, so it was a draw game. Gen. [Ludwig] Blenker had command of the left wing. The Dutch did not know how to fight bush whackers.[16] The loss on both sides was very heavy. The Bucktails, 108 strong, were protecting the Pierpont Battery, 4 rifled cannon & two of our boys were hit with pieces of shell, of Co G probably. 300 shells & balls

---

12. *O.R.*, 12/1:676, Report of Brig. Gen. George D. Bayard, June 20, 1862. See also Angelo's letter above.

13. *National Tribune*, Dec. 10, 1881, reproduction of an article by "F.A.B." in the *Philadelphia Times*. The anonymous author claimed that Johnson told him this personally.

14. *O.R.*, 51/2:570, General Order No. 30, Headquarters Ewell's Division, June 12, 1862; Thomson and Rauch, *History of the Bucktails*, 160.

15. *O.R.*, 12/1:675, Report of Capt. Hugh McDonald, June 9, 1862. The victim was a member of the 27th Pa. It is not known if Angelo witnessed the soldier's demise, but he surely heard about it.

16. The "Dutch" to whom Angelo referred were Germans. "Dutch" was an Anglicized version of the German word "Deutsch."

passed over us, some of them bursting right over us. A bullet out of a shell struck within 6 inches of my head in the ground. A Rebel regiment tried to flank us & take the battery but we soon put them to flight, killing & wounding about 60 of them.

Monday we started on after Jackson, but he got away. Genl. [James] Shields headed him at Port Royal & tried to burn the bridge but was repulsed with the loss of two cannons & I know not how many men. I saw the Rebels' baggage train at Port Royal. It was 1 mile long or more, but it was safe for we could not get to it. We stayed all night & the next day commenced falling back.

It is 35 miles from here to Port Republic & 21 to Strasburg. The wounded were all brought to this place. There is 3 very large hospitals here full of sick and wounded. It seems too bad to lose so many of our noble men but the Rebels paid dearly. They lost General Ashby & 1 captain & one lieutenant & over 100 killed & wounded, so one of the prisoners told me that was with the Rebel battery Friday night . . . I think their loss was more for we had good shots & I shot 15 shots. I know some of them done their work for I was perfectly calm and took good aim.

In his last paragraph, weariness and fear haloed his words.

Well, enough of this, Laroy. I have not received any money yet & can't tell how soon I shall. Sometimes I think I shall get killed before this war is ended & that will be a long time the way things are working now. I am thankful that I have been spared &came off without a scratch. I saw one Rebel shoot at me & the ball came very close. Never mind all this. I am ready to meet them again tomorrow.[17]

After Cross Keys, there was time to rest from their "regular wild goose chase after old Stonewall Jackson," as one of Angelo's comrades put it. By then he had probably received the twenty-three bucktails Laroy had sent him on May 13, along with a bill for twenty-seven cents postage.[18]

Angelo was now a veteran of three battles. Two had been losses, but he had fought well. Indeed, Colonel Kane had listed him among those deserving a "reward" for his conduct at Dranesville.[19] He had

---

17. Angelo to Laroy, June 14, 1862, KLC; *O.R.*, 12/1:799, Report of Isaac R. Trimble, June 11, 1862. Trimble assumed the Bucktails had been "cut to pieces" and complimented them by saying that their "gallantry deserved a better fate."

18. Means, *Corporal Brewer*, 215; Diaries of Laroy Lyman.

19. Letter from the Secretary of War, Feb. 28, 1862, Executive Documents Printed by Order of the House of Representatives, 37th Congress, 2nd session, 1861–1862, vol. 5, 18. Angelo's name was on a long list of men Kane cited for special mention.

been calm at Cross Keys, he asserted, and professed that his resolve to fight was still strong. Viewing his claims in hindsight, it seems he was trying to fool Laroy or, more likely, himself. The Rebels had nearly trapped the Bucktails at Harrisonburg. Several of his friends had fallen there, and more had gone down at Cross Keys. Amid the fury of battle, killing is a soldier's duty, which Angelo insisted that he had done well. He had fought fellow Americans against whom he felt no animosity and barely escaped being shot. Now that the fighting had ended, there was time to reflect on the growing possibility of death.

Angelo had written often of how Union forces were whipping the Rebels across the country.[20] Now he considered that a lie, and he was not alone in those feelings. The Union army overall was collapsing Confederate territory and causing damaging supply shortages, but that strategic assessment escaped soldiers fighting in Virginia where things were not going well.[21] Morale plummeted throughout the Army of the Potomac. The lads in blue had been confident that George McClellan's drive on Richmond would end the war. Instead, the Army of Northern Virginia's new commander, Robert E. Lee, had stared McClellan in the eye, and McClellan blinked. Men buried hopes of a quick return home along with comrades in the thousands of shallow graves that dotted the Virginia landscape.

Recruits were becoming increasingly rare as a war that was to last a few months dragged into its second year with no apparent conclusion in sight. Body counts and the return of damaged boys were too appalling to entice men to set aside their lives and risk death. With the recruiting flood slowed to a drip, talk reached the men of instituting a draft as the South had. Many soldiers doubted that men dragged into the army would make good fighters. Angelo held the opposite view but more from growing bitterness than reason, as he explained to Laroy.

> Oh when I think how some of our people at the North talk it makes my blood boil. Thousands of their friends are fighting to protect their rights & freedoms. They will stay at home & plan battles & whine & growl over the losses they have to pay. They do not think of the poor soldiers who are undergoing all kinds of hardships. I think it is high time to crush this rebellion. If men will not fight without drafting, do it at once. Bring out

20. Angelo to Laroy, Mar. 1, 1862, KLC; Angelo to his father, May 8/9, 1862, Pension of Angelo M. Crapsey. These letters are but two of many examples.
21. Richard D. Goff, *Confederate Supply*.

the petticoat guard. Put them in the front rank & then let them fight for their sweethearts.[22]

Increasing homesickness, apprehension, and the realities of war tempered his anger but took their toll in morale, as his letter to Laroy demonstrates.

You will have to put off that hunt until one year from this present fall, if you wish me to accompany you. I hope we can enjoy a good hunt. The wild deer, not man. Well, time will tell.

I suppose you have heared the fate of our army in front of Richmond. The [other] 6 companies of Bucktails were all cut to pieces & so was the whole army or at least the Pennsylvania Reserve Corps & I presume some of the Roulette boys have been killed. I hope not but fear it is true. I wish you would write me how the boys were the last time you heard from them. I do not know where to direct letters to them or I would write.

Well Laroy, I did not know when I was up the [Shenandoah] Valley but Angelo would be numbered among the many Bucktails that have met a soldier's burial. Slowly and sadly they laid him down from the field of his fame fresh & gory. They carved not a line but left him alone with his glory.[23] Things seemed to grow heavy but it seemed my time had not come to go under. All thanks for the preservation of my life to the God that watches over us. No one knows how soon some of us will give up our lives for the glorious old Stars & Stripes & the Union & the freedom of our children & friends who are near & dear to us.[24]

✺

A new general burst onto the scene, one destined to have a brief but profound effect on Thomas Kane's battalion of Bucktails. Blustering and irritating almost everyone, Maj. Gen. John Pope took command of an army that Abraham Lincoln had cobbled together from pieces of George McClellan's command.[25] These were men who had known only defeat, and that would not change under Pope's tutelage. His light would flicker out as fast as it flipped on, and Stonewall Jack-

---

22. KLC, Angelo to Laroy, July 24, 1862, KLC.

23. Angelo should have put quotes around this and the previous sentences. He was citing the last stanza of Charles Wolfe's poem "The Burial of Sir John Moore at Corunna." See Charles J. Rawlings, *History of the First West Virginia Infantry* (Philadelphia: J. B. Lippincott, 1887), for another use of this then well-known poem.

24. Angelo to Laroy, July 24, 1862, KLC.

25. *O.R.*, 12/3:435, Order of Pres. Abraham Lincoln, June 26, 1862.

son would do much of the extinguishing. The generals' one-sided
adversarial relationship began in the shadow of a promontory called
Cedar Mountain. Locals called it Slaughter Mountain, a far more
appropriate name on August 9, 1862. Before that day ended, Jackson
added a section of Pope's army to his expanding trophy case.[26]

The Bucktails arrived too late to fight at Cedar Mountain, but the
refuse of battle was there for all to see. "There has not been such a
desperate battle since the war," Angelo told Laroy. Friends from the
46th Pennsylvania, two companies of which came from Potter County,
had been "cut all to pieces." Merrick Jackson, Angelo's stepuncle, had
been "knocked down but got away safe and sound."[27] The day after
their arrival, Angelo joined a burial party and kept a keen eye for the
bodies of acquaintances. He wrote Laroy listing the dead and missing.

> Daniel Clark was wounded very bad, I think fatal, & Charles [N.] Barrett
> is missing & is thought to be killed. He may be a prisoner. None can tell.
> Merrick & I day before yesterday went out to look for him but did not find
> him.[28] The Rebels would not let us go all over the field. We [went] with-
> out arms with a burial party for the Rebels held the battlefield. It was a ter-
> rible sight. I saw hundreds of dead men. The Rebels were burying their
> dead & I talked with many of them. They said their loss was very heavy . . .
> Well it will not do any good to try to write the particulars. The Rebels have
> retreated. Where they have gone is more than I can tell.

After a last visit with his uncle Merrick Jackson in the camp of the
46th Pennsylvania, he noted, "I know how to pity them men. There
is 100 men fit for duty." He followed that with what sounds like wish-
ful thinking. "I think the Rebels will get dressed out soon for the new
troops will soon get in the field." Yet, even after witnessing all the carnage, he reminded Laroy, "You must send me a buck tail."[29]

Cedar Mountain seems to have been the turning point for Angelo.
Dranesville and Harrisonburg had planted the seeds, and Cross Keys
had fertilized them. At Cedar Mountain, they popped to life. From

---

26. *The Image of War: 186–1865,* 2:361. Slaughter Mountain was named for an inhabitant, Dr.
Philip Slaughter. Confederates also called the battle "Cedar Run" after a nearby stream.

27. *Bates;* Angelo to Laroy, Aug. 13, 1862, KLC. Pvt. Merrick Jackson, Co. H, 46th Pa. Inf.,
was Lura Crapsey's brother.

28. CMSRs of Daniel Clark and Charles N. Barrett, Co. H, 46th Pa. Inf.; U.S. Census, 1860,
Pa., Potter and McKean counties. Pvt. Daniel Clark, a resident of Potter County's Hebron Township, died of his wounds August 20, 1862. First Sgt. Charles N. Barrett, an 1870 resident of Liberty, McKean Company, survived to muster out July 16, 1865, at the rank of second lieutenant.

29. Angelo to Laroy, Aug. 13, 1862, KLC.

then on, his letters would never again contain his old jaunty attitude, and there would be no more humor. Increasingly, his writing reflected a growing fury against those whose support of the war he deemed to be weak. Those feelings were not unique to Angelo. As a Pennsylvania newspaper bluntly put it, after all the death and misery of wounded men "we may congratulate ourselves that the army is now safe and Washington safe; but so alas is the enemy, so is Richmond. There were 'great expectations,' little results."[30]

In retrospect, we can see the raw material of Angelo's destruction. The blessing of good health he had enjoyed since enlistment had already disintegrated and would continue on a downward spiral. However much he deluded himself that the Confederacy was nearing its end, his words show that he had begun to realize that his enemy would not give up easily, if ever.[31]

By the time the Bucktails left Cedar Mountain, Angelo Crapsey was well down the pathway to hell.

---

30. *Indiana Messenger,* Sept. 10, 1862.

31. Bell Irvin Wiley, *The Life of Billy Yank: The Common Soldier of the Union,* 275–95. Accounts of drooping morale in the Union army during 1862–63 are many, but the venerable Dr. Wiley's account adequately covers the topic.

7

Closer to Darkness

All is well, provided the light returns and the eclipse does not become endless night.

—Victor Hugo

CATLETT'S STATION WAS JUST A CLUSTER OF BUILDINGS IN CENTRAL VIRginia that comprised a rail station along the Orange and Alexandria Railroad. As with most railroads and the stations that served them, war had elevated its significance. Gen. John Pope pitched his headquarters there on the evening of August 22, 1862, but spent the night elsewhere, a fortuitous move for the general as events were about to prove.

The night remained deep black following a recent thunderstorm, and another rumbled in the distance. Another wave of thunder and lightning was approaching, but the real threat remained unseen and walked on two legs. Jeb Stuart and his cavalrymen were about to descend on Catlett's Station. A week before, John Pope's men had stolen Stuart's favorite hat and had come within an inch of stealing him. Retrieving the hat would provide a little dessert to the main course of striking down the hated Pope.[1]

Thomas Kane, fresh from captivity, was getting around on crutches while recuperating from the injuries he suffered at Harrisonburg. Breathing was not easy either after a Rebel soldier gun-butted him in the chest there. He had responsibility for security that night but put

---

1. *O.R.*, 12/2:50–52, General Orders, Headquarters, Army of Virginia, July 10–23, 1862. The South hated Pope because of a series of harsh general orders he issued. One told his men to live off the land but compensate only loyal Union citizens. Another held residents of the Shenandoah Valley financially responsible for damages to federal resources within a radius of five miles from any destructive incident. A third ordered the arrest of Southern males refusing to sign an oath of allegiance. *The Wartime Papers of Robert E. Lee,* ed. by Clifford Dowdey and Louis H. Manarin, 240. Robert E. Lee called Pope a "miscreant," a virtual profanity coming from the usually reserved Lee. William Willis Blackford, *War Years with Jeb Stuart,* 96. Blackford labeled Pope an "inflated gas bag."

only fifteen of his Bucktails on guard duty. General Pope later said he had thought that "amply sufficient," but he and Kane were both wrong. Stuart's men snatched the hapless fifteen before any of them could sound an alarm. That left 1,500 eager Rebel cavalrymen with nothing between them and a Union camp of 300 clueless Federals who were innocently polishing off a last cup of brew before crawling into their tents for a night's sleep that would never be.[2]

A bugle call raped the calm, and Stuart's horsemen roared into camp. Panicked Union soldiers raced for their weapons or dived for cover. "Supper tables were kicked over and tents broken down in the rush to get out, the tents catching them sometimes in their fall like fish in a net."[3] A soldier in Angelo's company scrambled out of his tent while trying to pull on his trousers at the same time. He stumbled and fell shoulder-first against a log. The injury forced him to shoot left-handed the rest of that night and for a long time to come.[4]

Charlie Robbins, his arm still smarting from his Harrisonburg wound, "came out of his tent in time to encounter a raiding horseman who slashed him in the hand with a saber and knocked him down near the bank of a creek." Charlie rolled into a ditch and decided that was enough fighting for one evening. He waited there until morning, suffering pain in his broken hand. Eventually he would require surgery to remove a piece of the shattered bone.[5]

At the first sound of the raid, Thomas Kane forgot about his crutches and limped out of his tent, his lungs straining for air. Enough of the Parisian rebel remained to override physical ailments. He rallied all the men he could find and formed in a wooded area near the station.[6]

What happened next is lost in the confusion inherent to battle and confounded by officers' chest-beating and cover-ups in after-action reports. A Southern officer wrote that the Bucktails got off only one volley. It had been "withering," he admitted, but insisted that his force routed the Pennsylvanians from the rail station.[7] Kane said that

2. *O.R.*, 12/2:60, Report of Maj. Gen. John Pope, Aug. 23, 1862; Blackford, *War Years*, 101–2; Thomson and Rauch, *History of the Bucktails*, 171.

3. Blackford, *War Years*, 102.

4. Pension of Charles P. Rice, Co. I, 1st Pa. Rifles.

5. Robbins interview.

6. Thomson and Rauch, *History of the Bucktails*, 172; Pension of Thomas L. Kane. Kane claimed that his leg remained weak the rest of his life, sometimes forcing him "to drop on one knee."

7. Blackford, *War Years*, 103.

was some other regiment and that his men, always cohesive and under control, routed the Southerners from the bridge. Whatever happened and whoever can be believed, the numbers were lopsided in the South's favor. The Bucktails had little choice but hide, shoot at what they could see, and hope.[8]

Stuart's men chopped up the camp, set fires, and took shocked Yankees prisoner. A few seconds with a sharp knife killed telegraph lines. A panicked railroader fired his locomotive and tried to escape, but a Confederate officer shot him down in the cab. The train raced away with no hand at the controls.[9]

A booming roll of thunder announced the arrival of a new storm. Walls of rain "as if poured from buckets" doused all fires. From then on, lightning and firing muskets offered the only illumination. Herds of terrified mules and horses stampeded through the blackness while officers shouted orders that went unheard or unheeded. Stuart's men reached the wooden railroad bridge and went to work. Firing a rain-soaked bridge is impossible, and it stoutly resisted their axes. For one of the few times during the war, Jeb Stuart left a bridge in one piece.[10]

The skirmish ended with something to offer both sides. The intact bridge offered the Union side a clear escape route, while Jeb Stuart had possession of the military papers and personal belongings of the hated John Pope. Stuart also had another victory to polish his still growing reputation.[11]

Thomas Kane, on the other hand, had to write an after-action report that began, "I am sorry to report that my little command was surprised." He claimed that he had been able to rally "68 men in an adjoining wood." Whatever happened after Stuart's attack began, Kane's security force had allowed a raiding party to wreck a camp, take prisoners, and steal General Pope's property.[12]

---

8. Ibid., 103; *O.R.*, 12/2:400, Report of Thomas L. Kane, Aug. 23, 1862. Kane claimed the Purnell Legion was the unit routed at the station.

9. Blackford, *War Years*, 103.

10. Ibid., 103–4; John J. Hennessy, *Return to Bull Run: The Campaign and Battle of Second Manassas*, 74–81. There is disagreement as to whether it was raining when the battle began. Rauch says it was, and Thomas Kane's report implied that. Charles Rice said he had just crawled into his tent when Stuart struck. Had it been raining beforehand, Rice would likely have been in his tent already. Blackford scouted the camp before the attack and reported seeing "innumerable fires" in the Bucktail camp, and Kane reported how Stuart's men started fires during the fight. Fire and driving rain are incompatible, so most likely it had been raining earlier but was not raining—or not raining hard—when the attack began.

11. *O.R.*, 12/2:730–32, Reports of Maj. Gen. J. E. B. Stuart, Feb. 23, 1863.

12. *O.R.*, 12/2:400, Report of Thomas L. Kane, Aug. 23, 1862; 12/3:630, John Pope to Henry Halleck, Aug. 23, 1862; 12/2:31, Report of Maj. Gen. John Pope, Jan. 27, 1863. Before he learned the details of Catlett's Station, Pope wrote, "I have just learned . . . that the damage

4. Catlett's Station. Courtesy of the Library of Congress.

If Angelo left an account of this night—it would have been out of character if he hadn't—it was not uncovered. All we know is that he was there and escaped unscathed from the skirmish at Catlett's Station. It was just another night of terror on the pathway to hell.

Nine days after the affair at Catlett's Station, Thomas Kane's section of the Bucktails arrived at the tail end of another John Pope debacle that made Cedar Mountain seem pale by comparison. Northern soldiers were streaming off the battlefield, and orders told the Bucktails to restore stability to a potentially chaotic situation. When the stream turned into a flood, the boys reluctantly snapped bayonets

---

done by the enemy is trifling; nothing but some officer's baggage destroyed." After he learned it was his baggage, he called the attack "most disgraceful to the force which had been left in charge of the trains." He criticized his 1,500 men for not having done better against 300 Rebels, a reversal of the actual head counts.

onto rifles and pointed them at comrades. A few hundred bayonets did not strike fear into men who had just experienced hell, so Kane asked some artillery boys to turn their cannons around. That made a better impression and fooled the Rebels, too, who hesitated to follow in darkness without knowing what power might lay behind those bucktailed fellows.[13]

After all had passed who could, the Bucktails burned a bridge and got out of there. The trek to Washington was much too reminiscent of the first Bull Run debacle. All the while they prayed the war would not drag them back to Bull Run a third time or anywhere else that John Pope commanded an army.

With the Bucktails' arrival in Washington, Thomas Kane ended his association with the regiment. The brass said it was a promotion, and it was—to brigadier general. But politics and rash decisions had dimmed the glow that once led the Bucktail officers to name the regiment in his honor. Kane realized that he would never command "his" regiment. The brigade command and brigadier's stars he accepted should have assuaged some of his grief.[14]

With Kane gone, Hugh McNeil assumed unfettered control of the Bucktails. With that ascendancy came a flash of inspiration that may well have been rolling around his mind for some time. The bucktail insignia had made such a sensation that McNeil suggested to Governor Curtin that the state should recruit an entire brigade of Bucktails.[15] Curtin raved about the idea, and few doubted that he would select McNeil as brigade commander, especially after Gen. George Meade gave him a rave review for his performance at Second Bull Run.[16] Two Bucktail captains headed back to Pennsylvania to recruit new regiments and accept colonels' commissions. Thomas Kane protested, but he was no longer relevant to the Bucktails.[17] Pennsyl-

---

13. Wallace Brewer to his parents, Sept. 4, 1862, Means, *Corporal Brewer,* 316; *O.R.,* 12/2:344, Report of Maj. Gen. Irvin McDowell, Nov. 6, 1862. The original bridge over Bull Run had not survived the first battle. A crude wooden span replaced it.

14. *O.R.,* 19/2:265, 265, Special Order 235, Sept. 11, 1862.

15. *Tioga County Agitator,* Aug. 6, 1862.

16. *O.R.,* 16:399, Report of Brig. Gen. George G. Meade, Sept. 5, 1862.

17. Thomas Kane to Andrew Curtin, Sept. 12, 1862, HCWRTC. Kane criticized the two new colonels, Roy Stone and Langhorne Wistar for recruiting instead of "remaining with their own regiments to share the privation and exposure of their comrades." There are four reasons to assume Hugh McNeil would command the proposed Bucktail Brigade. First, McNeil pushed the idea with the governor and reasonably expected to be rewarded. Second, Stone and Wister, named to command two of the new regiments, were both McNeil supporters. Third, George Meade's commendation boosted McNeil's reputation. Fourth, a letter written at the camp of the 150th Pa. had "Camp McNeil" in the letterhead. See Herman L. Burlingame, Sept. 2, 1862, typescript, McKean County Historical Society.

vania offered these two new regiments no special names, and Washington took the next two numbers available: 149 and 150. When these new boys showed up wearing bucktails, the originals took to calling themselves "Old Bucktails" to distinguish themselves from the Johnny-come-latelies who had swiped their beloved emblem. Many of them would make that distinction until they lay in their graves.[18]

Angelo, however, welcomed the new regiments. They added strength to the Army of the Potomac just as he had been preaching. Some of the names on the rolls of the 149th Pennsylvania were acquaintances from Potter County. Their presence did give him competition in the bucktail market because some of them were also asking Laroy to supply them with the beloved appendage. For a time, it did not matter to Angelo. The heart had gone out of his salesmanship when he realized how many men had bought tails on credit but could not pay from the grave. He gave away his remaining stock free of charge.[19]

Angelo and Laroy had long discussed taking a hunting trip to Laroy's Wisconsin relatives, and now Laroy talked in his letters about making a return visit during 1862. By necessity, the trip could not include Angelo. With that news, the journey became a dream that would weigh on his mind for the next two years.[20]

> I am well and hope this will find you the same & hope you will have good luck up west. How I wish I could go with you. I am not sick or tired of serving my country as long as the war is against us or the Rebels are in Maryland, but I hope the war will close. I am not ready to have it close in the Rebels favor. No, never, as long as there is a drop of blood in my veins. If we hold them two weeks we are all right.[21]

The Union would last another two weeks, but that fortnight would culminate in the worst day in the history of the American military. It remains so to the writing of these words.

---

18. Third Annual Reunion—Regimental Association of the Bucktail or First Rifle Regt. P.R.V.C, 1890; MG #7, folder #0278, Pennsylvania State Archives; Brig. Gen. Thomas Kane to Lt. Col. Lewis Richmond, Jan. 25, 1863, and Maj. Gen. John F. Reynolds to Headquarters, 1st Corps, Jan. 31, 1863, ms. 28437, Chester County Historical Society. The Bucktail Brigade never happened, and the new regiments never joined the Pennsylvania Reserve Corps. Kane tried to transfer his old Bucktails to his brigade, but their corps commander had other ideas and a higher rank.

19. Angelo to Laroy, Sept. 8, 1862; Sgt. Joseph J. Carey (Co. K, 149th Pa.), to Laroy, July 10, 1863, KLC. While a patient in hospital at Chester, Pennsylvania, Carey asked Laroy to send him a new bucktail to replace the one he had lost at Gettysburg.

20. Diaries of Laroy Lyman. Laroy had taken several trips west starting in 1845 and would take more in the future. He did not travel in 1862, possibly due to the prolonged illness and death of his brother Harris.

21. Angelo to Laroy, Sept. 8, 1862, KLC.

8
Bloodiest Day

The tyrannous and bloody deed is done, the most arch deed of
piteous massacre that ever yet this land was guilty of.
    —William Shakespeare, *Richard III*, act 4, scene 3

FOLLOWING THEIR SUCCESSES DURING THE SUMMER OF 1862, THE SOUTH
prepared to make its first major offensive into the North. Robert E.
Lee's men were tired, hungry, ragged, and often shoeless, and the
inadequate Confederate Commissary Department offered little hope
for immediate improvement. Union bullets, disease, straggling, and
"French leaves" all had shrunk brigades to the size of regiments and
regiments to company size. But the always audacious Lee convinced
Jefferson Davis that the political bickering between the McClellan
and Pope camps had weakened the Army of the Potomac. The time,
if not the matériel, seemed ripe for attack. Speed was vital. For the
plan to work, the larger, better equipped Union army had to remain
inert and disorganized.[1]

The Union army did neither. Abraham Lincoln exiled John Pope
to Minnesota to fight Indians and, over strong protest from Radical
Republicans, restored George McClellan to command. McClellan
was not Lincoln's first choice, but he was the only choice available.
"Little Mac's" return instantly invigorated the Army of the Potomac.
They soon were marching with new resolve through Maryland to con-
front Lee's invasion force.[2]

Pennsylvania directed a wary eye toward Maryland, never knowing
if the Rebels would cross the Mason-Dixon Line. That possibility trou-

---

1. Goff, *Confederate Supply*; Robert E. Lee, *The Wartime Papers of Robert E. Lee*, 292–94, 301–3,
307; Edwin Porter Alexander, *Fighting for the Confederacy*, 92. Porter, an artillery commander in
the Army of Northern Virginia, criticized the decision.

2. Sears, *George B. McClellan: The Young Napoleon*; T. Harry Williams, *Lincoln and the Radicals*,
178–80. See also Bruce Catton, *Mr. Lincoln's Army*, 30–35, for a colorful depiction of McClellan's reunion with his army.

bled Angelo. He pleaded with Laroy to "turn out & lay your head at shooting Rebels" should the enemy move into Pennsylvania. If his pacifist mentor would be willing to defend his home state with a gun, it would have validated Angelo's decision to enlist. He needed validation just then. Anxiety had become a constant companion. He closed a September 8 letter to Laroy with the words, "I trust and hope my life will be spared to see you once more. Receive this from a soldier. Write soon. Write soon."[3]

The two sections of Bucktails reunited on September 9. The gathering raised spirits until the men realized how many comrades' faces were not present. Barely four hundred of the original one thousand remained, and many of them were too sick or injured to fight.[4] But the six companies had elevated the regiment's firepower. They had spent a bloody June day outside Richmond fighting beside a select force of sharpshooters under the command of Hiram Berdan. His men used a breech-loading rifle that could fire more often than the typical muzzleloader's three shots per minute. The Bucktails let it be known that they were also in the sharpshooter class, bragging they had a man "who can hit a mark six inches square nine times out of ten at a distance of 1,000 yards." The Ordnance Department came through with a firearm worthy of a rifle regiment. The Bucktails were going to need them soon.[5]

On the morning of September 14, George McClellan's army uncoiled in the valley below South Mountain in central Maryland. Two roads wound their way up the slope, one toward Fox's Gap to their left and the other straight ahead to Turner's Gap. The Bucktails' segment of the Union army went to the right of the line to attack Turner's Gap from the flank. History remembers this area by no unique name, but the men there endured combat as terrible as anyone that day. Once more, Angelo escaped without a physical scratch and was able to relate his experiences to Laroy.

---

3. Angelo to Laroy, Sept. 8, 1862, KLC.

4. Letters and Telegrams Sent June–Aug 1862, Army of Virginia, 1862, RG-393, 67, NARA; Muster Rolls of the 1st Pa. Rifles, morning reports. Kane's battalion counted 201 on August 15; the other six companies counted 230 on September 5. The number available for combat duty was undoubtedly less. Special Orders No. 2, Letter and Telegrams Sent June–Aug. 1862, Army of Virginia, 1862. As early as July 24, Washington had tried to return Bayard's force to the Army of the Potomac and reunite the Bucktails, but John Pope refused, stating, "[Bayard] cannot be dispensed with . . . in the front of our lines."

5. The quote on the Bucktails' marksmanship is from *Adams Sentinel and General Advertiser,* Aug. 14, 1861. The accuracy of the claim remains unproven.

Well, Laroy, I will tell you a little of the great battles which I have been engaged in of late in which so many of our noble men have been laid cold in death & so many thousands are crippled for life. The 12th [of September] we drew new Sharps Rifles, breechloaders & good ones too. The 14th I tried mine at the battle at South Mountain. Artillery dueling commenced in the forenoon. The Rebels had command of the pass in the mountain & had their army upon the mountain. General [Ambrose E.] Burnside engaged them on the left slightly & at 4 o'clock P.M. [Maj.] Gen. [Joseph] Hooker engaged them on their left, being our right. The Pennsylvania Reserve was under Hooker & we were the extreme right.[6]

The Bucktails were thrown forward as skirmishers. It looked like a task to storm the mountain for it was very steep & more than one mile to the top of it. In we went. Company I was reserve awhile & the Rebels shelled us, wounding 3 of our men, 2 of which died that night. My right hand man was one to fall. Soon after this we were deployed & 3 with me were posted behind a rock wall. [Cpl.] W[allace] Brewer & [Pvt.] L[eslie] Bard & [Pvt.] Hero Bloom were with me. The Rebels were behind a fence & rocks. Bard was wounded & Brewer helped him away & soon Bloom was shot by my side. He died that night. [Pvt. A. Delos] Northrop fell a few yards to the left. [Pvt. William M.] Maxson fell dead within a few feet of him.[7] Well, it was close work. I only got my face and eyes full of bark for there was a tree just on the rock. That's all of this.

Up comes the reinforcements & the Rebels were flanked & they fell back slowly fighting all the way to the top when their left was turned. [Brig. Gen. James Brewerton] Ricketts' & [Brig. Gen. Rufus] King's divisions move upon the center & Burnside on the left & the battle raged until 8 o'clock in the evening. Our Army had gained the crest of the mountain. The rebel host was retreating in confusion towards Boonsboro.[8]

Robert E. Lee's army was retreating but not in "confusion" as Angelo thought. But their situation was perilous. Lee had only part

---

6. Jacob D. Cox, "Forcing Fox's Gap and Turner's Gap," in *Battles and Leaders of the Civil War,* vol. 2, 586. Shelling at South Mountain began around 7:00 AM, but the Bucktails did not move into position on the Union right until early afternoon. Angelo's claim that Burnside had engaged "slightly" is an understatement.

7. CMSRs of all members of Co. I, 1st Pa. Rifles. Wallace W. Brewer, Leslie S. Bard, Hero Bloom, A. Delos Northrup, and William M. Maxson were all members of Co. I. Northrup died of his wounds three days later.

8. *O.R.,* 19/1:169–80, Organization of the Army of the Potomac, Sept. 14–17, 1862. Brig. Gen. James B. Ricketts led the 2nd Div., 1st Corps, and Brig. Gen. Rufus King, the 1st Div., 1st Corps. King, however, was relieved of command that day for prior questionable performance, succeeded by Brig. Gen. John P. Hatch who was wounded, and in turn replaced by Brig. Gen. Abner Doubleday. Maj. Gen. Ambrose Everts Burnside supposedly commanded both the 1st and 9th Corps, but George McClellan had removed the 1st Corps from his responsibility. Angelo to Laroy, Sept. 30, 1862, KLC.

of his army with him, which was why he was eager to reach a town six miles from Boonsboro and a ford that offered an escape route into Virginia. They made it unscathed, thanks in part to Jeb Stuart's rear guard. Once Lee learned that Stonewall Jackson had captured Harpers Ferry, he stopped his army on the ridge outside Sharpsburg, Maryland, and stared back at George McClellan. It was a risky move. Lee's back was to the Potomac, his army still scattered, and McClellan had more manpower and superior ordnance. Had McClellan turned loose his army on September 15 or 16, history might have reported that the war in Virginia ended at Sharpsburg. But turning an army loose was not what George McClellan was about. His characteristic caution permitted Lee just enough time to coalesce his forces.[9]

During the afternoon of September 16, the Union 1st Corps, Bucktails in the lead, moved to their right in search of the Confederate army. To get there, they had to cross a creek called Antietam.[10]

At noon our regiment crossed the creek & was on picket until 4 o'clock. The divisions of Hooker were crossing & at 5 o'clock we moved forward & soon commenced driving in the Rebel pickets. Just as we emerged from a belt of woods into a plowed field, the Rebels fired across the field. We moved forward double quick & lie down behind a little knoll & commenced firing at the Rebels. Soon they opened with grape & canister. It seemed as if they would blow us from the ground.

It was soon dark. We kept firing so fast that they could not stand it. My gun was so hot I was afraid to load it but kept stuffing it & firing at the flash of their guns. We charged & drove them out of the woods & they poured in the grape again but to no effect. We were determined to hold the woods & did all night.[11] Col. [Hugh] McNeil was killed & [1st] Lt. [William] Allison also.[12] I fired 70 times & was well satisfied to stop for the night. We slept upon our arms & the Rebels fired several volleys into the

9. Stephen W. Sears, *Landscape Turned Red: The Battle of Antietam;* James V. Murfin, *The Gleam of Bayonets: The Battle of Antietam and Robert E. Lee's Maryland Campaign, Sept. 1862.* See also Mark A. Snell, *From First to Last: The Life of Major General William B. Franklin,* for an account of General Franklin's failure at Crampton's Gap that allowed many of Lee's separated forces to escape and join Lee at Sharpsburg.

10. *O.R.,* 19/1:268, Report of Brig. Gen. George G. Meade, Sept. 24, 1862. Meade reported he was "indebted" to the Bucktails for locating the Confederate army.

11. The Rebels facing the Bucktails, located in what history would later dub "the East Woods," were from Col. Evander McIver Law's brigade, in the division of Brig. Gen. John Bell "Sam" Hood.

12. Thomson and Rauch, *History of the Bucktails,* 205. Hugh McNeil reportedly shouted, "Forward, Bucktails! Drive them from their position!" and then took a bullet in the heart. CMSRs of the 1st Pa. Rifles. Angelo actually wrote "Lt. Ellison," who could only be 1st Lt. William Allison, Co. B.

woods & kept us awake. The general sent orders to [1st] Lt. [Frank J.] Bell to take 10 men & creep up most to the Rebel pickets and lie there until morning. Bell took 10 of us & we laid down behind a log & waited until morning.[13]

As soon as it was light the Rebels sent in their sharpshooters & tried to drive the 1st Pennsylvania [Reserve] Infantry Regiment. We let them advance & when within 12 rods we just commenced to upset them. I knocked several of them & they tried to kill us but we could hold them off as long as our ammunition held out. I only had 20 rounds & we soon were in a ticklish position for the 1st Regiment fell back & the rebels got so they shot past the end of the log & wounded Lt. Bell, [Pvt.] Peter Close & [Pvt.] Joseph Hayter & shot through my knapsack not more than I'm from my back.[14]

Well we just skedaddled & soon picked up some ammunition from the dead & wounded & went in again & soon drove them out of the edge of the woods & away from the fence. We advanced & in came the reinforcements by division & the battle soon roared like claps of thunder. I saw the Rebels come in by brigade with their flags floating in the breeze. I fired until my cartridges were all gone & then withdrew for breakfast. It was about 9 o'clock.

Shot and shell & grape & canister was flying like hail. Men fell like weeds. The battle raged all day with a deafening roar. Ground was lost & won. Victory was ours. 35 stand of colors were taken from the Rebels. The slaughter was terrible on both sides. I think our men killed two to the Rebels one & the Rebels wounded two to our one for they fired buck shot plenty too. This regiment did not have to go in again that day.[15]

The 18th was spent burying the dead & no fighting and the Rebels retreated during the night. The game was lost. They had crossed the Potomac safe & sound.[16]

---

13. CMSR of Frank J. Bell, Co. I, 1st Pa. Rifles. Wounded again at Gettysburg, Bell received a discharge by surgeon's certificate October 19, 1863.

14. CMSRs of Peter Close and Joseph Hayter, Co. I, 1st Pa. Rifles. Pvt. Peter Close survived his wound. Pvt. Joseph Hayter survived Antietam but would die at Fredericksburg three months later.

15. Sears, *Landscape Turned Red*, 294–96. Once again, Angelo inflated casualty rates in the Union's favor. *O.R.*, 19/1:200, 810–13, Return of Casualties. The Army of the Potomac reported 12,410 casualties (2,108 killed, 9,549 wounded, 853 missing) at Antietam and 15,220 for Sept. 3–20. The Army of Northern Virginia reported 10,291 losses (1,567 killed, 8,724 wounded, missing not reported) for the entire campaign. Barrett Tillman, *Brassey's D-Day Encyclopedia: The Normandy Invasion A–Z*, 60. American losses for June 6–20, 1944 (1st and 29th Inf. Div., 82nd and 101st Airborne Div., and all nondivisional troops) were 24,162, of which about 8,000 were captured. In other words, American casualties in one day at Antietam equaled two weeks at Normandy.

16. Angelo to Laroy, Sept. 30, 1862, KLC.

Angelo looked for a scapegoat and found one in Col. Dixon S. Miles, commander of the garrison at Harpers Ferry that Stonewall Jackson captured on September 15.

Laroy, these battles have been victories & would of destroyed the Rebel army if the traitor [Col. Dixon S.] Miles at Harpers Ferry had not of surrendered.[17] As it is, [there will be] no end to the rebellion for a winter campaign is not practicable in Virginia, at any rate with success. I fear so at least.

Fighting, hellish as it was, may not have been Angelo's worst experience at Antietam. He worked burial detail and helped dump the bodies of compatriots into shallow graves. Whenever possible, they carved the victim's name on a rough wooden headboard. Sometimes it was difficult to tell what body parts belonged in which grave.

The day after the battle, George McClellan made a halfhearted effort to chase Lee's army as it recrossed the Potomac into Virginia.[18] When that failed, he planted his army around Sharpsburg and complained to Washington how poorly supplied he was. The respite gave Angelo plenty of time to contemplate his own mortality.

The Army is quietly resting along the Potomac but you may not think [it] strange to hear of a forward move into Virginia & probably a heavy battle. Many of our company are laid cold in death by the leaden & iron storm, 13 in number. Since the 6th of June our company had 14 killed & wounded in the late battles. 6 of them are now dead. It makes me feel lonesome. So many killed & wounded & some taken prisoners. Our company numbers 22 now here. The rest are sick at the hospitals & on extra duty & 7 prisoners not exchanged & several have deserted.

Well, Laroy, I don't know how I have escaped death or a wound. I thank my Heavenly Father for my life being spared this far. I know not how soon I will follow my comrades who now lie slumbering in an unknown grave.

---

17. Cranky, excitable Dixon Stansbury Miles was a career soldier and West Point graduate who had been accused of drunkenness at First Bull Run. Although absolved, the army relegated him to command of Harpers Ferry and never offered him general's stars. Dixon lost Harpers Ferry partly because his position was untenable but also because an inexperienced officer failed to hold high ground across the Potomac. A Confederate shell took Miles's life shortly after he had ordered the surrender flag waved. He was imperfect but not the traitor Angelo assumed.

18. This affair was the battle of Shepherdstown where the 118th Pennsylvania "Corn Exchange" Regiment received its baptism of fire. Crossing the Potomac at Boteler's Ford at Shepherdstown near Sharpsburg, they climbed the steep banks but were driven back in a rout. Many fell to their deaths, and more were shot down as they tried to run or swim to safety through the Potomac River. In 2006, the battle site was preserved.

5. An Antietam burial detail. Courtesy of the Library of Congress.

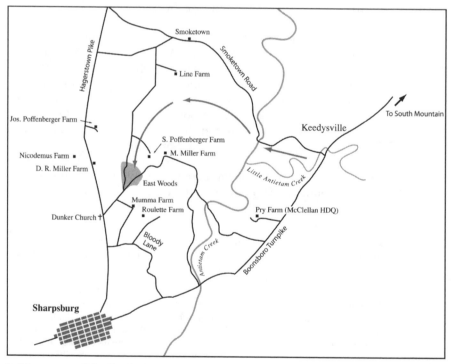

6. Movement of the Bucktails at Antietam.

One consolation: They died fighting for their country & freedom. I can't see any end to this war but hope for the best. I am ever ready to do my duty. Let it go as it will. Many a traitor has fallen by my aim. I know it.[19]

Gov. Andrew Curtin tried to rescue his depleted Reserve Corps by asking the army to send them home for rest and refit. The War Department did not want to set precedent and refused. An escape from war then might have saved Angelo. Instead, he looked forward to another shivering winter locked in mud and watching friends die of disease, ever fearful that might happen to him next.[20]

⁘

While they waited, Jeb Stuart executed another ride around McClellan's army. A frustrated Abraham Lincoln visited Sharpsburg and stood with George McClellan for some of their best photo opportunities, but the president could not goad the reluctant general into action. After five weeks, Lincoln issued McClellan a direct order to move. The Army of the Potomac slogged thirty-five miles in eleven days while Lee's army marched twice as far in half the time and got between McClellan and Richmond. The day after a national election ensured a Republican Congress, Lincoln dropped the ax on McClellan.[21] His dismissal naturally became the overriding topic of conversation in camp. The general's departure gnawed at Angelo, as he explained to Frank Sibley.

> I suppose you are aware of the removal of Gen McClellan. He reviewed the troops yesterday for the last time & he was cheered all through the army & his removal caused great indignation among the officers & men. I am afraid the removal of McClellan will have a bad effect upon the army for this reason. The men have so much confidence in him. But I think Burnside or [Maj. Gen. Franz] Sigel or Hooker are good generals & for all what we know they may be just as good as McClellan. The best man in the world cannot win a victory if the men do not have confidence. I hope it will be satisfactorily explained. I think there must be some good reason

19. Angelo to Laroy, Sept. 30, 1862, KLC.

20. Executive Correspondence, Andrew G. Curtin to Abraham Lincoln, Sept. 30, 1862, Colonel H. G. Sickels to Andrew G. Curtin, Dec. 26, 1862, and George D. Ruggles to A. G. Curtin, Jan. 12, 1863, Commonwealth of Pennsylvania, RG-26, Department of State, Pennsylvania Historical and Museum Commission, Boxes 61 and 63; *O.R.,* 21:878, Recommendation of Maj. Gen. John F. Reynolds, Jan. 10, 1863.

21. Sears, *Young Napoleon,* 338.

for his removal. As for myself I will fight as good under Gen. Burnside as any other man.[22]

An inert army pays for immobility with boredom and sickness. Angelo had set out on McClellan's slow march still battling a case of diarrhea and pining for home and that hunting trip west. Growing increasingly defeatist, he wrote Laroy, "Those scenes will never be enjoyed by you & I." The one piece of positive news was Angelo's promotion to sergeant and the extra four dollars of monthly pay that went with it.[23]

Angelo was not the only one in the regiment due a new rank. Hugh McNeil's death had created a need for a new colonel. Twenty-three-year-old Charles Frederick Taylor, onetime University of Michigan student and world traveler allegedly fluent in both French and German, this time sought the colonel's position. Governor Curtin had given up on electing officers and appointed him. The young man from Chester County, the farthest removed from the Wildcat District in geography and upbringing, would become the Bucktails' most respected commander to date and perhaps ever.[24]

The Army of the Potomac likewise needed a new commander, and President Lincoln put that job on the unwilling shoulders of Maj. Gen. Ambrose Everts Burnside. President Lincoln previously had offered him command, but the bewhiskered general turned it down. After McClellan's dismissal, Burnside assented to the president's wishes.[25]

Lincoln and the entire North would soon regret the decision. By the end of the next battle, the North knew that another disaster had befallen their army and another general had failed them. It took historians some time to realize that early in the battle an opportunity

---

22. Angelo to Frank Sibley, Nov. 10, 1862, KGC.

23. Carded Medical Records Volunteers, Mexican, and Civil Wars, 1846–65, Entry 534, NARA; Angelo to Laroy, Nov. 9, 1863, KLC; CMSR of Angelo M. Crapsey; August V. Kautz, *The 1865 Customs of Service for Non-Commissioned Officers and Soldiers,* 287.

24. *Pennsylvania Magazine;* Thomson and Rauch, *History of the Bucktails,* 27–28; Executive Correspondence, George G. Meade to S. S. Williams, Oct. 20, 1862; Department of State, RG-26, message from Governor Andrew G. Curtin to the Pennsylvania Senate and House, Jan. 12, 1863, Pennsylvania State Archives, Harrisburg, Pennsylvania. The election system for officers ended June 1862, but Andrew Curtin felt constrained by the law that had created the Reserve Corps and would not immediately approve officers' appointments. Thus, Fred Taylor did not receive a colonel's rank or pay until three months after his promotion to command even though he inherited a colonel's responsibility. CMSR of Angelo M. Crapsey. Angelo's official promotion date was November 25, 1862, but his comments to Frank Sibley in his letter of November 10 show he had been operating in that capacity for several weeks.

25. William Marvel, *Burnside,* 99.

had presented itself that, for a few tantalizing moments, had opened a door to victory. One general recognized the opportunity, but only one colleague supported him and then not in time. Had more officers taken initiative, the dreadful slaughter in front of a famous stone wall would never have happened. That door slammed on the Union army and finished Burnside's chance at immortality before it started.

It finished thousands of soldiers, too. One of them was Angelo M. Crapsey, who was about to reach the point of no return on the pathway to hell.

9
Hell Itself

What hour of terror comes to test the soul, and in that terror's
name obeyed the call?

—William Butler Yeats

THE BUCKTAILS DID NOT FARE WELL AFTER LEAVING SHARPSBURG. BEL-
lies rumbled for food, and exposed skin often lost the battle with
frostbite. Some men broke ranks in defiance of orders and roamed
the countryside foraging for anything that might add a modicum of
pleasure to their miserable lives. Angelo struggled with a severe cold,
and diarrhea often sent him racing to the side of the road before he
soiled himself.[1] Thus, he was anything but positive when he wrote
Frank Sibley.

> Well, Frank, I think we will march before night for it looks like it . . . What
> direction we will march is more than I can tell. I think if we move on we
> will have a battle on the Rapidan [River]. Well I hope for the best if things
> go wrong. I think the Rebel army has been reinforced & probably it num-
> bers more than our army. This war is carried on in a strange manner &
> I fear for the army is a large one we have to contend with & the men in
> the ranks are discouraged, or part of them, while many are mad because
> McClellan is removed.[2]

Angelo's negative attitude is striking compared to the boasts he
had made a year and a half earlier. Where once he said of the enemy,
"Let them come," now the best he can offer is, "I hope for the best if
things go wrong." He may as well have said *when* things go wrong. He
had bought into George McClellan's fallacy that the Confederate
army outnumbered the Union, which was never true. He was, how-

---

1. Wallace Brewer to his parents, Nov. 29, 1862, Means, *Corporal Brewer,* 376–77; Thomson
and Rauch, *History of the Bucktails,* 225–26; Angelo to Frank Sibley, Nov. 10, 1862, KGC.
2. Angelo to Frank Sibley, Nov. 10, 1862, KGC.

ever, right about an impending battle along a river. He just picked the wrong river.

War led the Army of the Potomac to Falmouth, across the Rappahannock River from the quiet Virginia town of Fredericksburg. It was an old city by American standards. Scores of the famous and wealthy had visited and remained, including George Washington's family. Its strategic location along rail and stage lines equidistant between the two capital cities virtually guaranteed its annihilation.[3]

Maj. Gen. Ambrose Burnside's goal was to get his huge army across the Rappahannock and wedge it between Richmond and Robert E. Lee's forces. Problem was, there were not enough fords in proximity to Fredericksburg, and bridges had long since gone to kindling. Burnside ordered pontoon bridges and then paced for ten days waiting for Washington to deliver them. Meanwhile, Lee's army kept growing larger and better entrenched on the heights beyond town. By the time the pontoons arrived, Confederate defenses were so formidable that it seemed foolish to order an assault against them. In the political wake of McClellan's demise, Burnside felt he had no choice but to attack. Many afterward granted him the title of fool for doing so.

ᗧ·ᗝ·ᗧ

The men of the Army of the Potomac surely had mixed emotions when orders arrived to gear up for battle. Anything was better than shivering in a crude camp and waiting for the next disease to strike. That did not ease their anxiety. A member of the 9th Pennsylvania Reserve, a schoolteacher in calmer days, made a diary entry he would need three days to fully appreciate: "If one might be permitted to indulge in expectations at all, he might expect a fight of no small consequence before long."[4]

The Pennsylvania Reserves marched into the Fredericksburg area while Burnside's artillery was doing a fair job of pounding the town into rubble.[5] The next morning, Angelo and thousands of others lined up along the ice-rimmed Rappahannock and prepared to cross.

---

3. That geographic location still makes Fredericksburg a target for invasion, except today it is urban sprawl that threatens to macadamize much of the Chancellorsville battlefield. Much of the Fredericksburg battlefield is lost forever.

4. Diary of Robert Taggart, Dec. 10, 1862, John Taggart Papers, 1861–1864, MG-124, Reel 4021, Pennsylvania State Archives, Harrisburg, Pa.

5. John W. Haley, *The Rebel Yell and the Yankee Hurrah: The Civil War Journal of a Maine Volun-*

They negotiated two swaying pontoon bridges and formed line of
battle east of town. That teacher in the 9th Reserves, ever the sophis-
ticated master of understatement, was moved to write, "The sight of
the strong fortifications in front of us, the huge cannon glistening in
the sunlight, and the reflection that they are to be used . . . against
us, are not calculated to enliven the spirits."[6]

From a distance, the ground they would have to cross appeared
almost flat, but experienced observers recognized it would provide
an ordeal for an attacking force. Fences, ditches, hedgerows, a road
bordered by earthen parapets, and a railroad track all cut across their
line of march. These were minimal obstructions in peacetime, but
enemy gunfire would grant them alplike stature. Rebel skirmishers
had places of cover to contend a charge all the way across the field.
Behind that on a tree-covered ridge, more unseen enemy waited
behind well-constructed breastworks. Until it reached the trees, any
army crossing those fields would be a wide-open target for artillery. A
Maine volunteer saw what he would face in the morning and went to
sleep "with dismal foreboding."[7]

December 13 began a third day of unseasonably warm weather that
gave birth to thick fog.[8] As soon as he received the orders, the Bucktails' division commander, George Gordon Meade, marched his
three brigades nearly a half mile downstream before turning ninety
degrees to the right and marching toward an elevated road a third of
a mile distant. They then aligned under cover behind the road.[9] Jeb
Stuart's cavalry harassed the Bucktails from the left, and they called
for help in driving the pesky Stuart away. As soon as they formed and
without orders from Meade, the division and its supporting artillery
moved across the road and prepared for battle.[10]

---

teer, 55. Burnside was justified in shelling Fredericksburg because Rebel sharpshooters were lodged there.

6. Diary of Robert Taggart, Dec. 12, 1862; O.R., 21:521–23, Report of Lt. Col. Robert Anderson, Dec. 18, 1862.

7. O.R., 21:449, Report of Maj. Gen. William B. Franklin, Jan. 2, 1863; 21:510–11, Report of Maj. Gen. George G. Meade, Dec. 20, 1862; Charles Carleton Coffin, *The Boys of '61: Four Years of Fighting*, 156; Justin R. Sypher, *History of the Pennsylvania Reserve Corps*; Haley, *Rebel Yell and Yankee Hurrah*, 57; O'Reilly, *Fredericksburg Campaign*, 134–35, 142.

8. O'Reilly, *Fredericksburg Campaign*, 127. A Georgetown weather observer reported the temperature as 34 degrees at 7:00 AM and 60 degrees by 1:00 PM.

9. Battle of Fredericksburg Map 1, Fredericksburg National Military Park. The Bowling Green or Old Richmond Stage Road is today's Route 2. It is entirely developed, leaving nothing of the vista the Bucktails saw at the time. O'Reilly, *Fredericksburg Campaign*, 141–42. Meade's division aligned about one hundred yards in the rear of the road.

10. O.R., 21:518–19, Report of Col. William McCandless, Dec. 18, 1862; 221:91–92, series of

Suddenly, a fog-concealed Rebel cannon on the left sent lead sleeting through Union ranks. Infantrymen dropped to the muddy ground and tried to disappear into it. This close embrace with nature continued for an hour, enough time to give Stonewall Jackson valuable intelligence on the Union strength and fortify his positions. All efforts to dislodge the gun went for naught.[11]

About 11:00 AM, Union artillery opened and blasted Confederate positions for more than an hour without return fire. No one then knew that the barrage had been essentially useless, which was why General Meade gave his infantry the order to move forward. For once, a charge would not include the Bucktails. Their brigade commander decided they could do their best work if broken into squads and assume picket duty supporting the artillery. They watched as the rest of the Pennsylvania Reserve Corps and supporting forces aimed for a finger of woodland that stretched into the open plain and engulfed a section of the railroad tracks. Confederate guns remained silent. The only sound was that of thousands of feet stomping through mud and officers shouting orders.

At eight hundred yards, Confederate artillery opened, chopping large holes in the Federal lines. Fire came from right, left, and front in a deadly crossfire. As one soldier put it, "Hell itself had broken through." Meade called his men back behind the line of artillery. Once more, human beings tried to assume the skill of worms by burrowing as deeply into the muddy ground as possible. Confederate cannoneers saw their enemy retreating and went "wild with joy."[12]

Union guns opened a second time, this time in a bitter struggle with their enemy counterparts. Shells flew in every direction. Some ripped furrows in the mud and created shrapnel out of the frozen earth below. Trees shattered. Men and animals on both sides died,

---

dispatches from Gen. James A. Hardie to Ambrose Burnside; Fredericksburg Map 1; O'Reilly, *Fredericksburg Campaign*, 142–43. This almost spontaneous move angered Meade, but he made the best of it. The 121st and 142nd Pennsylvania were new, untested infantry regiments recently added to the Reserve Corps' division. The 121st served in the Bucktails' brigade at Fredericksburg. Col. William Sinclair was the Bucktails' brigade commander.

11. O'Reilly, *Fredericksburg Campaign*, 147–49, 152. Maj. John Pelham commanded the single twelve-pound napoleon gun. An additional gun later sent in support got off only one round before Union guns destroyed it. A side benefit of Pelham's audacious attack was instilling the idea of a Confederate flanking movement. This neutralized a six-thousand-man Union force, effectively removing them from the upcoming attack. Its commander was Abner Doubleday (who had nothing to do with baseball).

12. *O.R.*, 21:547, Report of Robert E. Lee, Dec. 14, 1862; 21:632, Report of Thomas J. Jackson, Jan. 31, 1863; O'Reilly, *Fredericksburg Campaign*, 153–54.

torn to pieces by screaming, hot metal. The duel lasted about an hour. Throughout the ordeal, Angelo Crapsey and his brethren lay helpless on the ground as the world burst open around them.[13]

When Meade saw two Confederate caissons explode on the hill and the Rebel cannoneers run away, he decided the time was now. He ordered his men up and out of the mud. Forward they went, shoulder to shoulder in tight formation exactly as the tactics manuals taught it. The Reserves hadn't marched more than a few hundred yards when Meade saw the Bucktails standing firm. Furious, he galloped over and demanded to know why they were not advancing. Fred Taylor informed him of the orders to stick with the artillery. Meade tersely countermanded them. Taylor rounded up his Bucktails and hustled them toward the right of the brigade. When he saw a gap on the brigade's left, he took the initiative to divert his regiment leftward to fill it.[14]

Charlie Robbins was back in ranks, closing out a bad year. Smallpox had struck while he convalesced from his Harrisonburg and Catlett's Station wounds, and a reluctant attitude had put him before a court-martial that stripped him of ten dollars' pay. A trip to the hospital for a syphilitic condition could hardly have improved his attitude. This day, angst was being provided by something more deadly than courts-martial and social diseases.[15]

Meade's men struggled through ditches and deep mud to reach the elevated railroad tracks. Now, they had to deal with Rebel skirmishers posted behind. Ranks had gone from parade ground perfection to jumbled, so Meade halted his men in the midst of a battlefield, the enemy only a few yards away, and dressed his ranks. Once they crested the railway, the Confederates opened with musketry and

---

13. O'Reilly, *Fredericksburg Campaign*, 154–65. The Union artillery this time did some damage to the Confederate guns, knocking out thirteen of them and killing many Rebel artillerists.

14. Frank A. O'Reilly, *Stonewall Jackson at Fredericksburg: The Battle of Prospect Hill*, Dec. 13, 1862; *O.R.*, 21:511, Report of Maj. Gen. George G. Meade, Dec. 20, 1862; 21:933, Order of battle; 21:518–19, Report of William McCandless, Dec. 18, 1862; Thomson and Rauch, *History of the Bucktails*, 233. The Bucktails were assigned to the 1st Brigade, 3rd Division, 1st Corps, Left Grand Division, but their late movement put them into action with the 3rd Brigade.

15. Robbins interview; Pension records, CMSR and Carded Medical Records of Charles H. Robbins, Co. I, 1st Pa. Reserves. Two days after the battle of Antietam, Charlie asked the regimental surgeon to relieve him of duty due to illness. The surgeon refused. When the regiment was ordered on the march, Charlie refused to go, claiming he was too sick. The army charged him with "misbehavior before the enemy," a serious charge that his court-martial obviously took lightly given the easy punishment they delivered.

artillery. Men fell singly and in clumps. Yet, somehow, someway, they kept going.[16]

Meade's division actually had fallen into unbelievably good luck. Fire battered them from right and left, naturally squeezing men toward the center. There, only light small arms' fire challenged their passage. A Confederate commander had committed the nearly always fatal error of leaving a gap in his line, and this one was at least four hundred yards wide.[17] Meade's center regiments climbed the wooded hill and stunned an unsuspecting line of Confederate reserves. The Bucktails swung left, cutting their way through brush and brambles. A bullet felled Fred Taylor's horse, and shortly another tore through his shoulder. But his boys continued and helped to drive Tennesseeans and Georgians from their rifle pits in deadly hand-to-hand combat, the most vicious and personal of all fighting.[18]

It was "a fearful price to pay," as one Bucktail put it, but George Meade's division had gouged a gaping wound in Confederate defenses. The fresh troops to follow would rupture Robert E. Lee's right flank and roll up his line.[19]

The only reinforcements to arrive were Confederate. Meade twice sent a subaltern to ask another general to send help. Both times he refused, claiming he would only heed an officer with a higher rank. Meanwhile, Angelo and comrades were exhausted and out of ammunition. Their gallant inroads could not stand without assistance. When that failed to happen, Confederate reinforcements rained all hell down on them. The Union boys fell back fighting, leaping from tree to tree until it was time for each man to make for the rear as best he could.[20]

---

16. *O.R.*, 21:632, Report of Lt. Gen. Thomas J. Jackson.

17. O'Reilly, *Fredericksburg Campaign*, 129–30. Maj. Gen. Ambrose Powell Hill was the area commander reporting to Stonewall Jackson. He considered the land too swampy to sustain an attack. Before the battle, Robert E. Lee inspected and approved the line, including the gap.

18. *O.R.*, 21:91–92, series of dispatches from Gen. James A. Hardie to Ambrose Burnside, Dec. 13, 1862; report of Lt. Gen. Thomas J. Jackson, Jan. 31, 1863, 21:632; Report of Maj. Gen. George G. Meade, Dec. 20, 1862, 21:512–13; Report of Maj. Gen. Ambrose P. Hill, Jan 1., 1863, 21:646; O'Reilly, *Fredericksburg Campaign*, 177–85; CMSR of John Frederick Taylor. The Bucktails had help from the new 121st Pennsylvania, who acquitted themselves well.

19. O'Reilly, *Fredericksburg Campaign*, 185. Bucktail veteran Jonathan V. Morgan, Company E, said this more than sixty-two years after the battle.

20. *O.R.*, 21:512, Report of Maj. Gen. George G. Meade; 21:647, Report of Maj. Gen. Ambrose P. Hill; 21:512–13, Report of Maj. Gen. George G. Meade; 21:480–81, Report of Brig. Gen. John Gibbon, March 7, 1863; 21:1072, Order of battle; Haley, *Rebel Yell and Yankee Hurrah*, 58; *Report of the Committee on the Conduct of the War*, part 1, 693, 705; Krick, *Lee's Colonels*, 38;

Angelo did not make the trip. Charlie Robbins saw that his old friend seemed "completely done out and could not run as the rest did to get away from the Rebels." Angelo said he had "felt heavy" at Cross Keys. Here, his legs must have seemed like lead.[21]

Charlie did not have that limitation. He raced across the field until he reached a ditch he remembered as a "walled-up canal." He tried to spring over, but the ditch was too wide and Charlie, too fatigued. He smacked hard against the opposite side. Stunned, he hunkered down and awaited what he thought was the inevitable. Other men were leaping in every second, some of them Rebels he wrongly assumed were deserters.[22] Charlie escaped capture thanks to the arrival of reinforcements. Official accounts list Angelo as wounded at Fredericksburg. Charlie may have reported that fact to superiors because everyone knew that Angelo would never give up.[23]

Everyone would have been wrong. No bullet had touched Angelo. He had conceded defeat. The Rebels had given him no choice. The lad who once vowed never to compromise had thrown up his hands and shouted, "I surrender!"[24]

A bullet in the head would have been more merciful.

O'Reilly, *Fredericksburg Campaign*, 204; Warner, *Generals in Gray*, 175–76. Gen. John Gibbon's division entered the woods to Meade's right but could not exploit his gains. Brig. Gen. David Bell Birney was the general who twice refused to accept orders from a subordinate. The unit that drove out the Reserve Corps units in the Bucktails' area was Lawton's Brigade, a group of Georgians commanded by Marietta native Edmund Nathan Atkinson, who was subbing for the wounded Alexander Robert Lawton.

21. Pension of Angelo M. Crapsey, deposition of Charles H. Robbins, undated.

22. Robbins interview. Charles Robbins's memory must be questioned since he gave the interview nearly seventy years after the fact. He recalled fire from Union gunboats having saved him from capture.

23. *O.R.*, 21:512, Report of Maj. Gen. George G. Meade, Dec. 20, 1862; 21:518–19, Report of Col. William McCandless, Dec. 18, 1862; 21:454–55, Report of Maj. Gen. John F. Reynolds, Dec. 21, 1862. Robbins interview; Pension of Charles H. Robbins, deposition of Charles H. Robbins; Muster Rolls. The Bucktails' muster roll lists Angelo's status as missing in action, but both Bates's *History of Pennsylvania Volunteers* and Sypher's *History of the Pennsylvania Reserve Corps* claim he was wounded. Sypher further distorts the account by listing him as "M. Crapsey Angels."

24. CMSR of Angelo M. Crapsey; Angelo to Laroy, Aug. 31, 1861, and Jan. 11, 1863, KLC. Angelo's service records do not mention a wound, and in his January 1863 letter he wrote, "[I] arrived in Libby Prison without a scratch." Angelo made the "no compromise" statement in the August 1861 letter, writing, "Compromise will not be uttered by any Union man." The supposition of what Angelo said at his surrender is based on events after his return home and comes later in the story.

7. Frederickburg from the Union artillery's perspective. The Reserve Corps' charge took place several miles downstream (left). Courtesy of the Library of Congress.

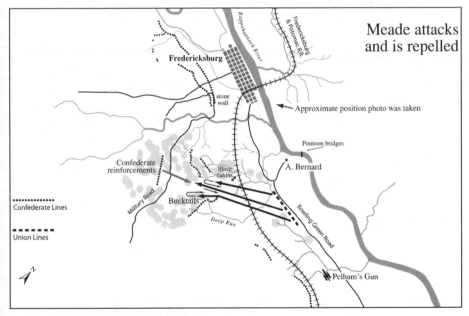

8. The battlefield at Fredericksburg.[25]

_____

25. Obviously, George Meade's men were not the only Union forces on the field. I have simplified the map for clarity.

10
Top of the Slide

It is a silent, screaming slide into the bowels of ultimate despair
. . . a man hanging by his fingernails over the edge of chaos, feeling his fingers slowly straightening . . . [a] stripping away of every
sense and fibre of body and mind and spirit that make us what we
are . . . a mutant creation filled with fear, loathing, guilt and death-
wishing.
—Brian Keenan describing his experience as a hostage of Iran

The train huffed into Richmond and disgorged its dirty Yankee
cargo. Men stumbled off the cars, grateful to unpack stiff bodies.
Those who were injured asked healthier friends to lend a shoulder.
All were weak from hunger. Rebel guards threatened them into formation and set them on their way to a three-story brick warehouse
located at 20th and Cary streets. Behind the building, the Kanawha
Canal lumbered by, its gentle sounds drowned out by the roar of the
James River just beyond. Trembling Yankees filed into the building,
stood for an inspection not always gently performed, and then lurched
upstairs.[1]

Libby and Sons had been the warehouse's prewar name. Confederate authorities had given the occupants forty-eight hours to vacate
and turned it into Libby Prison.[2] The lingering stench of hemp,
tobacco, and fish mixed with the reek of diarrhetic, unwashed men
to batter the senses. Vermin reveled in Libby's fare. One man
reported with just a touch of hyperbole that "lice you can scrape up

---

Epigraph is from Brian Keenan, *An Evil Cradling* (London: Hutchinson, 1992).

1. Sandra V. Parker, *Richmond Civil War Prisons,* Virginia Civil War Battles and Leaders Series,
12; Recollections of Michael Heiman, *York Gazette,* July 9, 1891; Charles E. Gotwalt, "Adventures
of a Private in the American Civil War," manuscript collection, York County Heritage Trust,
York, Pa.

2. Parker, *Richmond Civil War Prisons,* 9; *Gettysburg Compiler,* Jan. 19, 1863, on the parole of
Pvt. Thomas T. Shellenn, Co. K, 12th Pa. Regiments.

on Libby's floor by the peck." Those small creatures competed for space with more than thirteen-hundred captive human bodies.[3]

What food Confederate authorities issued was of horrible quality, and the occasional soup or meat ration stopped after an imprudent joker drenched the prison commandant with water. Only a six-ounce bread ration issued twice daily remained to quell hunger. Angelo sold his boots for sixteen dollars in Rebel scrip to buy food from sutlers eager to sell overpriced wares to a literally captive clientele.[4]

Men could only wait, cold and hungry, enduring each other's stench. Angelo looked for a "sign of getting released." But the South's fury over the hanging of a New Orleans man and a Union general's insults to Southern womanhood had brought a temporary halt to prisoner exchanges. An agreed-upon ten-day limit for imprisonment came and went.[5] More prisoners swelled the population—81 on New Year's Day and 125 more the next day, according to Angelo's count. When prisoner exchanges began anew on January 6, he watched jealously as others left for the exchange point at Aiken's Landing. His turn came January 9 at 7:00 AM.[6] Miserable though his prison experience had been, his three weeks of incarceration was insignificant compared to what men would have to endure later that year and through the end of the war.

Three weeks had been quite enough to tear apart the mind of Angelo M. Crapsey.

On January 12, 1863, Angelo arrived in Camp Parole, Annapolis, Maryland, the rendezvous point Washington had established to house released prisoners until officially exchanged. It would be his home for the next five months. He wrote a letter to Laroy as soon as he arrived.

Well, I guess you will be surprised when you receive this. I suppose you think I am very fortunate in escaping death. I am thankful to be thus

---

3. CMSR of Angelo M. Crapsey; Parker, *Richmond Civil War Prisons,* 22. Libby was actually three identical brick buildings abutted together.

4. Diary of Angelo M. Crapsey, 1863; Pension of Angelo M. Crapsey.

5. *O.R.,* ser. 2, 5:802, James Seddon to Lt. Gen. J. C. Pemberton, Dec. 31, 1862; 15:753–54, Gov. Thomas O. Moore (La.) to Jefferson Davis, June 12, 1862; 15:906–8, Proclamation of Pres. Jefferson Davis, Dec. 24, 1862. Gen. Benjamin Butler, military commander of occupied New Orleans, hanged William B. Mumford for tearing down an American flag that was flying over the mint. When women openly defied Butler's men, he threatened to treat them as prostitutes. *O.R.,* ser. 2, 3:880–85, Alexander Walker to Jefferson Davis, Sept. 13, 1862. Walker called Butler, "[A] brutal tyrant who has been sent by the United States government to oppress, rob, assault and trample upon our people in every manner which the most fiendish ingenuity and most wanton cruelty could devise."

6. Diary of Angelo M. Crapsey, Jan. 9, 1863.

9. Libby Prison. Courtesy of the Library of Congress.

spared to write to you. Our regiment lost a great many killed & wounded. I know not how many. 16 were taken prisoners who were not wounded, probably as many wounded . . . [I] arrived in Libby Prison without a scratch . . . 500 came down in the Steam Ship N[ew] Y[ork]. Some of the men were seasick last night. I am well & hope this will find you all [well, too]. Give my love to all. I will write you soon again & full act of my experience while a prisoner.

If Angelo ever wrote Laroy describing his experience in Libby Prison, that letter has sadly disappeared. Given that the Lyman family steadfastly maintained his letters over the years, it is possible he never wrote one.

Angelo watched camp life pass by and made diary notations as if he were a mere observer. Assigned as sergeant of 4th Company, 1st Battalion, he assumed duty drawing clothing for his assigned unit and apparently did so without difficulty. That did not stop him from

10. The steamer *New York* docked at Aiken's Landing on the James River approximately thirteen miles downstream from Richmond. Angelo boarded the *New York* here for his return to freedom. Courtesy of the Library of Congress.

resenting the duty and considering Camp Parole to be "a dog's life."[7] Desperate to see home, he pleaded with authorities to grant him a furlough. When they told him none would be forthcoming, he wrote President Lincoln begging for the permission Camp Parole would not grant. He became so insistent on escaping that he fell in with the 77th Pennsylvania when they left Camp Parole, only to wish them good-bye at the train station and walk back to camp through rain and snow.[8]

Resigned to remaining at Annapolis, he poured out his thoughts to Frank Sibley.

---

7. Ibid., Jan. 13 and 16, 1863.
8. Ibid., Jan. 24 and 27, 1863.

I have been very negligent about writing for this reason. I expected to come to see you in person, but as I receive no furlough I again communicate with pen and am thankful to still be in the land of the living. I was today thinking of those killed and wounded in Company I. They number as follows: 16 killed, 61 wounded. What a change.

Well, Frank, I am glad you are so fortunate in getting a school and hope you will continue to prosper as well as you have since I joined the army.[9] Many times I look to the past and say if I had only improved my time in study for several years past I could converse with friends and learned men without having them say, "He is a blockhead." Therefore, you will not expect to find any grammar in my letters.

You probably have a faint idea of the life I have led since I joined the army for no one except he has been a soldier can imagine what one has to endure providing he is in active service. One thing I have to congratulate myself is I have tried to do my duty as an American & a soldier.

Angelo then made a chilling and prophetic observation to Frank Sibley. "How many young men are ruined by this war? Many are gamblers and drunkards forever ruined. How long it will continue is more than one can imagine."[10]

Frustration with the dull life of Camp Parole forced this bitter diary entry.

I am not well this morning & went & got some medicine. 3 men got their discharges today & two of them did not have anything ail them. Sick men can't get a discharge but slinks can. That's the style in the army.[11]

He released more pent-up emotion to a friend and Laroy's relative, Almaron Lyman, himself just discharged from the army for health reasons.

Almaron, its a long time since I have heared from you & this is a request for you to write a few lines and tell me how the people use you and how your health is. I heared you were discharged, an act of ill health.[12] If I have not written to you, rest assured you were not forgotten. Many times I think

9. John Minard, *Civic History and Illustrated Progress of Cuba, NY*. Angelo is referring to Frank Sibley's forthcoming matriculation at Alfred Academy, later Alfred University. Sibley's subsequent importance to Cuba is proven by his thirty-six mentions in Minard's Cuba history. See index compiled by Samuel M. Bush at www.rootsweb.com/~nyallega/civicindex.html

10. Angelo to Frank Sibley, Feb. 7, 1863, KGC.

11. Diary of Angelo M. Crapsey, Feb. 27, 1863.

12. Pension of Almaron N. Lyman, Co. G, 53rd Pa. Lyman received a discharge after losing the hearing in one ear.

& say I would like to hear from the other comrades of Roulette . . . I fear some of them are dead. Oh how fortunate your friend has been in the many battles. Many of my comrades who were near & dear to me now lie cold in death, 18 by the Rebel bullets.

I hope for peace but not until the Rebels lay down their arms & return to the Union. That is honorable and nothing short of that. What good would it do to make peace with them now? It would not be three years before it would break out again. The nation is not exhausted yet, nor never will be. "Of the people" will sustain the Government.[13] Who could live under Southern tyranny? We have seen enough of them.

The Rebels began the war. They would of taken the capital & driven us from our peaceful homes. They forced the war upon us & now I say bring every man into the field. Give every one a chance to save the nation. It's not for Negroes we're fighting. If the Negro were swept from this nation it would suit me. Put them out. Make it a free white nation. They do not belong in this country. Put every lover of them out with them and hang every person who is caught shipping them to this nation. Let every state pass a law to keep them out of the state & I will risk their getting far to the North . . .

Well Almaron, what is to be did about that debt I owe you? I hardly know what to say about it. I guess probably I had better keep it a little longer, that is if you can wait for your pay until I return or get killed. If I should, Laroy will settle it with you. Please write soon and tell me what you think of it . . .

I shall join my regiment as soon as exchanged. I have tried to get a furlough but did not succeed. I am usually well and hope this will find you well. Tell Laroy I can't see his letters now a days. What's the reason? . . . No more at present. Hoping some day to shake you by the hand in my own dear native land.[14]

"Usually well" is as positive a description as Angelo will ever again apply to himself. His view on the Negro race had flip-flopped from his previous mention of the issue. That was in a letter written after only one battle, before he began dwelling on death and had seen the inside of a Rebel prison camp, before he had fallen into a deep depression.[15] Abraham Lincoln had just issued the Emancipation Proclamation that some Union soldiers saw as extending the war and adding a cause to the conflict that had not motivated them to enlist.[16]

---

13. The quotation marks are original around these three words Angelo wrote more than nine months before Abraham Lincoln used them to close his Gettysburg Address.

14. Angelo to Almaron Lyman, Mar. 1, 1863, KLC.

15. His state of mind will be further examined later on.

16. For additional study of Union soldiers' reactions to the Emancipation Proclamation's

One Crapsey characteristic endured, though: his Lyman-like disapproval of bad behavior, especially drunks. If we can believe his diary, there were many of them at Camp Parole. Three of them were tent mates who regularly staggered in late at night making enough noise to wake up everyone. He was happy when they returned to duty.[17]

A letter from Laroy at last arrived on April 9. With it came an issue of the *Potter County Journal* with an article describing one of his typically successful three-day hunts. Angelo perked up at word from his old mentor. He even managed a paragraph of banter, albeit a brief one. And the bucktail trade again took on at least some significance.

> Well, Laroy, you have had exceedingly good luck hunting this last winter. How I wish I could of been with you & if Providence continues to smile upon me for the next two years, I will then go west with you & we will have something of a time hunting & chasing the wild buffalo & now & then a skirmish with the Indians. Probably you would not like that part very well, but I guess you would shoot some of them before you would let them raise your hair. You know what I mean. But we will make no calculations upon that.
>
> How uncertain is life. I have given up all hopes of ever returning home until the war closes or my term of enlistment expires . . . That is 13 months longer & if we have the fighting to do, there will not be but few left to tell the tale for the Bucktails. When I look back & think of the past it seems strange how I have escaped the bullets for I have had them cannon balls fall & explode killing men who were beside me & many times little fellows ripping my knapsack or clothes. I say little but not so very little neither, for you know a musket ball is not very small. All I have to say I thank high heaven only for my protection & hope trusting in God for the future.
>
> Those Bucktails you sent me last winter arrived at the regiment & were disposed of somehow. I wrote to the Adams Express agent at Washington this morning to forward the box of buck tails to Annapolis. You did wrong in sending them to Washington, but I will probably get them soon. I think we will be exchanged soon. I hope so at least.
>
> Well I guess I will have to write. Hate a letter. I receive many letters & it is no little trouble to write so many, but rest assured a letter from Roulette is welcome any time. I received one from Cuba with yours & receive one from there every week & one from Harrisburg nearly every week.[18] They

---

effects, see Dennis W. Brandt, *From Home Guards to Heroes: The 87th Pennsylvania and its Civil War Community* (Columbia: University of Missouri Press, 2006), 161–66.

17. Diary of Angelo M. Crapsey, Mar. 26, 1863.

18. Ibid., Feb. 9, 1863. Angelo's Harrisburg correspondent probably was "Miss Mary Gill." The 1863 Harrisburg city directory lists an unmarried schoolteacher named Maria E. Gill living on North Second Street near Walnut, and the 1860 census shows that she was nineteen

are always welcome. How I would like to be with you this summer & even this spring. I guess I could break another bobsled drawing sap.[19]

Angelo then made a plea to Laroy that might have changed the course of his life had Laroy acted on it.

Laroy, if you do not go west this summer come & see me. I will pay one half of your expenses & you can see the Army & get some trophies. It would be a delightful trip for you & it would do you good to hear them pocket pistols fired in time of battle.[20]

Laroy could have fulfilled Angelo's wish because he did not travel west that year. Traveling long distances was something Laroy did often. He routinely visited New York City and Philadelphia to sell deer meat to restaurants and had traveled to Wisconsin before there were trains to ride.[21] A trip to Annapolis would have been nothing unusual, and there was rail service all the way from northern Pennsylvania. Had he done so, he might have saved Angelo's life and spared the Lyman and Crapsey families a summer of terror. At the very least, he ignored a plea from a young friend in desperate need of his companionship.

Life slogged forward in Camp Parole, dreary and boring. The most exciting event in Angelo's life was the day they dismantled their tent and killed an infestation of rats.[22] The army officially exchanged him on May 6, but he made no mention in his diary until May 9. By then, the Army of the Potomac had endured another humiliating defeat at a rural Virginia crossroads called Chancellorsville. Its new commanding general, Joseph Hooker, had bragged how he would bring the war to the Rebels. Instead, he brought the same frustrating results as his predecessors and emboldened the South to attempt another invasion of the North.

At 11:00 AM on May 16, Angelo left Camp Parole, bound for the regiment and friends he had not seen for six months.[23] Had he remained with the Bucktails after Fredericksburg, he would not have been anymore content than he had been at Camp Parole. Washing-

years older than Angelo. She may have been related to a Gill family that once had been neighbors to the Crapsey family in Tioga County.

19. Angelo to Laroy, Apr. 9, 1863, KLC.
20. Ibid.
21. Diaries of Laroy Lyman.
22. CMSR of Angelo M. Crapsey; diary of Angelo M. Crapsey, Apr. 20, 1863.
23. Diary of Angelo M. Crapsey, May 16, 1863.

ton had detached the regiment from the Pennsylvania Reserves and assigned them to guard duty at Fairfax Station, Virginia. The boys had set up as pleasant a camp as possible but took full advantage of their relatively free time. Col. Fred Taylor returned from convalescing from his Fredericksburg wound and saw many men obeying orders when and if the spirit moved them. He immediately instituted new rules.[24]

Angelo hit the Bucktail camp on May 18. "The officers & men seemed well pleased at our return," he wrote.[25] That was probably true, but it is here that wartime accounts of Angelo's appearance and behavior are best documented. There is no reason to believe that he had behaved any differently at Camp Parole.

Charlie Robbins rushed to greet his old friend but pulled up short. Thirty years later, he recalled that meeting and their subsequent days together.

> When he first came back I remember that he did not appear as he had before his capture appeared sort of strange and as if he wanted to be by himself. If I went to speak to him sometimes he would make answer and then again he would not say anything. I know that he used to say that he was unfit to be seen in decent company. [He] complained that his clothes and himself were lousy and called our attention to the matter when we knew that he [only] imagined what he was talking about. Once in a while he would get a spell when he would talk about how the prisoners had to suffer and about the vermin that they had to encounter while he was a prisoner. I know that he always acted strange after his return.[26]

Although freed from Libby Prison, he was still struggling to leave its putrid confines.

No matter how he had withdrawn from those around him, Angelo maintained rational thought about the war and a credible knowledge of military and political events. He wrote to Laroy on a congressional watchdog subcommittee called The Committee on the Conduct of the War.[27]

---

24. Angelo to Frank Sibley, May 23, 1863, KGC; Order Book of Co. K, 1863–64, P.S.A., 276, entries for Mar. 20 and 23, 1863. During this time, the Bucktails tried filling their depleted ranks, but recruiters failed.

25. Diary of Angelo M. Crapsey, May 18, 1863; Angelo to Frank Sibley, May 23, 1863, KGC.

26. Pension of Angelo M. Crapsey, deposition of Charles H. Robbins, Jan. 18, 1893.

27. The Joint Committee on the Conduct of the War was formed in December 1861 of three senators and four representatives. It was partisan Radical Republican, highly anti–George McClellan, and very powerful. It investigated anything it wanted whenever it wanted.

The report of the committee appointed to investigate the conduct of the generals since the war begun is very interesting. Everything goes to show [Maj. Gen. George B.] McClellan & [Maj. Gen. Fitz-John] Porter were determined to defeat [Maj. Gen. John] Pope in front of Washington.[28] McClellan sent many insulting requests to the President calling for troops when he knew they could not be had & he asked for more troops than there was organized at the time & he delayed taking Richmond when he could [have done] that. All of the generals say he could of gained a victory at Antietam if he had fought them the next day, the 18th. If [Maj. Gen. Philip] Kearney was alive he would set McClellan forth in the correct light.[29] I am not down upon McClellan, an act of politics for that has no abode in my brain. I say death to traitors & out with generals who are so selfish & contrary who will not do when they can. Laroy, read that report for it is correct, sound facts, not suppositions. It is founded on orders.

A letter to Frank Sibley provides another example of his still robust patriotism, but it also reflects sadness tinged with bitterness.

Once more I write to you from my regt. I arrived here last Monday & have been very busy building and fixing quarters. Therefore you will excuse me for not writing sooner. I suppose you know that Reserves are in the defense of W[ashington]n. The 1st Brigade is here at Fairfax Station 18 miles from Alexandria & three miles from Fairfax Court House . . . We have a new division general [Brig. Gen. Samuel Wylie Crawford] and it's quite probable we will be ordered to join the Army of the Rappahannock, but none can tell.[30] This is a very nice camp. It's on a hill & the company streets are shaded by cedar trees & it makes it quite pleasant.[31]

It made me feel sad to just think what a company we had at one time & compare it with the number now remaining. Many of the best men have been killed. There is only one man beside myself who has been in all of the battles which the company has been engaged in left to tell of the many

28. George McClellan and John Pope carried on a mutual hate affair. By the time Angelo had written this letter, Fitz-John Porter, a friend and supporter of McClellan, had been court-martialed and cashiered for his behavior at Second Bull Run. John Pope had pressed the charges. A court would exonerate Porter more than two decades later, in part thanks to the testimony of former Confederate general, James Longstreet.

29. Warner, *Generals in Blue*, 258–59. Philip Kearny, whom Winfield Scott labeled the bravest man he ever knew, lost an arm in the Mexican War and afterward spent years in Europe fighting as a mercenary. One of the Union's first commissioned brigadiers, he died at the battle of Chantilly (Ox Hill), September 1, 1862.

30. Angelo meant the Army of the Potomac.

31. Warner, *Generals in Blue*, 99. Samuel Wylie Crawford, a native of Franklin County, Pennsylvania, was a doctor in civilian life. He took command of the Reserve Corps days before this letter.

bloody scenes, and there is a number who have never been in a single battle such as teamsters and ambulance drivers. But if you was to talk with
them you would think they had been in every engagement & even know
more about the battles than those that participated in them. The company mustered 29 for duty, but if we must march ten miles & go into battle we would not have over twenty for actual service.

I can look back upon years past & gone and think of the many enjoy-
ments that I did not realize at the time. One is not apt to think of it at the
time, but he will see after a few years where he enjoyed the pleasures of
the world.[32]

That March, Laroy informed Angelo that he had a new baby half
brother. Even that life-affirming event led to negative thoughts
wrapped in patriotism.

I am . . . glad to hear of that little newcomer. Probably he will live to avenge
the death of his brother if he should fall fighting to protect the flag of our
Union & our homes & a nation's honor. That flag is now red with the
blood of her sons who have died fighting to protect it. Hoist up the flag
and long may it wave o'er the land of the free and the homes of the brave.

By June, the three-month-old baby incredibly still lacked a name,
and John and Lura Crapsey asked Angelo to supply it. Oddly, they did
not make the request directly to Angelo but through a relative of
Laroy's, Otis Lyman. Angelo granted his parents' request and dipped
into his army experience for his brother's name.

Otis Lyman's letter had arrived stating your visit up to Roulette and also
your request for me to name that boy. I will give him a name if it will suit
Mother and you. I will name him after a brave officer & a good man & a
dashing general. That was George Bayard who was killed at Fredericksburg. Please name him George Bayard Crapsey but call him Bayard.[33]

The Crapseys did exactly as Angelo requested except that the family
would always call his half brother by his first name.[34]

---

32. Angelo to Frank Sibley, May 23, 1863, KGC.

33. Angelo to his father, June 5, 1863, Pension of Angelo M. Crapsey.

34. Angelo's half brother, George Bayard Crapsey, never married or sired any children as far
as his family knows, but he did perform a roller-skating bear act with a traveling circus. That tid-
bit is courtesy of Angelo's grandnephew, Kenneth Crapsey, via telephone June 17, 1998. The
author enjoyed being repeatedly called "Skipper" by Mr. Crapsey. Mr. Crapsey died December
23, 1999, at the age of eighty-seven. A photo of George and his bear can be seen on Miriam Robbins Midkiff's blog at http://ancestories1.blogspot.com/2007/11/crapsey-photosand-roller
skating-bear.html

It is not certain, but his parents may have begun hounding him to get a discharge. It is possible they had received information on Angelo's mental condition from comrades. Angelo offered a clue of that in a letter to his parents, one in which he also hints at friction with his biological mother's family, the Barnums.

> I don't want you to say anything to me about discharges. I am bound to see this war through with if I don't get killed, and if I do you may know I have did my duty to my country & to the parents who bore me. The Barnums will never say they were disgraced by me.[35]

The Union army's sturdiest soldier may have been "broken down in body and mind," as Charlie Robbins described him, but he was not a quitter.[36] How could a man who had accused the Potter County boys of cowardice for going home put himself in the same position? How could he give up on his ideals when he was raised by two men who routinely risked everything, even their lives, for their beliefs? Laroy and John had done their work well. Confused though his mind may have been, it retained the tenacity that was a trademark of his mentors.

Angelo procured an "old Springfield musket" and polished it into working condition. The Springfield may have been a much-coveted musket elsewhere, but it was not good enough for a Bucktail. He wanted a Sharps carbine just like the rest of the regiment. When the army was not forthcoming with one, he spent forty dollars of his money to order a new one directly from the factory.[37]

In mid-June, he found time to sneak in a bit of pleasure with an acquaintance from Roulette, another of Laroy Lyman's many wartime correspondents. The friend had recently returned from recruiting duty at Coudersport and undoubtedly brought welcome news from home. They attended the theater and stayed overnight at a pleasant hotel, a night of recreation that cost Angelo $25. It was money well spent because it may have been the last bit of pleasure he ever experienced.[38]

---

35. Angelo to his father, June 6, 1863, Pension of Angelo M. Crapsey.

36. Pension of Angelo M. Crapsey, deposition of Charles H. Robbins, Jan. 18, 1893.

37. Diary of Angelo M. Crapsey, June 4, 1863; Angelo to Laroy, June 1, 1863, KLC.

38. Reuben Roberts to Laroy Lyman, several letters in KLC; U.S. Census, 1860, Pennsylvania, Potter County, 194; Diary of Angelo M. Crapsey, 1863, June 17. Angelo's friend was 1st Lt. Reuben Z. Roberts, Co. G, 53rd Pa. The 1860 census reports Roberts living with Laroy's brother Harris, probably as a hired hand.

11
Depths

Our greatest foes, and whom we must chiefly combat, are within.
—Miguel de Cervantes

ROBERT E. LEE SET HIS ARMY INTO MOTION AGAIN. WHERE HE WENT, THE
Army of the Potomac must follow. On June 25, 1863, the day after
Angelo attended the theater, the Bucktails latched on to the hind end
of the Union 5th Corps and marched for six days through the mug-
giest weather that part of the country could offer. To make everyone
just a little more miserable, it rained three of those days. No one knew
exactly where he was going except that the direction was north.[1]

The Pennsylvania Reserve Corps crossed the Potomac River at
Edwards Ferry and soon were marching into Frederick, Maryland.
News awaited, the same tired announcement the men of this under-
achieving army had come to expect. Joseph Hooker was out as commander of the Army of the Potomac. President Lincoln had given the
job to George Meade, the fourth commander in seven months. Meanwhile, the Army of Northern Virginia leadership hierarchy had
remained solid for the last year until recently shaken by the death of
Stonewall Jackson.[2]

The Bucktails neared Pennsylvania soil for the first time in many
months. In spite of marching twenty-three miles that day, the brass
ordered a special muster. In part, it was for payroll purposes, but it
was also as an esprit de corps gimmick in true nineteenth-century
romantic tradition. The Reserve Corps stood for a reading of a general order that asked each man to "nerve himself for the conflict and
to drive the invader of our sacred homes from the soil which his dis-
loyal tread has polluted." The Reserves obligingly cheered and threw

---

1. Diary of Angelo M. Crapsey, June 25–30, 1863. Angelo mentions rain on June 26, 29,
and 30.
2. Ibid.

their hats into the air. We cannot know if Angelo's hat went airborne. He did not mention the event in his diary, possibly because his company was in the rear guard and not present with the others.[3]

At daylight on July 1, they pressed forward, stopping at the state line for inspection of arms and again at a stream to refill canteens. The band appropriately struck up "Home Again" when they crossed the Mason-Dixon Line.[4] The Bucktails settled down at midnight just beyond Hanover near McSherrystown, in the realization that they would have to defend their home soil just as the Confederates had been doing for two years. The daylong sounds of battle to the west had made that point clear.[5]

The next day they arrived at the southern end of this latest battlefield. Ahead of them stood two hills, the left one being the higher. Both hid the visual details of the fighting, but intense noise and gunsmoke floating above the two summits betrayed its existence. Some of the men may never have heard of the town that lay a mile or two to the north, but its name was about to burn into their memories. The town had no special qualities, just an inconsequential Pennsylvania crossroads community where a handful of skirmishers inadvertently started one of the greatest battles the world would ever know.

At the order, "Fall in, Bucktails!" the boys leaped to their feet. They were going to climb the lower of those two hills, Colonel Taylor said. Their commander, his face so boyish that even a wisp of a beard failed to age him, walked among his men offering words of encouragement, and they believed. When it came their time, they "moved into position in column by regiment, . . . Bucktails on the left, . . . forward to the crest."[6]

There, on a hill they would come to know as Little Round Top, Angelo Crapsey prepared to walk farther down the pathway to hell.

꧁꧂

At 4:00 PM, July 2, 1863, the fields south of Gettysburg, Pennsylvania, exploded. Rebel infantry stormed through a peach orchard bristling with Union artillery and carved a bloody swath through once-

---

3. *Lancaster Daily Express,* July 13, 1863, unknown author but obviously a member of the Pennsylvania Reserves; Harry W. Pfanz, *Gettysburg: Culp's Hill and Cemetery Hill,* 16.

4. Account of Frank J. Bell, Co. I, 1st Pa. Rifles, Library of the Gettysburg National Military Park.

5. Ibid; *O.R.,* 27/1:652–53, Report of Brig. Gen. Samuel W. Crawford, July 10, 1863.

6. Account of Frank J. Bell.

peaceful farm fields. Union soldiers were spread too thin to offer sufficient resistance and fell before the flood of Confederates charging through "plunging shot . . . everywhere tearing up the ground in a terrific rain of death." A Georgia soldier said, "The slaughter in our front was simply beyond description," and another Georgian could "hear bones crash like glass in a hailstorm." A Confederate force pushed over the crest of a wooded ridge and into a valley peppered with boulders. On the opposite side, Union cannons spewed death from a rocky height and from behind stone walls at the base of the hill. Yet, so loud was the din of riflefire and shouting that some men could not hear the cannons' roar.[7] Recent rains and severe fighting had turned the valley into a bloody swamp. Muddy ground tried to snatch their shoes, for once giving barefooted men a small advantage. They leaped a tiny stream tinted red with blood and started toward the crest of the rocky hill. Others before them had died in the attempt, but this group smelled victory when they saw frantic Union artillerists preparing to pull out.[8]

About an hour into the attack, the Pennsylvania Reserves, Bucktails on the left of the second line, uncoiled from the northern slope of Little Round Top. The Reserves knew nothing about Union heroes named Chamberlain, O'Rourke, and Vincent, men who had already carved their niches in history preserving this hill for the Union side. They did know that whatever had gone before them would be for naught unless they held now.[9]

The Bucktails swung left up the hill. Some men hesitated to maneuver through the hail of bullets, but Fred Taylor goaded them up the slope. The boys reached deep for courage, kept their heads low, and asked those shaky artillerymen to hold on a little while longer.

7. *O.R.*, 27/2:358–59, Report of Lt. Gen. James Longstreet, July 27, 1863; Captain George Hillyer (9th Ga.) to the *Southern Banner*, July 29, 1863, vertical file 7-GA97; "Tout Le Monde" to the *Savannah* [Ga.] *Republican*, letter dated July 7, 1863, vertical file 7-GA17; William Thomas Fluker Jr. (15th Ga.), "A Graphic Account of the Battle of Little Round Top Hill at Gettysburg," produced by Terri Lee Fluker, 7-GA15; Maj. M. J. Bass (59th Ga. Res.) to unknown, vertical file 7-GA59, all vertical files located in the library of the Gettysburg National Military Park (GNMP).

8. Samuel Crawford to Brig. Gen. J. C. Rice, Dec. 11, 1863, to Professor M. Jacobs, Dec. 1863, and to Col. J. W. Fisher, Dec. 22, 1863, Letters of Samuel Crawford, GNMP.

9. Letters of Samuel Crawford; *O.R.*, 27/1:652–56, Report of Brig. Gen. Samuel W. Crawford, July 10, 1863; 27/2:401–2, Report of Maj. Henry D. McDaniel, July 8, 1863. The 98th Pennsylvania, a 6th Corps regiment separated from its command, fell in on the left of the Bucktails. Some reports state they charged downhill through the Bucktails. See Pfanz, *Gettysburg: The Second Day*, 396–98, and Gary Kross, "To Die Like Soldiers: The Retreat From Sickles' Front, July 2, 1863," *Blue and Gray*, vol. 15, issue 5.

The Reserves' first line let loose a volley of musketry that stalled the weary Rebels. Then came the order to charge. Fred Taylor shouted, "Up boys and at them!" Throughout ranks, officers echoed Taylor's order. Cheering Union soldiers leaped to their feet and waded into the enemy.[10]

Two armies smashed together. Men pounded each other with fists and gun butts. Union men were fresher and moving downhill, so the tide rolled in their favor. The exhausted Rebels summoned what energy remained and fled back across the valley, over the wooded knoll littered with dead and wounded, Federals in pursuit. The Bucktails swung left, pushed forward to a stone wall atop the ridge, and leaped over. "We drove them like sheep $1\frac{1}{2}$ miles," Angelo wrote afterward. Col. Fred Taylor knew that his shepherds had gone too far and were in danger of being cut off. He ordered them back to the stone wall where he assumed they would find a degree of safety.[11]

Charlie Robbins didn't find it safe. The bullet that struck him pierced "his diary and a tintype and lodged against one rib." He crouched down behind "a pile of rubbish" and prayed this war would spare him further pain. There would be no divine intervention this day. A shell exploded close by—or so they told him later. He only recalled that he woke up in a hospital five miles from the battlefield, left leg broken, and body numbed by a hip contusion that would keep him bedridden for months. The explosion also had initiated a lifetime of roaring inside his head that at times grew so loud it rendered coherent thought impossible.[12]

Darkness had nearly descended when Colonel Taylor saw "two or three hundred Rebels" appear at the edge of the woods to his left. He tried to shout an order, but the thick smoke had so parched his throat he could hardly speak. In his stead, one of his officers shouted a demand that the Rebels surrender. The Southerners had a different

---

10. *O.R.*, 27/1:657, Report of Col. William McCandless, July 9, 1863; Account of Frank J. Bell.

11. Capt. John P. Bard, "Pennsylvania in the War: The 'Old Bucktails,' 42d Regt., P.V. at the Battle of Gettysburg," *Philadelphia Weekly Press,* Apr. 1888. See also "The Bucktails: The Famous Rifle Regiment of Pennsylvania; The History of One of the Best Known Regiments in the Army of the Potomac," in *Grand Army Scout and Soldiers' Mail,* Jan. 6, 1883, for an account of the events on Little Round Top; Angelo to Frank Sibley, Aug. 3, 1863, KGC.

12. CMSR and Pension of Charles H. Robbins. Charlie Robbins spent the next seven months in the hospital, three of them at the facility on Penn Commons in York, Pennsylvania. The artillery blast obviously caused tinnitus.

idea and took aim. "Tree!" somebody in a blue uniform yelled. Everyone leaped for the widest trunk available. Fred Taylor did not move fast enough. The twenty-three-year-old colonel fell into the arms of one of his men and whimpered, "Mum." Within moments, the Bucktails needed another colonel.[13]

The Bucktails held that stone wall for the remainder of the night, keeping their heads down and firing at any perceived enemy motion. The proximity of an unseen enemy so rattled some men that they sneaked off to the rear.[14] Finally, the two sides agreed on "an involuntary truce" to retrieve the wounded from no-man's-land. As soldiers assumed humane duties, a Southern voice began the strains of a familiar hymn. Both lines fell silent and savored the boy's music. He rendered several other selections, closing with *When This Cruel War is Over*, a sad tune with lyrics describing the separation from loved ones and the hopes of meeting them again. When it ended, both lines applauded the talented Southerner. Tomorrow they would begin killing each other all over again.[15]

The next morning began with a skirmish between the Bucktails and Confederates lodged in Devil's Den, but the day's main activity did not involve the Bucktails. All along the Confederate line, hundreds of guns erupted and answered in kind from the Union side. One Southern soldier called it "the most terrific cannonading that has ever shook American hills."[16] Yet, it was merely the preliminary round for that day's fighting. Angelo never mentioned if he could see much of the immortal charge wrongly assigned to George Pickett. Anyway, he was too concerned about what was going on in front of him. Before the day ended, the Pennsylvania Reserves pushed the Confederates back a considerable distance in a fight forever over-

---

13. Account of Frank J. Bell; Thomson and Rauch, *History of the Bucktails*, 270; Account of Cpl. Adam Baker, Co. H, 1st Pa. Rifles, Robert L. Brake Collection, U.S. Army Military History Institute. Baker insisted that Taylor died within two minutes of his wounding. Gary Kross in "To Die Like Soldiers" claims that Taylor died later that night. Other accounts have Taylor dying wordlessly. The flank markers on the modern-day Gettysburg battlefield delineate the Bucktails' position, and a marker honors the site of Taylor's death.

14. Account of Frank J. Bell.

15. *Confederate Veteran*, Aug. 2, 1904; George Hillyer, "Battle of Gettysburg, Address Before the Walton County Georgia," vertical file 7-GA9, Gettysburg National Military Park, original at the University of Georgia library. See also Hess, *The Union Soldier in Battle*, 113, for a similar episode of music shared between enemy lines.

16. Gabriel Shank to Annie Amelia Shank, July 8, 1863, Virginia GenWeb Project, Gabriel Shank and Aldine Keiffer Collection: Military Records, Articles, Letters, and Diary of Gabriel Shank, Co. G, 10th Va. Inf., www.rootsweb.com/%7Evarockin/shank/Gabriel_Shank.htm

shadowed by the carnage to the north. In spite of the confusion swirling in his mind, Angelo felt proud that the Bucktails had "saved the left wing of the Army."[17]

Angelo slept on a pile of rails that evening. Without knowing it, he had fought his last battle. He had killed his last man. From then on, his personal struggle would make the battle of Gettysburg seem nothing by comparison.[18]

The next month was the most difficult time of Angelo's life to that point. On July 7, the Bucktails marched twenty-eight miles; on July 15, twenty-five, with little rest in between. Heat and humidity sucked strength and threatened heatstroke with every step. Days began predawn, and what sleep they could grab often had to happen in the rain. He called on a reserve strength—"grit," he called it—that few today without Special Forces training can comprehend. When fever struck, he took quinine and kept going until his body utterly failed.[19]

He maintained his daily diary entries until July 18 but then abandoned that chore for three weeks. Not until August 3, while a patient at Carver U.S. General Hospital in Washington, was he strong enough to write a letter to Frank Sibley to explain what had happened. He described the battle of Gettysburg from his perspective but with nowhere near the detail of previous battles. What happened to him afterward was even worse.

> Well, Frank, your letter found me at Berlin MD & very sick too with chill fever . . . Well, I can't write so I will not try to tell you any more [than] this. I think I stood the march well until the 15th of July when I was taken sick. The 14th we marched from Williamsport[, Maryland,] to Middletown [, Maryland,] across South Mountain. It was a terrible warm day & we marched 25 miles. I ate a hearty supper & went in bathing & I suppose I chilled my blood for the next day I was very sick & had chills & fever and the sick was not sent off at Berlin but were dragged along in ambulances day after day & I was terrible sick. If it had not been for my comrades getting chickens & berries for me to eat and a little bread, I should of died. That was four days I did not eat anything.
>
> There was a battle expected at Manassas Gap & all sick were left in the woods & and the nurses left with us were lazy & would not cook or fetch

17. Angelo to Frank Sibley, Aug. 3, 1863, KGC. Sgt. James B. Thompson, Co. G, earned the Medal of Honor for capturing the 15th Georgia flag.

18. Diary of Angelo M. Crapsey, July 4, 1863.

19. Angelo to Frank Sibley, Aug. 3, 1863, KGC.

11. Little Round Top as the Conferates saw it. The Bucktails charged from the right of the crest. Courtesy of the Library of Congress.

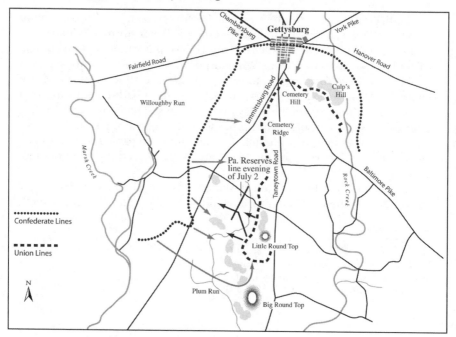

12. Gettysburg, situation on the late afternoon of July 2.

water for us. But I got a teamster to fix me a tent & get water & and some berries for me. The 25th they took us to Warrenton[, Virginia], 25 miles. Oh how sick I was! The 26th we lay in the ambulances & the 27th we were taken down most to Rappahannock Station where the division was. I was perfectly helpless.

Our doctor put up a hospital & took care of us. The 28th they sent us in ambulances to Warrenton & there we were put in the cars like so many hogs in a freight car & we were laying along the road at by-stations waiting for trains to pass. We arrived in Washington that night & lay till morning in the cars. When I arrived here the 29th [?] I was nearly gone under but I have recovered very fast. I can walk a little. My fever is broke. I shall soon be well. Many poor fellows died. I saw one die while we lay in the woods. If I had not kept up my grit I should have died too.

Well, I don't know as you can read this for its most impossible for me to write. What's the reason my folks don't write? Are they mad or what is the reason? I hope you will not delay writing. So long this time. Good by, write soon.[20]

Hospital meals included farina, gruel, and an occasional treat of toast brought to him by a kindly nurse. Quinine was the medicine most often administered, as it was for any patient exhibiting his symptoms. Nonetheless, his condition worsened. "My bowels . . . [are] all upside down," he wrote in his diary when he returned to it on August 15. He composed a letter to Laroy but only managed a few lines that painted an unrealistically positive picture of his condition. His diary contains a more honest description: "I have got the diarrhea terribly. It's the chronic diarrhea. I have to run from 8 to ten times in 24 hours. Nothing but slime & blood passes my bowels."[21]

That was the last diary entry he made for more than a month. There is one on August 27 that is not in his handwriting: "Angelo's father arrived . . . His son is very sick with the diarrhea." Carver Hospital had wired John Crapsey that he should come immediately if he wanted to see his son before he died. Angelo must have known about the telegram because it did not go to his parents' home but to a friend in Cuba, who gamely rode nearly forty miles at night to deliver it to Crapseys. Typical of John Crapsey, the friend had to advance the reverend twenty-five dollars for train fare, which Angelo repaid from his army wages.[22]

---

20. Ibid.

21. Diary of Angelo M. Crapsey, Aug. 15 and 20, 1863; Angelo to Laroy, Aug. 17, 1863, KLC.

22. Pension of Angelo M. Crapsey, deposition of John Crapsey, Jan. 29, 1887, and statement of Harriet N. Scott, Apr. 11, 1889; Diary of Angelo M. Crapsey, cash account entry dated Oct.

John Crapsey was stunned to behold a son shriveled from the wasting effects of diarrhea and deranged by fever. Angelo's physical condition would be the smallest shock John would receive. Lucid moments came and went for Angelo only to be swamped by behavior John described as "quite violent and delirious." John concluded that his son was "out of his mind." Angelo offered evidence for his father's unprofessional diagnosis each time he grabbed his head and screamed, "My head is as big as a half-bushel!"[23]

The reason for what happened next cannot be known. John later claimed that Angelo had asked him to apply faith healing, which is reasonable. If so, Angelo may have mistaken John's Pentecostal incantations for something evil, or long-held resentments surfaced in Angelo's weakened mind. Perhaps John may have simply been in the wrong place at the wrong time.

Angelo attacked his father, striking him, screaming throughout the assault. Hospital stewards had to pull him off. John Crapsey was devastated.[24]

Carver sent Angelo to Philadelphia's Mowrer U.S. General Hospital, aka Chestnut Hill. On September 23, Angelo's home became ward 13, bed 28, and Dr. Hanly, his assigned physician. Chestnut Hill had no more success than Carver, and this time a frustrated John Crapsey demanded action. According to John, doctors took one look at Angelo and said, "Take that man away. He is insane."[25]

John's memory coincided with Angelo's diary entry for September 28, the first he had made in four days.

> Sep 28   I am very weak. They took me before the board & they decided to discharge me from the service. They say I will not be fit for the field again this winter.

1, 1863. The stalwart friend from Cuba was forty-eight-year-old innkeeper and farmer Abel M. Scott. Scott's niece, Cora Lodencia Veronica Scott, was a well-known spiritualist and trance medium who may have known John Crapsey. Married four times, she is also known by the surnames Hatch, Tappan, Daniels, and Richmond. See Cora L. V. Richmond Archives, www.interfarfacing.com

23. John Crapsey to E. B. French, Sept. 11, 1865, Pension of Angelo M. Crapsey; Pension of Angelo M. Crapsey, depositions of John Crapsey, Feb. 3, 1889, and Nov. 7, 1892.

24. Pension of Angelo M. Crapsey, depositions of John Crapsey, Jan. 29, 1887, and Nov. 7, 1892; Miller, *Modern Pentecost*, 44–45.

25. Diary of Angelo M. Crapsey, Sept. 22–30, 1863; Carded Medical Records of Angelo Crapsey; *Pennsylvania Magazine;* Indexes of Philadelphia Hospitals, RG 94, Entry 544, NARA; Frank H. Taylor, *Philadelphia in the Civil War;* John Crapsey to Pension Commissioner Black, Feb. 3, 1889, Pension of Angelo M. Crapsey. Chestnut Hill was a twenty-seven-acre medical facility located 9.5 miles northwest of Philadelphia "between Abington and Springfield Avenues and

Sep 29   I am getting worse every day I stay here. It is so cold here, no fire
         in the wards. This is written after date. I was too sick to write at
         that time.

Sep 30   I was up 12 times within the last 24 hours. I am very sick.

John prepared to return home with his son on October 1, but the
trip nearly did not happen. Angelo looked at his father and announced that he would not go anywhere with a stranger. John called
on all his persuasive powers to convince his son of his identity and
coax him onto the train. Throughout the trip, Angelo maintained his
daily diary entries but made no mention of his father's presence.
They arrived in Cuba on the morning of October 3. This time the
pathway to hell was going to take a circuitous route.[26]

༺ஒ༻

Joseph Josia Robbins was feeling his age. The patriarch of the Robbins family had traveled to California during the gold rush and served
in the Mexican War. He decided to emulate his son and in late September 1861 enlisted with Company E, 58th Pennsylvania. After two
years of duty, liver and lung ailments forced him into the hospital at
Fortress Monroe. The army next sent him to Germantown Hospital
near Philadelphia, where they admitted and discharged him the
same day. Surgeons told Private Robbins that a rest was all he needed
and issued him a twenty-day furlough.[27]

Joseph must have felt relieved when the train finally arrived in
Olean, New York. All that remained was a twenty-eight-mile journey
to his home near Liberty. Apparently, he was penniless because he
started walking home, no easy feat for a man in his condition. By luck,
a stagecoach happened by, and the generous driver offered a poor
soldier a lift. When he climbed in the coach, he found John and
Angelo Crapsey on board. Conversation revealed that they had all

---

the Chestnut Hill track of the Reading Railroad and County Hill Line Road." It opened January
17, 1863, with a patient capacity of 2,820, later expanded to 4,000. During Angelo's stay, patients
overflowed into churches and firehouses.

26. Diary of Angelo M. Crapsey, Oct. 1–3, 1863; Pension of Angelo M. Crapsey, depositions
of John Crapsey, Jan. 29, 1887, and Harriet N. Scott, Apr. 11, 1889.

27. Robbins interview; Pension records and CMSR of Joseph J. Robbins, Co. E, 58th Pa. Robbins was forty-two years old when he enlisted. His health did not improve, and the army granted
him a twenty-day furlough extension.

arrived on the same train from Philadelphia without encountering each other. Robbins tried to make conversation, recalling, "When I spoke to Angelo he did not seem to recognize me, sort of waved his arms and looked at me in a strange way and muttered something, but I could not understand what he said. Only when the wagon jolted he would say, 'O dear.'"[28]

The stage pulled into the station at Allegany Bridge (modern-day Eldred), eighteen miles from Olean, where Joseph Robbins started for home on foot.[29] Angelo and John clearly did not continue the journey because Angelo's diary entry for October 1 states that the army was going to send his discharge to Cuba. He kept his diary mysterious by revealing no reasons for that, but Josia Robbins's deposition proves the Crapseys had been homeward-bound. Robbins clearly stated where and when he met them on the stage, and his furlough date matches the time of Angelo's return. Since the Robbins and Crapsey families lived virtually next door, they should have finished the journey together. As far as Angelo's fevered mind was concerned, Cuba was home, and they returned there.[30]

Angelo may have felt more secure in Cuba, but his body was being savaged. "I am in great pain," he wrote virtually every day. Food as harmless as mashed potatoes set his bowels aching, and a sore throat made swallowing difficult. "I am clear off my hooks," he wrote on October 12. "My guts ache like split. Oh what a devilish disease this is."[31]

Chestnut Hill Hospital discharged Angelo to date October 13 for the official reason of "chronic diarrhea." Although his records display "disability—none," just as prominent are the words, "Disqualified for the Invalid Corps." The army put men with missing limbs into the Invalid Corps, yet Chestnut Hill would not grant Angelo that possibility. Nothing on his discharge states his disqualification was due to his mental condition. Based on his erratic behavior, hospital officials could hardly have concluded anything else.[32]

---

28. Pension of Angelo M. Crapsey, deposition of Joseph J. Robbins, Apr. 2, 1891.

29. Ibid.

30. Ibid.; Pension records and CMSR of Joseph J. Robbins; Diary of Angelo M. Crapsey, Oct. 5, 1863. John Crapsey returned home October 5. That was the only mention Angelo made in his diary concerning his father during that time.

31. Diary of Angelo M. Crapsey, various entries Oct. 4–12, 1863.

32. CMSR and Pension of Angelo M. Crapsey, Certificate of Disability for Discharge; *O.R.*, ser. 3, 3:170, General Order No. 105, Adj. Gen. Office, authorization to create an Invalid Corps,

In late October, John Crapsey returned to Cuba to retrieve his son, and this time they finished the trip home. We may never know how difficult that trip was for John Crapsey.

As the time for their arrival neared, Lura Ann Crapsey focused her eyes down the road waiting for the wagon to appear in the distance. Two and a half years without seeing your son, even a stepson, is too long. Her stomach churned both with eagerness and more than a scrap of anxiety. John's descriptions of Angelo had unnerved her. Surely, John must have exaggerated. Even if Angelo were as bad as her husband described, a few weeks' rest and a mother's love would cure anything. When at last the rattling of the wagon came into earshot, Lura rushed to greet the travelers. When she saw Angelo, she froze. That was not her stepson but a "scarecrow [so] weak and ema-ciated" as to be almost unrecognizable. A few moments of attempted conversation convinced her that John had *understated* Angelo's con-dition. Alice Crapsey gave a terse evaluation of her half brother: "He looked wild."[33]

Josia Robbins visited the Crapseys several times during his furlough and encountered more strange behavior.

> [I] always found [Angelo] beside himself. [He] seemed to be looking for the enemy, seemed to think that his clothes were unclean and was fre-quently raving and always seemed to be motioning with his hands. He never seemed to recognize me [even] though we had lived near each other so long and he had known me so well before he went into the army . . . In the thirty days I was home on a furlough, I saw him several times, and I know that he was violently insane.[34]

Angelo felt well enough to visit the Lymans on November 12, but Laroy wrote nothing more in his diary than Angelo had arrived for a

Apr. 28, 1863; ser. 3, 3:668, General Regulations for the Recruiting Service and Organization of the Invalid Corps, Aug. 12, 1863. The Invalid (later "Veteran Reserve") Corps was formed "by taking those [infantry] officers and enlisted men . . . who, from wounds received in action or disease contracted in the line of duty, are unfit for field service, but are still capable of effec-tive garrison duty, or such other light duty as may be required."

33. Pension of Angelo M. Crapsey, depositions of Lura Ann Crapsey and Alice Crapsey McBain, Nov. 7, 1892, and Viola Girtrude Peck Robbins, Jan. 17, 1893.

34. Pension of Angelo M. Crapsey, depositions of Joseph J. Robbins, Apr. 2, 1891, and Jan. 18, 1893.

visit. On the 17th, Angelo had to return to Philadelphia to retrieve his medical discharge, a round trip that should have taken four or five days. It required eleven. When Angelo returned, Laroy thought that his young friend appeared "quite smart now," a cryptic description that failed to reach the truth that Angelo was too far down the pathway to hell to ever return.[35]

---

35. Diaries of Laroy Lyman. Someone tore out the pages of Angelo's diary dated October 22 through December 28.

13. Angelo M. Crapsey. Young, handsome, and ready for anything. An antebellum image. KLC.

14. A sheepish-looking Angelo. The image was probably taken at Harrisburg, 1861. KLC.

15. Sgt. Crapsey at Camp Parole, battle-hardened, depressed, and psychotic. KLC.

16. Rev. John Crapsey Jr. Courtesy Raymond Handy.

17. The Lyman Family c. 1870: seated: Thankful and Laroy; standing: Isabella, Celestia, Milo, and Sybil. KLC.

18. The Lyman house, supposedly an antebellum image. Thankful and Laroy sit on the porch. KLC.

19. The Lyman fireplace c. 1940. This is where Angelo's bier stood and Laroy died. KLC.

20. Bennett House, Smethport, PA. Laroy's favorite hotel, where Thomas Kane's first company of Bucktails organized. Courtesy of the McKean County Historical Society.

21. Thomas Leiper Kane. Courtesy of Ronn Palm's Museum of Civil War Images.

22. Hugh McNeil. Courtesy of Ronn Palm's Museum of Civil War Images.

23. Charles Frederick Taylor. Courtesy of Ronn Palm's Museum of Civil War Images.

24. Charles and Viola Robbins. Courtesy of Bertha Robbins.

A WILD WOLF!

Just Caught in a Steel Trap, and a

PORCUPINE,

Will be Exhibited by a Hunter of Potter Co.,

Pa., on

He will also relate some Hunting Excursions, and answer most questions concerning the Hunting of Bears, Wolves, Elk, Deer, and Wild Cats. Having killed all of the above named animals, and residing near them and understanding the nature of them, he feels confident that he can give a correct history of their habits, &c. **LAROY LYMAN.**

25. Poster. Potter County's answer to P. T. Barnum, except Laroy ended his tours by killing and skinning the performers. Courtesy of the Potter County Historical Society.

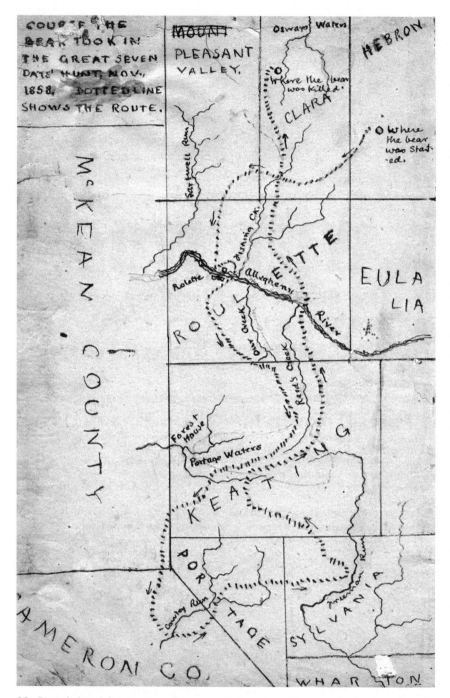

26. Laroy's hand-drawn map of a seven-day-long hunt for one elusive bear. Angelo was a participant. KLC.

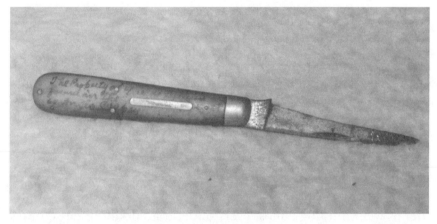

27. Angelo's knife, uncovered after his death. Courtesy of the Potter County Historical Society.

12
Home, Where the War Never Ends

The veteran expects little change when he returns home, but
finds substantial; those to whom he returns expect little change,
but find much.

—Joel Osler Brende and Erwin Randolph Parson

ANGELO MOVED BACK WITH THE LYMANS, AND HIS HEALTH IMPROVED
due to Thankful's cooking and being among friends in familiar surroundings. November 30 must have been a glorious day for Angelo.
He and Laroy put rifle under arm and stepped into the woods
together for the first time since he had joined the army. Angelo soon
felt well enough to "help with the butchering, cut one drag of wood,
and help . . . do the chores." Best of all, he assisted in harvesting deer
for Laroy's venison supply business that sold meat to several New York
City restaurants. During the last two weeks of December, the two
friends went hunting almost every day and no doubt discussed that
western hunting trip that was so important to them.[1]

Angelo's body started a slow journey back toward normalcy, but his
mind was not making the same trip. "He was sort of wild and wandering in his memories all the time," an acquaintance recalled. Stepsister Viola recalled that "he acted so queer. Sometimes he would talk
and then again he would not say anything. Sometimes he would eat
and then again he would not eat a thing." "Perfect wreck in mind and
body" was a common description of Angelo. "Shattered" was another,
the same word Angelo had used to describe the Bucktail sergeant
who had shot himself three years earlier.[2]

Epig.: J. O. Brende and E. R. Parson, *Vietnam Veterans: The Road to Recovery*, 48.

1. Diary of Angelo M. Crapsey, Oct. 13, 1863; Diaries of Laroy Lyman; Laroy to Thankful,
Mar. 19, 1864, KLC.

2. Pension of Angelo M. Crapsey, depositions of Isaac Sears, Apr. 2, 1891, John Crapsey, Nov.
7, 1892, Viola Robbins, Jan. 18, 1893, Stephen P. Reynolds, May 5, 1893, and Thankful Lyman,
Nov. 30, 1883.

Sybil Lyman, Laroy's eldest daughter, asked Angelo to drive her and some friends to Olean, New York, for a day of shopping. They had taken the trip together before the war, and she did not hesitate to ask this time. Perhaps she thought that their old friendship would put life back into Angelo. Instead, his behavior forced Sybil to make certain that others were always nearby. It was the last trip they ever took together.[3]

Laroy's sister, Prudence Lyman Boyington, had always enjoyed Angelo's letters with their "vivid descriptions of the army" and was eager to hear his tales firsthand. She invited him to her home but immediately saw "that he was changed in his manner" and "not inclined to talk to me on anything like the manner he showed in his army letters . . . He told me he was a sharpshooter and that he had shot many men and this seemed to affect him. Not long after he was at my house I began to hear remarks about his peculiar actions." Prudence decided shortly afterward that she could not visit Laroy as long as Angelo was around.[4]

Angelo's solitary conversations were often incomprehensible, but some odd words came through clearly. "Nits make lice," he said often, sometimes followed by a pronouncement that "[I] went down to fight the Rebs." The "nits" comment started a rumor. Folks began to say that he had shot children in the war, behavior unacceptable even to the most rabid Yankee. In Roulette, where Union allegiance was questionable, the accusation was damning. Without one shred of evidence, public opinion turned against him.[5]

Seneca B. Pomeroy was a lumberman who lived a short distance from Laroy. Sim, as friends called him, had long worked for Laroy and as a young man helped build the Lyman's house. Twelve years Angelo's senior, Sim perhaps served in a big brother role. The two had hunted and worked together often and passed many social hours in the Pomeroy home. At first, Angelo's strange behavior did not concern Sim, who noticed only that the once "lively and cheerful" lad appeared to be "more melancholy and sober." He chalked it up to the war and assumed the old Angelo would return eventually. His opinion changed after one event.[6]

---

3. Pension of Angelo M. Crapsey, deposition of Sybil Lyman Burdick, Nov. 5, 1892.

4. Pension of Angelo M. Crapsey, deposition of Prudence Lyman Boyington, Nov. 22, 1892; Diaries of Laroy Lyman. Prudence was as independent as Laroy and took no guff from her brother.

5. Pension of Angelo M. Crapsey, deposition of William S. Brine, May 5, 1893.

6. U.S. Census, 1860, Pennsylvania, Potter County, 193, shows Angelo living with the Pomeroys.

Sim heard a Roulette man declare that "he wished to God Crapsey had been shot." When he related that to Angelo, the reaction surprised Sim. Angelo "dropped his head and turned away and seemed to be thinking. Finally he turned to me & said he didn't know why [the man] wanted to say that about him. I thought his actions at the time was strange, as at any time before his army service that remark would have stirred him up. He would have been fighting mad."[7]

There would be no more fists thrown at detractors, no more arguments over politics, no more gates ripped from their hinges.

If Laroy considered Angelo a burden, he did not mention so in his diary. Laroy seldom expressed inner feelings that did not involve religion or criticism of others, so he may have been behaving kindly in his inimitable fashion. Indeed, he granted Angelo's fondest wish. On May 9, 1864, two days after the remnants of the Bucktail Regiment suffered hell at the battle of the Wilderness, the two men rose at 3:00 AM, settled on Angelo's overdue pay, and prepared to depart on that long-awaited hunting trip west.[8]

Olean, New York, was the trip's jumping-off point. Along the way, they visited Laroy's relatives in Toledo, Ohio, and toured the state house in Lansing, Michigan, which Laroy considered inferior to Potter County's courthouse "by a good deal." They improvised their travel itinerary, doing what they wanted as long as they wanted to do it. As Laroy wrote Thankful, "What is the use in hurrying back until we are satisfied?"[9]

Michigan appealed to them until they reached Grand Haven, where they spent a night at a tavern so rough they had to sleep with loaded pistols under their pillows. The experience rattled Angelo, who awoke "as gritty as fury" and spent the day behaving "as tough as an old bear." Angelo disappeared that day and did likewise at various times on the trip. Laroy naively supposed that he was off writing let-

Pension of Angelo M. Crapsey, deposition of Seneca Pomeroy, May 13, 1893. "Sim" Pomeroy's nickname courtesy of descendant Lyle R. Slingerland. Pomeroy testified that Angelo "was at my house a good deal before he went in the Army." The 1860 census also shows Angelo living with his parents in McKean County. The 1850 census (New York, Cattaraugus County, Humphrey Township, 117–18) lists the family twice, one as the Crapsey's daughter Angela.

    7. Pension of Angelo M. Crapsey, deposition of Seneca B. Pomeroy.

    8. Diaries of Laroy Lyman. Laroy paid Angelo one hundred dollars. Laroy's brother-in-law, John Taggart, accompanied them on the trip.

    9. A composite of Laroy's letters to Thankful dated May 14 and May 15, 1864, KLC; Diaries of Laroy Lyman. At Olean, they "got the bus" to the train station where they each paid a $7.85 fare. Presumably, that fare took them from Olean to the eastern shore of Lake Michigan.

ters to lady friends, which could be interpreted in hindsight as a state of denial.[10]

They booked passage across Lake Michigan and at Milwaukee entrained for La Crosse, where they rented sleeping berths for a boat trip up the Mississippi River. The town of Prescott came next, followed by another boat ride up the St. Croix River. They finished their long journey with a stagecoach ride to New Richmond, Wisconsin, the home of Laroy's aunt and uncle. Laroy reported their health as "tip-top" but admitted that Angelo was "a little sick" but eating "like a hungry man."[11] They found Wisconsin wildlife no more able to dodge bullets than their Pennsylvania kin and bagged many trophies. After several days of hunting and visiting, they bid their hosts good bye and traveled to St. Paul, Minnesota, to tour Fort Snelling and see Indian and Rebel prisoners.[12]

Angelo fell ill on May 11. Once more pain slashed his bowels. They pressed on by stage to Belle Plain, Minnesota, where they suffered a dreadful dinner at an "awful tavern" and a night's lodging in a "dirty house." Winnebago was the next port of call. From there, Laroy went off to check into a land deal, but Angelo did not accompany him. Instead, he went to the nearby town of Fairmont. No extant document explains why they separated. Perhaps Laroy did not wish to suffer Angelo's erratic behavior while transacting business.[13] Neither do we know why Angelo chose Fairmont or what happened while he was there. If anything did take place in that southern Minnesota town, it had to have been a damning experience because their extended vacation suddenly imploded. Laroy called an immediate halt to their travels and started for home. By the time they reached home on June 1, Angelo had reached the lowest ebb of his life to date.

Diarrhea ravaged him as hard as it had the year before. Any mention of the war sent him into fits of rage. Flashbacks became recur-

---

10. Diaries of Laroy Lyman; Laroy to Thankful, May 15, 1864, KLC.

11. Richmond, Wisconsin, is now New Richmond, although a local historian claims it was always "New Richmond" to distinguish it from another Richmond in southern Wisconsin. The town is in western Wisconsin thirty-five miles northeast of Minneapolis, Minnesota. Sam Palmer to "Dear Brother and Sister," Apr. 8, 1845, KLC. Laroy first traveled to Wisconsin in 1845, preceding his aunt and uncle.

12. Laroy to Thankful, May 21, 1864. The commander of the department in which Fort Snelling was located was none other than Maj. Gen. John Pope.

13. Diaries of Laroy Lyman. The story of the trip west came from Laroy's diary and several letters he wrote home during that time. He purchased land in Blue Earth County.

ring struggles as his mind brought phantom army comrades in and
out of his life. When not waving his hands in the air, he continuously
rubbed imaginary lice from his body. People, once leery, shunned
him completely, and that added to his despair. He began telling
friends and family, "Even the grasshoppers hate me" because he had
killed so many men. Thankful Lyman called on Seneca Pomeroy to
assist with Angelo. Sim once found him sitting in bed, sobbing, "terribly grieved about something. He seemed to think that everybody
was against him and would try to injure him." Sim had some success
quieting Angelo's behavior but was unsuccessful in easing the tor-
ment in his mind.[14]

Laroy demanded John Crapsey take Angelo home. When John and
Lura arrived at the Lyman home, they found Angelo "raving" and
threatening to jump through a closed window. Laroy already had
summoned a doctor and, through everyone's efforts, Angelo eventually calmed. The doctor warned them all to keep a close watch on him
from then on, or he might try to kill himself. According to Lura
Crapsey's testimony, John Crapsey "didn't seem to realize Angelo's
condition, however, & we left him there at Lyman's after he got a little better."[15]

❧

The year 1864 was a busy one for Laroy. He traveled to New York
and Philadelphia several times and in July made plans to return to
New York. For the first time, Thankful and son Milo were going along,
surely grateful to get a break from the emotional upheaval Angelo
was causing at home. That meant Laroy was preparing to leave his
three teenaged daughters alone in the house with a mentally disturbed ex-soldier who could not stop fighting the war. While that is a
hindsight observation, it surely must have occurred to Laroy and
Thankful at the time.[16] Laroy got only as far as Coudersport before
he began having second thoughts and there made a diary entry that
drips with guilt: "Angelo is worse but we left him." That is the first
written indication that Laroy recognized Angelo's mental state. He

14. Pension of Angelo M. Crapsey, depositions of Lura Crapsey, Nov. 7, 1892, Sybil Lyman
Burdick, Nov. 25, 1892, and Seneca B. Pomeroy, May 13, 1893.

15. Pension of Angelo M. Crapsey, deposition of Lura Crapsey, Nov. 7, 1892; Diaries of Laroy
Lyman. The doctor was Richard V. Post, although the 1860 census lists farmer as his profession.

16. Diaries of Laroy Lyman.

wrote a quick letter home—probably to daughter Sybil—asking Ike Sears to "keep everything straight while I am gone." He did not explain why he had failed to make those arrangements before he left.[17]

Sybil coped as best she could and kept a watchful eye on Angelo. She tried to reason with him during his distraught periods, but the teenage girl was no Seneca Pomeroy. Darkness offered her and her sisters no relief. Angelo's screams woke her in the middle of the night, and she rushed downstairs to see what had happened. What she saw made her gasp. The Lymans thought they had locked away all lethal objects, but Angelo had a knife in his hand and was threatening to kill himself. Sybil watched in horror as he raced across the room and leaped through the closed front window. Shards of glass and wood clattered onto the porch. Angelo rose, moaning, stunned, bloodied, yet somehow not seriously injured. He started toward the river to finish his suicidal intentions, slowly at first, then faster, still shouting, still clutching the knife.[18]

Sybil ran to the Pomeroy house to fetch the only person she knew could calm Angelo. By now, Sim was losing confidence in his counseling ability and brought help. The men treaded cautiously as they neared the river, ears open for a rustle of bushes, eyes scanning for movement in case Angelo's tortured mind mistook them for an enemy. They found him in the brush on the riverbank, still sobbing suicide threats. Sim disarmed Angelo and calmed him somewhat, but "they had considerable trouble to get him back in the house."[19]

That afternoon, Sim hitched the Lymans' wagon and did what John Crapsey should have done: he took Angelo home. "On the way down," Sim remembered, "he was not rational [and] was talking in a wild manner."[20] John Crapsey was not home when they arrived, and Lura asked a neighbor man to stay with her until her husband returned. She also hid all knives and made certain the children were never alone with their half brother.[21]

As days passed, Angelo vacillated between raving madness and silent depression. Occasionally a degree of lucidity returned, but those periods only deepened his pain. For those few moments, he

17. Laroy to unknown, July 12, 1864, KLC.

18. Pension of Angelo M. Crapsey, deposition of Sybil Lyman Burdick, Nov. 25, 1892.

19. Pension of Angelo M. Crapsey, depositions of Seneca Pomeroy, May 13, 1893, and Sybil Lyman Burdick, Nov. 25, 1892.

20. Pension of Angelo M. Crapsey, depositions of Seneca Pomeroy, May 13, 1893.

21. Pension of Angelo M. Crapsey, depositions of Seneca Pomeroy, May 13, 1893, and Lura Ann Crapsey, Nov. 7, 1892.

could realize what was happening. The embarrassing memory of each psychotic incident sent him deeper into melancholy, especially the recent event at the Lymans.

The louse infestation that Angelo's mind had created grew worse. When scraping his arms did nothing, he rummaged through a shed and found a broken scythe blade. He raised it over his head and brought it down to hack off the infested arm. The blade cut him badly but was too dull to effect the desired amputation and amazingly caused neither permanent damage nor infection.

During one wild spell, he leaped down the length of the stairs. Most likely, his mind had sent him back into battle. But the Rebel standing at the bottom of the stairs was only his little sister. He escaped without broken bones, but his sister did not escape a terrifying experience. He drank poison as he had seen comrades do three years before. His body, weak as it was, somehow retained enough strength to survive. He saw a Rebel coming at him, picked up a rock, and pitched it at the enemy "in a savage way." The Rebel was his sister Hattie, and the rock, fortunately, just a piece of tree bark. For a long time afterward, Hattie woke in the night screaming with her own nightmares. On several occasions, Angelo would unexpectedly leap to his feet, throw his hands into the air, and shout, "I surrender!"[22]

The killing fields of Fredericksburg had followed him home.

The Crapsey house sat a few dozen yards from the Allegheny River, which is no more than a fair-sized creek in that part of the state. The day was bright and hot, and no one thought it strange when Angelo removed his hat and coat and laid them on the ground, neatly folded. He stared at the river, took a deep breath, and walked toward it. When Angelo reached river's edge, John shouted for him to stop and rushed to his son. Angelo turned on his father and motioned for him to stay back, freezing him with glaring eyes.

"You want me to kill you, do you?"

John Crapsey stood firmly in place and watched Angelo leap into the river and sink below the surface. John hesitated, fearful of what might happen if he intervened, yet knowing he must. When he saw that Angelo was losing strength, he waded in and pulled his son's head above water. Angelo flailed his arms, fighting to get back below the surface. John struggled for his son's life and shouted for help,

---

22. Pension of Angelo M. Crapsey, depositions of Alice Crapsey McBain and Lura Crapsey, Nov. 7, 1892, John Crapsey and Joseph Josia Robbins, Jan. 18, 1893, and William S. Brine, May 5, 1893.

which came from two of his daughters and a woman neighbor. Together, they dragged him into the house.

"After that," John recalled, "he seemed to get more rational for a while."[23]

John Crapsey took his son to three doctors, but their only suggestion was to put Angelo into a mental institution. That was not going to happen to the son of John Crapsey, who concluded that Angelo only needed to be restrained. Had he not always calmed after friends and family subdued him? John plotted with Lura and Viola to take Angelo by force. It would be easy, they thought. Angelo was too sick and weak to fight back, they thought, as if the recent experience in the river had never occurred.[24]

John grabbed his son, but Angelo shucked him off with surprising power. He again turned on his father, glaring. Before courage deserted them, the three seized Angelo and held on with all their strength. They fought to get him upstairs. The house shook as they wrestled their insane son into a bedroom and tied him to the bed. No one slept through the screams that lasted all night and into the next day.

John had little choice but to free Angelo, and he calmed. The Crapsey's established an impossible twenty-four-hour vigil knowing that only time stood between the present moment and Angelo's next attempt to die. Or the next assault on one of the children during a flashback.[25]

On August 2, John Crapsey prepared to return Angelo to the Lymans, claiming that his son had expressed a desire to return to work. That was probably true, but the Lymans were no more able to cope than the Crapseys, and they were not Angelo's parents. To be fair, John and Lura did not know what to do. Angelo was too dangerous to be around small children. As they prepared to leave, Angelo jumped off the wagon.

"I won't ride after that horse!" he shouted, pointing to the horse as if it were an unearthly creature.[26]

John coaxed his son back on board and at last set off on their journey. The return to Roulette seemed to revitalize Angelo, and he

---

23. Pension of Angelo M. Crapsey, deposition of John Crapsey, Nov. 7, 1892. The neighbor's name was Mary A. Falkner.

24. Pension of Angelo M. Crapsey, affidavit of John Crapsey, Apr. 7, 1888. John Crapsey claimed a pension examiner told him, "I ought to be prosecuted for not sending my son to an insane asylum."

25. Pension of Angelo M. Crapsey, deposition of Alice Crapsey McBain, Nov. 7, 1892.

26. Pension of Angelo M. Crapsey, deposition of John Crapsey, Nov. 7, 1892.

immediately set to hoeing the garden. His "wild" and "curious" behavior continued, however, but Laroy would not comment more succinctly than that in his diary.[27]

John Crapsey stayed overnight at the Lyman house. When he left in the morning, he could not know that he would never again see his son alive.

⁓⁕⁓

Laroy learned of Angelo's death late on August 4 and went to Liberty to relay the news to the Crapseys. Incredibly, they did not go to Roulette until the following day after Laroy visited them "to see about the funeral." While John and Lura went to view Angelo's remains on August 5, John did not return for the funeral the next day.[28]

Laroy never dwelled on death nor became overly emotional about it. The death of young people was more familiar in his time. To him, the earthly loss of life was but a temporary condition the Second Coming would rectify. He simply paid Angelo's funeral expenses and went about his business. The only mention he made of Angelo in his diary in the next twenty years was the day of Angelo's memorial service. But on that dreary day of August 5, 1864, he penned five words that said more than an encyclopedia.

"I am nearly sick today."[29]

---

27. Diaries of Laroy Lyman.
28. Ibid. No documentation was found to indicate if Lura Crapsey attended the funeral.
29. Diaries of Laroy Lyman. The funeral expenses were $8.15 for the coffin, $2.00 to the gravediggers, and $5.00 to Dr. Post, the attending physician.

13
Analyzing the Dead

These heroes are dead. They died for liberty—they died for us.
They are at rest.

—Robert Green Ingersoll

How can we analyze the causes of Angelo's demise when there can be neither counselor to clear the psychological fog nor lab tests to diagnose his physical ailments? The only answer is that we must use at least some intelligent speculation, unsettling as that is to historians who necessarily rely on hard evidence. We can, however, follow Eric T. Dean's lead from his book *Shook Over Hell: Post-Traumatic Stress, Vietnam, and the Civil War* and view Angelo's well-documented behavior through modern medical and psychiatric lenses. Toward that end, two mental health professionals assisted me in analyzing Angelo. Both were understandably uneasy about diagnosing a paper patient, especially one who had lived in an era they have not studied in intimate detail. Nonetheless, both agree that anecdotal evidence of Angelo's case appears to be textbook with regard to events prior to the battle of Gettysburg. Disagreement came as to whether his condition after that battle was solely psychological or at least partially physiological.

It is clear that Angelo left Libby Prison suffering from severe depression and psychosis. After Gettysburg, it is most likely that he contracted a physical illness that ground away his remaining strength and exacerbated already severe mental problems. That dire combination led to worse aberrant behavior and ultimately, suicide. Joseph Josia Robbins, for all his ignorance of science, made a basically correct diagnosis when he said, "Angelo had been taken a prisoner of war and . . . his sickness in connection with his prison life had caused him to go crazy."[1]

---

1. Pension of Angelo M. Crapsey, deposition of Joseph Josia Robbins, January 18, 1893.

Comparing wars of different eras can be a daunting task. A unique combination of social, political, and military conundrums controls each conflict, and each possesses singular horrors. In the end, there is one constant: soldiers from Western cultures must set aside a lifetime of ethical teaching so that the taking of human life is not only possible but desirable. Joel Osler Brende and Erwin Randolph Parson call this phenomenon "dissolution of conscience," and it has to happen if an army is to be victorious. Nonetheless, during World War II, some U.S. soldiers admitted after the assaults on Makin and Kwajalein islands that they never had fired their rifles because America's moral code had instilled in them a powerful conviction against killing. The free world can be glad that most World War II soldiers overcame this reluctance, but many paid an emotional price in the doing.[2]

Moral values were no different for Angelo Crapsey eighty years earlier. His patriotism and sense of duty pushed him to fire ten rounds at Dranesville, fifteen at Cross Keys, seventy on the eve of Antietam, and twenty more the following day, after which he took cartridges from the dead and continued fighting. He told Laroy that at Harrisonburg "we picked them off like pigeons." At Cross Keys, his shots "done their work for I was perfectly calm and took good aim." At South Mountain and Antietam, he knew that "many a traitor has fallen by my aim."[3]

A World War I doctor would have diagnosed Angelo's pre-Gettysburg condition as "shell shock," under the misconception that prolonged shell fire physically damaged the nervous system. It was a reasonable assumption given that war's days-long artillery bombardments. Angelo had withstood a severe artillery assault at Fredericksburg. It was an hour in duration, not days, but it may have been sufficient to strip him of sanity. By World War II, psychiatrists called the condition "battle fatigue," but it was the same problem. Vietnam brought the condition to the public's attention as never before and sadly added too many case histories to advance science's knowledge. It also ultimately generated a typically weighty twentieth-century name: post-traumatic stress disorder, "PTSD" for short. Intense media coverage of Vietnam has led much of the public to conclude wrongly that PTSD sprang from that conflict.[4]

---

2. Brende and Parson, *Vietnam Veterans*, 91; see also chap. 5, "War: Its Effects on Identity"; Dean, *Shook Over Hell*, chap. 2, "Every Man Has His Breaking Point: War and Psychiatry"; Ben Shephard, *A War of Nerves: Soldiers and Psychiatrists in the Twentieth Century*, 236. Shephard notes that some experts have disputed the Kwajalein research.

3. Angelo to Laroy, Jan. 4, 1862, June 14, 1862, and Sept. 30, 1862, KLC.

4. On November 12, 2007, I searched the U.S. Army Military History Institute Research Cata-

Angelo clearly suffered PTSD. That is easily provable by comparing his symptoms and circumstances to the diagnostic criteria found in the standard mental health reference, *Diagnostic and Statistical Manual of Mental Disorders,* popularly known as *DSM.* Angelo's behavior fits every one of these criteria.

A.   Exposure to a traumatic event
B.   Reliving the traumatic event
C.   Estrangement from others and/or a foreboding of the future
D.   Inability to sleep or concentrate and/or the presence of exaggerated startle response
E.   The duration of symptoms exceed one month
F.   Impaired social functioning[5]

While hindsight shows his letters of late 1862 reflecting a mind and body prepped for failure, events during the battle of Fredericksburg and his subsequent confinement in Libby Prison were the devastating blows that smashed his psyche. Where once he had laughed at hardship and thrived in army life, imprisonment stripped him of all control. He could not rip Libby's gates off their hinges, and Lyman-like logic was of no value. He was the wolf now, like the ones Laroy captured, caged, and destroyed at his whim, a specimen dependent on his keepers for life's necessities and even life itself.[6]

Angelo no doubt had the same feeling of entrapment a British medical officer experienced during World War II during a lengthy Luftwaffe bombardment of Crete. He saw men and experienced himself having

> the sensation of an animal, trapped and helpless, sufficient to numb the stoutest heart. Men felt it whose courage was never in question, men who continued to give orders and to fight with no thought of surrender or withdrawal. What had changed in them was their spontaneity and their

---

log with "PTSD" as a parameter and found 151 references. *Shook Over Hell* is the only one that references the Civil War. Vietnam is the single most common war cited. See www.carlisle.army .mil/ahec/index.htm

5. *DSM,* 465–68. Alphabetic listing here conforms to the manual's jargon. One of the collaborating mental health professionals diagnosed Angelo's condition as "major depression, single episode, with psychotic features." "Single episode" means his condition had never occurred until the traumatic event. "Psychotic features" are exemplified by Angelo's struggle with imaginary lice and his phantom conversations.

6. Thanks to Keri S. Ullman, MSW, for the diagnosis and psychiatrist Dr. Thomas P. Lowry for agreeing. Brende and Parson, *Vietnam Veterans,* chap. 5, "War: Its Effects on Identity." See also Dean, *Shook Over Hell,* chap. 2.

power of decision. A lethargy gripped them. They spoke in low mono-tones, and replied to questions in sudden feeble irritations. They became unrecognizable to their friends.[7]

That was much the way Angelo's Bucktail comrades described him after his return from Camp Parole.

Further evidence of Angelo's prison breakdown comes from the testimony of Bucktail comrade Richard Atkin Rice, a fellow Libby inmate and Angelo's tent mate afterward at Camp Parole. Rice's room adjoined Angelo's, but the men had bored a hole through the wall to converse with those on the other side. Rice could hear Angelo grumbling constantly about his physical discomfort. Given Libby's wretched food and filthy conditions, that seems reasonable, yet it was something that Rice well remembered. He knew that Angelo was a tough soldier who seldom complained. This time he did, louder and longer than Rice had expected.[8]

After his Libby experience, Angelo clearly exhibited "episodic behavior," which we now know is a characteristic of PTSD. At times, the victim copes. During other periods, he must withdraw from the real world. Angelo could write long, lucid letters and continue mak-ing daily diary accounts, yet he often could or would not speak to companions. Charlie Robbins testified that sometimes Angelo would talk, other times not. Sometimes he would eat, other times not. Sometimes he would wander off, other times remain with his com-rades. Once home, Prudence Lyman Boyington did not immediately "notice that he was inclined to insanity . . . He was at times better and then worse." Before long, she "felt rather afraid of him and did not go where he was. I did not go to my brother's house on that account."[9]

Even as he struggled to connect with people, Angelo clung to his political and patriotic ideals. Psychotic and bedridden with a life-sapping illness after Gettysburg, he still could express pride and a

7. Shephard, *War of Nerves*, 230, citing I[an] McD. G. Stewart, *The Struggle for Crete, 20 May–1 June 1941* (Oxford: Oxford Paperback Reference, 1991).

8. Diary of Angelo M. Crapsey, Jan 12, 1863; Pension of Angelo M. Crapsey, affidavit of Richard A. Rice, date unstated; CMSR of Richard A. Rice, Co. I, 1st Pa. Rifles. Rice was a ser-geant at the time of capture and would rise to the rank of 1st lieutenant. Rice forgot that he had tented with Angelo after their release. Sgt. Lorenzo B. Prosser was Angelo's other Camp Parole tent mate.

9. Pension of Angelo M. Crapsey, deposition of Prudence Lyman Boyington, Nov. 22, 1892.

touch of braggadocio describing the army's accomplishments in a letter to Frank Sibley.

> The third [of July] we were skirmishing all day until four o'clock when our brigade charged on [Maj. Gen. John Bell] Hood's Rebel division. Their skirmishers made quite a sharp fight but we soon routed them & the whole division soon & we pressed after them and we drove them like sheep 1½ miles. You may guess our rifles were not silent. Our regt captured 10 prisoners & the battle flag of the 15 Georgia Regt. The rest of the brigade did full as well.[10]

Throughout his ordeal, Angelo closely followed the war's progress as if Fredericksburg and Gettysburg had never happened. "One thing I have to congratulate myself is I have tried to do my duty as an American & a soldier," he wrote Frank Sibley from Camp Parole. In hindsight, those words smack of whistling in the dark, yet his diary reflects joy at every Union success. "Bully for our men!" he wrote on receiving reports of Federal accomplishments in Arkansas and on the Yazoo River.[11] Even though his verbal communication skills had deteriorated, he had shown sound mental organization when he told Laroy about the work being performed by Congress's Joint Committee on the Conduct of the War.[12]

As he looked about him, however, he saw fellow parolees behaving badly, and that seemed to disgust him even more than before, as his diary reveals.

> There is plenty fighting & robbing & whiskey is plenty . . . Fighting is the main business and drinking whiskey. The exchanged men were out to drill or make as if to drill. It is a perfect farce. The men will not drill . . . Plenty of drunken soldiers. That is a common thing.[13]

His unrelenting attitude may have supported his mental downfall after he saw that reality and philosophy clashed so fiercely.

Angelo maintained what mental equilibrium he could by unconsciously resorting to a blocking mechanism modern health professionals call "numbing," a withdrawal from belief in an effort to sup-

---

10. Angelo to Frank Sibley, Aug. 3, 1862, KGC.
11. Diary of Angelo M. Crapsey, Jan. 16, Mar. 13, and June 11, 1863.
12. See pages 116–17.
13. Diary of Angelo M. Crapsey, compilation from entries of Jan. 17, 20, and 25, 1863.

press painful memories. Nervousness, depression, and the inability to relate to others are all characteristic symptoms of numbing and ones Angelo exhibited often. Lura Crapsey recalled how "he couldn't even tell a little story about his army experiences." When Sim Pomeroy told him how an acquaintance had wished him dead, the lad who once would have become "fighting mad" just sank deeper into depression and accepted the inevitable. Every witness commenting on his post-Gettysburg behavior reported how he regularly wandered off mentally and muttered gibberish.[14]

Many PTSD victims struggle with "survival guilt." Dr. Joel Osler Brende, a psychiatrist specializing in assisting Vietnam veterans' return to American society, and his coauthor, Dr. Erwin Randolph Parson, a clinical psychologist, were grunts in Vietnam and therefore doubly qualified to understand the mental trials of that war. They reported how one Vietnam veteran's struggle with survival guilt sent him spiraling into alcoholism. The man felt sincerely that he returned safely from Southeast Asia only because more worthy men had died in his place. With crushing frankness he asserted, "It was not right that I should be [alive]."[15]

Angelo experienced six battles and escaped death in all of them, sometimes by a hair's breadth. At Dranesville, "the bullets came pretty close to me . . . One of them struck the man behind me." At Cross Keys, "300 shell & balls passed over us, some of them bursting right over us. A bullet out of a shell struck within 6 inches of my head . . . I saw one Rebel shoot at me & the ball came very close." At Harrisonburg "the Rebels were within 5 rods of me when I climbed the fence." While climbing South Mountain under fire "my right hand man was one to fall . . . Bloom was shot by my side . . . [and] Northrop fell a few yards to the left. Maxson fell dead within a few feet of him . . . I only got my face and eyes full of bark." After release from Libby Prison he wrote, "It seems strange how I have escaped the bullets for I have had them cannon balls fall & explode killing men who were beside me & many times little fellows ripping my knapsack or clothes."

Worse, when the pressure of fighting was the greatest at Fredericksburg, he had failed in his duty, or so his confused mind concluded. "Compromise will not be uttered," he had once written to

---

14. Brende and Parson, *Vietnam Veterans*, 68–69; Pension of Angelo M. Crapsey, depositions of Lura Crapsey, Nov. 7, 1892, and Seneca B. Pomeroy, May 13, 1893.

15. Brende and Parson, *Vietnam Veterans*, 96.

Laroy.[16] But at Fredericksburg, he had compromised. It did not matter that all the Union forces in that sector had to flee or that surrendering or dying were his only choices. His mind told him that he had quit when others had fought and perished. All the bragging, all the patriotic words he had used arguing in Roulette were stripped of meaning, laying bare once hidden feelings of inferiority. He, from society's lowest station, the "blockhead" who was "unfit to be seen in decent company," he who had dared to decide when human life should end, had survived while others died. In that putrid cage called Libby Prison, the walls closed in, and imaginary lice conspired with the living creature to infest a body he now considered worthless.[17]

Modern-day psychiatry has given us tongue-twisting terms for Angelo's phantom lice: "delusional parasitosis" or "somatic type delusion." Soap and water ended Angelo's real scourge. Only death ended the imaginary one.[18]

☙❧

Fredericksburg was the top of Angelo's fatal slide, but clearly he hit bottom after Gettysburg. This time, however, the illness appears to have been physical. Angelo first noted his symptoms in his July 16 diary entry. He blamed it on taking a chill after swimming and dubbed the condition "chill fever," a term that described high fever accompanied by chills and shakes. He could have called it "ague," the disease he had feared most since joining the army.[19] His swim most likely did not cause his physical disability, but eleven consecutive days of hard marching in sultry weather, culminating on the 15th with a twenty-five-mile march, surely weakened the resistance of his diarrhea-wasted body. The causative event took place sometime around the battle of Gettysburg, whether from the bite of a malarial-laden mosquito or by coming in contact with fecal matter laced with typhoid bacteria or parasites.[20]

---

16. Angelo to Laroy, Aug. 31, 1861, KLC.

17. Angelo to Frank Sibley, Feb. 7, 1863, KGC; Pension of Angelo M. Crapsey, affidavit of Charles H. Robbins, Aug. 16, 1885.

18. The Bohart Museum of Entomology, "Delusional Parasitosis," http://delusion.ucdavis .edu/. Delusional parasitosis is a medical disorder in which the victim genuinely believes he is being infested by parasites. See also *DSM*, 325–26.

19. See earlier reference, Angelo to Laroy, May 30, 1861, KLC.

20. Diary of Angelo M. Crapsey, July 6–16, 1863; Angelo to Frank Sibley, Aug. 3, 1863, KGC.

Medical science now recognizes that typhoid fever and malaria have different causes and apply unique treatments. Many of the diseases' symptoms, however, can be strikingly similar. Even today the disease is certifiable only by laboratory analysis of blood and/or stool samples. Lacking such analytical tools, Civil War surgeons had to treat the two illnesses in similar manners because they could only deal with symptoms. Ergo, they lumped them together as "malarial" and often issued a diagnosis of "typhoid-malaria."

Angelo's indicators—fever, weakness, abdominal pain, sore throat, delirium, weight loss, and diarrheic releases the color of pea soup he described as "slime"—could have fit several diseases. (He made no mention of the roseate skin spots that would have pegged his illness as typhoid fever.) Abdominal pain and diarrhea were the symptoms he dwelled upon in his diary because they tortured him the most. Yet, the Mayo Clinic Web site lists diarrhea only as a *possible* symptom of malaria, while the Centers for Disease Control and Prevention (CDC) does not mention diarrhea at all. For typhoid fever, the Mayo Clinic claims constipation as a more common symptom in adult sufferers, and the CDC lists only constipation.[21]

I have read more than five thousand Civil War pension records to date and have noted exactly two soldiers reporting constipation. I recall them because their statements were shocking by comparison. On the other hand, "diarrhea" and "dysentery" appear in the vast majority of pensions, even those not alleging the illness as a contributing pension issue. One surgeon reported seeing every man in his command at least once for the "quick-step."[22] Funny as that name may seem now, the disease is not amusing, particularly to a soldier in the field with no access to toilet facilities. The disease went beyond inconvenience. Federal surgeons recorded fifty-seven thousand deaths from the wasting effects of diarrhea or dysentery, and no one knows how many Confederate soldiers died from it. It is likewise impossible to know how often the disease was a major contributing factor in deaths by other reported causes.[23]

---

21. *Medical History of the Civil War*, index, vol. 1, viii–ix. If blood were present in the stool, surgeons labeled the condition dysentery. Otherwise, they considered it diarrhea. They regarded dysentery as more serious but treated both with the same methods.

22. George Worthington Adams, *Doctors in Blue: The Medical History of the Union Army in the Civil War*, 16.

23. U.S. Department of Health and Human Services, Centers for Disease Control and Prevention (CDC), www.cdc.gov/ncidod/dbmd/diseaseinfo/typhoidfever_t.htm, and www.cdc .gov/malaria/disease.htm; Mayo Clinic, www.mayoclinic.com/health/typhoid-fever and www

At the same time, surgeons reported one in five cases under their care as malarial in nature. Enormous anecdotal and statistical evidence demonstrates that most soldiers diagnosed with malaria and typhoid fever also suffered with diarrhea or dysentery. This seeming dichotomy is explicable once we understand that diarrheic conditions were so prevalent that their presence in malarial and typhoid fever patients was coincidental rather than symptomatic. By observing patients with these simultaneous conditions, physicians wrongly, but understandably, concluded they were looking at one disease with multiple symptoms.

Typhoid and malaria both can create another symptom that may be relevant to Angelo Crapsey. Paranoid psychosis and delirium can occur if the diseases proceed to their severest forms, and whatever struck Angelo appears to have been an extreme form. But even without a bacterial, viral, or parasitic assault on his brain, his post-Gettysburg illness sapped whatever physical strength he needed to get him through the scourge of psychological trials.[24] He needed all the power he could muster to deal with the village he had left forty-one months before, and he had none left to do that.

"Atrocity" is word that many baby boomer Americans associate principally with the war in Vietnam.[25] Civil War-era morality generally forbade the dehumanizing factors that led to such events. Atrocities did occur but seldom in the gruesome form we think of today. Most often, the perpetrators were guerrilla sociopaths such as William Clarke Quantrill, "Bloody" Bill Anderson, or Champ Ferguson.[26] The Confederacy officially disapproved of such behavior but did little to

---

.mayoclinic.com/health/malaria. *Medical History of the Civil War*, index, vol. 1, viii–ix. Cholera, a disease accompanied by severe diarrhea, was rarely reported in the Civil War.

24. Mayo Clinic, www.mayoclinic.com/health/typhoid-fever/DS00538/DSECTION=7; CDC, www.cdc.gov/malaria/disease.htm#severe.

25. As of this writing, many of a certain political persuasion freely apply the term to almost any security activity associated with the war on terror.

26. James M. McPherson, *Battle Cry of Freedom: The Civil War Era*, 292. The Kansas-Missouri region was especially prone to violent reprisals. McPherson calls Civil War–era Missouri "a no-man's land of hit-and-run raids, arson, ambush, and murder." Mark Grimsley, *The Hard Hand of War: Union Military Policy Toward Southern Civilians, 1861–1865*, 197–98. After the battle of Saltville, Virginia, Confederate guerrilla Champ Ferguson killed a number of wounded soldiers still lying on the battlefield and murdered another in his hospital bed. Arrested and tried after the war, Ferguson justly died on the gallows.

stop it—assuming there was anything realistic they could have done to prevent it.[27]

Unlike America's Asian enemies in Vietnam, Korea, and World War II or today's Islamic terrorists, Rebels and Yankees shared common ancestry, the same historical heroes, worshipped the same deity, and spoke English (or soon would learn it). Men did "go off" in hand-to-hand combat, but that was from the natural course of life-or-death struggle, not planned brutality.[28] Even if a man wanted to commit mass murder, the absence of automatic weaponry and portable explosive devices limited the possibilities.[29]

By modern-day standards, both sides' prison camps were such hell-holes as to be atrocities by their mere existence. But they evolved largely from neglect and ignorance and not the systematic practice of abuse common in Japanese and North Vietnamese internment camps. Neither side beheaded, beat, or worked prisoners to death, although prisoners did die of malnutrition and exposure. Battles between the main armies, however gruesome the resulting carnage may have been, generally were stand-up affairs waged under an unwritten code of honor between men who often expressed admiration for their enemy's grit. Formal communication between adversaries commonly closed with "your obedient servant."

But atrocity was still possible, and accusations of it appear to have fallen onto Angelo's shoulders. Most likely, the cause was one cryptic statement he uttered upon his return. Roulette resident William Sherwood Brine essentially accused Angelo of barbaric acts. The English-born Brine was a member of Battery E, 1st Pennsylvania Light Artillery, a Reserve Corps unit that served with the Bucktails during the first part of the war.[30] He was also a member of the hunting party that ill-fated August day. He testified:

> I have always thought that Angelo shot some people or children while in the army when not in battle for he used to say that "nits made lice," that he went down to fight the Rebs. He might almost have said that he had

---

27. Grimsley, *Hard Hand of War*, 118; McPherson, *Battle Cry of Freedom*, 292, 787–88; George S. Burkhardt, *Confederate Rage, Yankee Wrath: No Quarter in the Civil War*, 197–98.

28. A racial component sometimes led to harsh consequences when black and white troops faced each other in battle. Both sides gave as much as they received. See Burkhardt, *Confederate Rage, Yankee Wrath*, 159–86.

29. The Gatling gun, an early hand-crank-operated machine gun, was used sparingly during the war and was too large to conceal.

30. CMSR and Pension of William S. Brine, Batt. E, 1st Pa. Light Art.; Angelo to Laroy, Oct. 30, 1861, KLC.

shot children as to say what he did. It was generally believed that something that he did in the army preyed upon his mind and wound[ed] him. That's the way it looked to me. He certainly was unbalanced.[31]

John V. Weimer, Angelo's former schoolmate and another member of the hunting party, kept the rumor mill churning. "Sometimes I thought he had done something in the army that troubled him or that he imagined he had," Weimer testified. "I remember that it was all about the army when talking to himself, and I never could see that anything else worried him."[32]

Both men's insinuations are weak. Brine, for example, met Angelo in the field in October 1861 but did not see him again until he returned to Roulette. He never mentioned that he had witnessed atrocities involving Angelo or anyone else.[33] Brine served in the army only one and a half years and about half of that inactive due to a knee injury. Battery E suffered only one man wounded and none killed during his tenure, so he was unlikely to have experienced the horrors that Angelo had seen.[34]

Weimer had even less contact with Angelo during the war. He made no personal observations of Angelo while in the army and surely had no idea of any specific cause for his breakdown. While Weimer may have been correct in assuming that Angelo "had done something in the army that troubled him," such events did not have to be more than what was routinely expected of a soldier.[35]

There is a plausible interpretation of Angelo's "nits" remark that does not involve an act of atrocity. Both armies had soldiers in ranks who should have been carrying schoolbooks instead of rifles. Angelo surely saw their young bodies bleeding on the field, some of whom died by his hand. In his first battle, he had witnessed three Confederates beheaded and burned to a crisp. It is hardly strange that such ghastly experiences would affect a moral man.

Roulette's civilians could not comprehend the truth of war. Suspicion and Angelo's inexplicable behavior were enough to turn the town against him. Politics played at least some role. Many in the town were Copperheads, a peace-at-all-cost movement equivalent to Vietnam-era hippies and the Iraq war's CODEPINK. Although the name actu-

---

31. Pension of Angelo M. Crapsey, deposition of William S. Brine.
32. Pension of Angelo M. Crapsey, deposition of John V. Weimer.
33. Angelo to Laroy, Oct. 30, 1861, KLC.
34. CMSRs of all men of Battery E, 1st Pa. Light Art. (43rd Pa.).
35. Angelo to Laroy, Oct. 30, 1861, KLC.

ally referred to the copperhead penny symbol worn by advocates, many Union soldiers preferred the reptilian reference. Roulette witnessed Copperhead demonstrations shortly before Angelo arrived home.[36]

Four months after Angelo's death, a veritable who's who of the town met in the red schoolhouse to "form ourselves into a club for the purpose of assisting each other hereafter in case of another draft." Each man put money into a pool. When drafted, a club member could withdraw up to five hundred dollars to pay a substitute. Although beyond draft age, Laroy Lyman donated three hundred dollars and then added one hundred more to cover the pledges of two donors who reneged. In all, fifty-six men pledged $3,146. Laroy made the largest single contribution.[37]

In spite of his association with the antidraft club, Laroy did not consider himself a Copperhead. Philosophy and religion formed the basis of his beliefs, not politics. In February 1863, he decried a strong showing of Copperheads at a town meeting and "did not go near them." If he paid attention to the war at all, it was because acquaintances were involved and sent him letters from the front. Not once did he propose civil disobedience. As a deputy marshal, he made it clear that he would arrest any deserter who refused to report to his unit.[38]

Roulette's antidraft club was neither illegal nor unusual because the law then permitted a drafted man to pay another to serve in his place. Nonetheless, it demonstrates the small community's attitude toward their young men serving in the army. Those who paid to get out of the draft were not necessarily Copperheads, but volunteer soldiers who were putting their lives on the line had other opinions. One Roulette soldier wrote Laroy, "I think those copperheads had ought to have their teeth extracted or their heads severely beaten . . . Some of the soldiers will with out doubt come back at the close of the war & then in my opinion will come the day of reckoning."[39]

---

36. Diaries of Laroy Lyman.

37. Minutes of meeting, Nov. 29, 1864, Potter County Historical Society; Diaries of Laroy Lyman. After the two men reneged on their dues, Laroy feared others might take the same path and affect the club's progress. He eliminated the problem by making a motion to deny voting rights to all noncontributors, and it carried. Laroy made a special note in his diary to remember those who disagreed with his motion, relatives included. Laroy Lyman to his uncle, Sam Palmer, Feb. 5, 1865, KLC. Perhaps the club was out of money when Laroy's nephew, Otis Lyman, received his draft notice and ran to Canada rather than serve.

38. Diaries of Laroy Lyman; Laroy to Mr. Blair, Dec. 20, 1864, KLC.

39. John D. Earl to Laroy Lyman, Apr. 16, 1864, KLC. For other letters expressing similar sentiments, see Wiley, *Billy Yank*, 286–88.

No one had felt that more strongly than Angelo, who had penned similar words on at least two occasions.[40] He returned home and heard acquaintances tell him that he had suffered for nothing and that his comrades had died without purpose. Worse, some suggested that he had killed wantonly. Ravaged in body and mind, he reacted badly—when he reacted at all—and Roulette responded in kind. In short, Angelo faced much the same circumstances as returning Vietnam veterans.

We must ponder if Laroy Lyman inadvertently made a major contribution to Angelo's suicidal tendency. Long before the onset of madness, Angelo offered a veiled hint of his need for Laroy's approval and used Prudence for leverage. "Prude wrote to me that she hoped the Union Army should come out victorious," he wrote Laroy. It is not difficult to sense the implication in Angelo's words to Laroy: If Prude can support the war effort, Laroy, why can't you? Angelo made similar oblique pleas in three other letters. He had pleaded with Laroy to defend his state if the Rebels invaded. He had suggested that Laroy might kill an Indian in lieu of losing his scalp once they traveled west. He had begged Laroy to visit him in Virginia so he could experience battle firsthand. Angelo was telling Laroy that if he would defend himself with violence, he would have realized why Angelo had chosen to do it. That could have eased the pain—or so he seemed to believe. While no documentation exists to confirm the two men engaged in heated discussions over the war, it is impossible to imagine the two of them *not* talking about it openly. Laroy spoke his mind no matter the consequences, and that surely led to lectures amounting to "I told you so." That had to sting Angelo. He had promised that had he died in battle, it would have been with Laroy's photo in his pocket. Yet, Laroy would never have done the same for Angelo. This is not to blame Laroy for what happened, but Angelo clearly sought benediction from his mentor and never received it.[41]

How much blame must John Crapsey bear for Angelo's demise? Had the reverend's religious excesses created a mental instability in Angelo? Angelo attacked his father at Carver Hospital and threatened him on at least one other occasion. Was John Crapsey the target of suppressed anger or merely an unlucky man in the wrong places at the wrong times? Suspicion will linger. Evidence indicates

40. Angelo to Laroy, Sept. 15, 1861; Angelo to Almeron Lyman, Mar. 1, 1863, KLC.

41. Angelo to Laroy, Aug. 20, 1861, Mar. 1, 1862, Sept. 8, 1862, Sept. 30, 1862, and Apr. 9, 1863; Laroy Lyman to Thankful Lyman, Dec. 19, 1861; Diaries of Laroy Lyman, KLC.

that Angelo threatened no one except his father and that he even failed to recognize him at Chestnut Hill Hospital.[42]

⁕

Lyman family lore offers a titillating possibility for Angelo's final mental collapse in Fairmont, Minnesota. While there, the story goes, he received a letter from his sweetheart, allegedly the daughter of Aaron Smith, revealing the devastating news she was to marry a man named Eli Kent and move into a Mormon colony. Lore concludes that this lost love is what sent him over the brink.[43]

There is no evidence as to what happened in Fairmont. While on their trip, Angelo and Laroy visited a Lyman relative, who, two weeks after Angelo's death, wrote Laroy to express shock over the suicide and how they had "liked him very much."[44] That means Angelo must have acted rationally while there. Yet a short time later, he made such a total break with reality that Laroy immediately brought him home. Laroy did not witness what happened in Fairmont, and Angelo may have never told him. Considering his mental state afterward, it is possible that little intelligent conversation ever again passed between them. Following Angelo's death, Laroy's diary contains several mentions of an Eli Kent and his wife. They were New York State residents who worshipped with him at times, but he never mentioned Mrs. Kent's first name. Mormon Church genealogical records contain no information on an Eli Kent/Smith marriage. Laroy never referred to them as being Mormon, something he surely would have noted given the nation's hatred of the religion and his own prejudices toward other faiths.[45]

One of Angelo's post–Libby Prison letters to Laroy offers another hint at possible woman trouble. "Laroy, I guess there will be no chance for me to get married when I return. What do you think about it? That $300 is gone. What gall! [Who] do you suppose would marry the soldier after three years or more service in the Army?" This may be a young man's lamentations of being fleeced by a supposed lover

---

42. The one exception is the bark-throwing incident related by his sister. While frightening to a young child, this did not appear to have been an attack on his younger half sibling.

43. Lyman, *History of Roulet,* 139; U.S. Census of 1850.

44. Willie Lyman to Laroy, Aug. 20, 1864, KLC; Lyman, *History of Roulet,* 27.

45. Diaries of Laroy Lyman. Popular genealogical Web sites such as *www.familysearch.org* and *www.rootsweb.com* contain nothing on an Eli Kent/Smith couple.

or simply the sentiments of a depressed psychotic. There are insufficient facts to know.[46]

Except for this one cryptic statement, Angelo never hinted at romantic involvements in his extant correspondence. Several witnesses agreed in pension testimony they were unaware of any affairs of the heart. It is a stretch to conclude that all witnesses lied or forgot such details because their testimonies occurred over a decade of time and in diverse locations. Laroy's diaries contain frequent comments on other men's dalliances but mention only a general interest in the opposite sex for Angelo.[47]

A recent book that reprints some of Angelo's letters (unedited) names the alleged mysterious love interest as "Purde."[48] Almost certainly, the author meant "Prude," Laroy's sister Prudence Lyman Boyington. Any sport is possible in the sexual arena, but an illicit love affair between Angelo and Prudence is unlikely. Whenever he mentioned her in his diary, it was as "Mrs. Boyington." He used "Prude" only in letters to Laroy.[49] Prudence was twelve years older than Angelo, married with several children, and well educated for her time and location. She surely would not have engaged in an adulterous relationship with a physically wrecked psychotic. If a dalliance occurred prior to the war, it would have been nearly impossible to hide in tiny Roulette, especially with snoopy brother Laroy around. If the big man had caught wind of such an affair, he would have thrown Angelo out of the house and mentioned the incident in his diary.[50]

Unless new evidence is uncovered, there will be no definitive answers, just questions with solutions that remain frustratingly out of reach. All that is certain is that after Fairmont, Angelo's pathway had come to an end, and hell loomed before him.

---

46. Angelo to Laroy, June 5, 1863, KLC.

47. Diaries of Laroy Lyman; Diary of Angelo M. Crapsey, 1863; Pension of Angelo M. Crapsey, depositions of John and Lura Crapsey, Nov. 7, 1892, and John V. Weimer and Prudence Lyman Boyington, Nov. 22, 1892.

48. Means, *Corporal Brewer*, 620.

49. Diary of Angelo M. Crapsey, Apr. 20 and 21, 1863.

50. Lyman, *History of Roulet*. Prudence was seventy-eight years old when she died on January 25, 1909.

14

Was Angelo Unique?

There can be no overstatement how frightening the experience
of war is.

—Joel Osler Brende and Erwin Randolph Parson

ON OCTOBER 12, 1863, PVT. GEORGE F. HURST, 25TH INDIANA INFANTRY,
entered Union Hospital in Memphis, Tennessee, racked with high
fever and diarrhea. Surely, he nor anyone else used exalted language
to describe his physical condition that day. But words were written
about him, as they were about thousands of others forced to endure
similar circumstances to those Angelo Crapsey had suffered. Today,
historians are the principle consumers of these words confined to
sentences void of lyricism and lofty sentiment, words so harsh they
can be an emotional challenge to read. Among them are a surgeon's
description of George Hurst, one that Angelo's doctor could easily
have written about him.

> He was greatly prostrated; his mind dull; countenance suffused [colored,
> probably red]; lips and tongue coated black; pulse 110 and quick; skin hot.
> Next day he was delirious. One ounce of brandy was given every hour. On
> the 14th the fever was found to remit in the morning, becoming increased
> in the afternoon. Mercury with chalk and rhubarb was given, and during the
> night the bowels were opened twice. Next day there was less fever; quinine
> was prescribed in three-grain doses three times a day. On the 16th there was
> less fever, but the patient vomited frequently. Ten grains of quinine were
> given at once, and the mercury, chalk, and rhubarb were repeated with car-
> bonate of soda. On the following day the bowels were opened several times,
> and the mind became clearer. The skin and conjunctivae [mucous mem-
> brane of the eyes] became yellow-colored on the 19th and on the 20th he
> had epistaxis [nose bleed], but was otherwise improving.[1]

---

1. *The Medical and Surgical History of the Civil War,* 5:114–15, Case 29, George H. Hurst, Co. D,
25th Ind.

For all the misery Hurst endured, he was luckier than Pvt. Joseph H. Nickless, 35th Wisconsin. A similar, if not identical, disease sent him to his grave. Nickless's death allowed medical science to study the effects of his common lower gastrointestinal illness. An autopsy revealed "diffuse inflammation of the mucous membrane throughout the whole extent of the small intestine . . . The large intestine was extensively ulcerated." Small wonder that men suffering with long-term diarrhea or dysentery endured such great pain.[2]

The descriptions of these two soldiers' physical conditions exist through the efforts of Dr. William Alexander Hammond, who spent sixteen months as Abraham Lincoln's surgeon general trying to revolutionize the army's health care system.[3] Never known for being tactful or humble, Hammond soon ran afoul of ignorance, bureaucracy, and strong-willed secretary of war Edwin McMasters Stanton. Hammond's military career crashed as a result of a headline-making court-martial that he had demanded in a vain attempt to clear his name of what may have been trumped-up charges.[4] Before all that happened, he issued an order that had a lasting effect on history: surgeons must keep detailed records of their cases. This documentation formed the basis for one of his brainchildren, *The Medical and Surgical History of the War of the Rebellion*. This seminal work contains detailed and, for its time, shocking rhetorical and pictorial illustrations of the war's medical practices, wounds and diseases, and a plethora of medical statistics. The voluminous collection consumes more than two feet of shelf space and challenges readers' eyesight with fine print that often further shrinks to Lilliputian dimensions.[5]

The Medical and Surgical History does not, however, contain the case of Owen Flaharty, 125th Illinois, or anyone like him. Eric T. Dean opened *Shook Over Hell* with Flaharty's trip down his own pathway to hell, one initiated by the battle of Stones River (Murfreesboro). After the battle, Flaharty desperately sought a furlough to escape war, but the army refused his request. He fell into a brooding silence and

2. Ibid., 3:253, Case 846, Joseph H. Nickless, Co. H, 35th Wis. Inf.

3. Bonnie Ellen Blustein, *Preserve Your Love of Science: Life of William A. Hammond, American Neurologist; O.R.*, ser. 3, 2:26, General Orders No. 48, Apr. 28, 1862.

4. Frank R. Freemon, *Gangrene and Glory: Medical Care During the Civil War*, 144.

5. Blustein, *Preserve Your Love*, 69. *The Medical and Surgical History of the War of the Rebellion* appeared in 1870 in six weighty, nonindexed volumes. In 1990, Broadfoot Publishing reprinted it in twelve smaller volumes and replaced *War of the Rebellion* with *Civil War*. The three indexes issued in 1992 should have Civil War historians blessing Broadfoot, especially because they retained original pagination. A cross-reference in the first index volume permits successful navigation of the original publication from the new indexes.

often would not respond when mates talked to him, then startled when they shouted to get his attention. His tent mate became concerned when Flaharty developed "a wild scared look" and his sleep grew troubled.

However bad his mental condition may have been, Flaharty had to fight in another battle or risk being labeled a coward. He again survived unscathed but witnessed numerous comrades' lives snuffed out of existence. After that, he isolated himself completely. Military life ended for Flaharty after he threatened to kill a friend for no discernible reason and shortly thereafter ran screaming from an enemy that was not there. Discharged, he returned home only to discover that the war had followed him and would not go away.[6]

Owen Flaharty's and Angelo Crapsey's cases are missing from *The Medical and Surgical History* because that huge collection of writing virtually ignores mental illnesses. Readers will find a mere two and a half pages on the subject of "nostalgia" that minimizes the condition we now know as depression (or worse) as little more than a bad case of homesickness. The article reports that nostalgia "patients were derived from two classes of soldiers: young men of feeble will [with] highly developed imaginative faculties and strong sexual desires, and married men for the first time absent from their families." The doctor-author did not consider that perhaps many cases went unreported from fear of being labeled "feeble-willed" and that most young men have "strong sexual desires," married or single. Otherwise, *The Medical and Surgical History* contains no case histories of emotionally troubled soldiers beyond those suffering the delirium attendant with intense fever. Suicides and insanity cases appear only in a series of departmental statistics without investigation of contributory factors. Of course, it published no postwar veteran suicide rates to shed light on war's aftereffects.[7]

The absence of psychiatric case studies is explicable. A general history of psychiatry typically contains but few prominent American names in the field prior to the Civil War and displays little genuine knowledge of the human mental condition. We remember Benjamin Rush principally for his signature on the Declaration of Independence and secondarily as a prominent Revolutionary War physician. Few recall him as the first American psychiatrist. For his time, Rush's

6. Eric T. Dean, *Shook Over Hell: Post-Traumatic Stress, Vietnam, and the Civil War*, 1–2.

7. *Medical and Surgical History*, 1:641, reported 301 white soldiers committing suicide, and 144 dying from known homicides.

attitude toward the mentally disturbed could, with charitable hindsight, be labeled "enlightened." He eschewed the cruelty typically
imposed on the mentally ill, but his knowledge was necessarily limited by the science of his day.[8]

Dorothea Lynde Dix, chief of Union female nurses during the war,
had been a strong advocate for the mentally ill for twenty years beforehand. Infuriated by traditional harsh treatment for mental patients,
Dix advocated a softer approach by caring for the mentally ill in "ther-
apeutic asylums" and had lobbied successfully for the opening of
many institutions for the mentally ill. Within her lifetime, however, statistical evidence proved that her espoused treatment was useless.[9]

The Civil War era had a few prominent physicians who delved into
the workings of the human nervous system. Silas Weir Mitchell pio-
neered the field of neurology and treated soldiers with nerve disorders, and Jacob Da Costa applied his theories of "irritable heart syn-
drome." Both functioned at Philadelphia's Turner's Lane Hospital
during the war. Mitchell insisted his patients "be strong" and reassert
their "masculinity." Part of his job was uncovering fakers and sending
them back to active duty, a task for which he contrived a number
of techniques. Da Costa dealt with heart issues such as chest pain,
digestive problems, and rapid pulse rate. The symptoms he reported
resembled anxiety attacks or cardiovascular conditions more than
post-traumatic stress, although that was no doubt a factor. The fact is
that no one knew what caused mental illness. Most physicians were
less progressive than Mitchell and Da Costa and considered the subject purely a morality and character issue. The enlightened era of psychological study would have to wait for psychiatrists such as Jung and
Freud, whose names would become familiar even to many laymen.[10]

Thus, when family and friends failed to understand the cause of
Angelo's mental breakdown, they were barely less ignorant than the
era's medical establishment. Indeed, it is difficult to use the word
"establishment" to describe the mid-nineteenth-century medical profession. Poor application of standards and a dearth of medical knowledge often made surgeons' ministrations more dangerous than help-

8. Franz G. Alexander and Sheldon T. Selesnick, *The History of Psychiatry: An Evaluation of Psychiatric Thought and Practice from Prehistoric Times to the Present*, 120–23.

9. Margaret Muckenhoupt, *Dorothea Dix: Advocate for Mental Health Care*, 111, 118.

10. Alexander and Selesnick, *History of Psychiatry*, 159; Silas W. Mitchell receives but one mention in this history. R. Gregory Lande, *Madness, Malingering, and Malfeasance: The Transformation of Psychiatry and the Law in the Civil War Era*, 172–78; Ben Shephard, *War of Nerves*, 65; Freemon, *Gangrene and Glory*, 165.

ful. Stodgy attitudes made even the best American medical schools hesitant to adopt modern methods. Harvard did not obtain its first stethoscope until 1868, thirty years after its invention. A year later, the school purchased its first microscope, a nearly two-centuries-old technology.[11]

Becoming a surgeon, as doctors were then most often called, was not a great challenge for anyone who was literate. No significant screening process existed to select the best and brightest candidates for a medical education. Physician-historians Thomas P. Lowry and Jack D. Welsh have described mid-nineteenth-century medical education as "nine months of lectures. To graduate, the student attended the same lecture series for a second time. There was little or no practical clinical experience." Amazingly, a man could become a "surgeon" without performing a single surgical procedure. Human dissection, a critical part of anatomical study, was then illegal in some states even though it was the norm in French medical schools. The subject of psychology, of course, was never broached.[12]

The sheer number of physicians required meant the army could not demand formal medical educations for men to gain the ranks of surgeon and assistant surgeon. Many surgeons took claim to that title only because they had apprenticed with a working physician, who himself might have been incompetent. The 29th Pennsylvania Infantry's assistant surgeon was a druggist who for three and a half years offered medical treatment he had no formal training to dispense. Pharmaceutical knowledge was so crude that surgeons routinely prescribed "remedies" with ingredients such as mercury, strychnine, turpentine, and creosote. Absent any concept of bacteriology, army surgeons "cleaned" surgical instruments by wiping them across their aprons before cutting into a patient on an operating surface covered with the remnants of those who had preceded him. Doctors considered pus forming on a wound to be a "laudable" sign of healing. Some still employed the medieval practices of bleeding, cupping, and application of leeches, and even the best medical minds considered liquor to have pharmacological value. A few of the more ignorant went so far as to cauterize the anal orifices of diarrhea patients to prevent evacuations.[13]

---

11. Adams, *Doctors in Blue*, 50.

12. Ibid; David Herbert Donald, *Charles Sumner and the Coming of the Civil War*, 48. Sumner became ill when, as an American medical student studying in France, physicians showed him the school's dissection rooms.

13. Wiley, *Life of Billy Yank*, 130; CMSR of Joseph A. Wolf, Asst. Surg., 29th Pa.; *Medical and Surgical History*, index 1, viii–ix.

Thus, when Angelo emerged from Libby Prison scraping imaginary lice from his body, he had no one in the medical profession who could help him through his crisis either physically or psychologically. Perhaps if Carver or Chestnut Hill Hospital had transferred him to the more enlightened Turner's Lane Hospital, he may have had a chance to recover. But ignorance cannot remove all blame from the army medical system, including the Bucktails' surgeons. No twenty-first-century level of medical sophistication was required for them to remove a man from active duty who was behaving in such a bizarre manner. While surgeons were overly sensitive to fakery, Angelo never had a reputation as a shirker.[14] Had the surgeons either discharged or transferred him to the Invalid Corps before the battle of Gettysburg, his chances of returning to normalcy would have increased. Doubtless, though, even the psychotic version of Angelo would have fought removal from active duty. No self-respecting soldier wanted to labor under suspicion of malingering, and he was especially sensitive to that issue. How could he return home after he had labeled the Potter County men "cowards" for doing the same thing in 1861?

His own words and ideals had helped trap him on the pathway to hell. And the army medical establishment missed its only opportunity to pull him back from the abyss.

༺ঽৡ৵ঽༀ

Modern-day America pays little more heed to Civil War mental disorders than the medical profession of that era. Most weekends see one or more living history demonstrations somewhere in the country, some of them huge in scope and played out before large audiences. Reenactors depict scenes of death, and actor-surgeons perform mock amputations in meticulously recreated field hospitals. But never does a reenactor assume the role of a wild-eyed psychotic scraping phantom lice from his body.[15] Even modern historians largely overlook mental health issues. Bring up Amazon.com on your computer, key "Civil War" and any other word referencing psychology in the search field, and perform as many searches as you wish. This giant book retailer will provide you with few books on the subject.

---

14. See Lande, *Madness, Malingering and Malfeasance,* especially chaps. 2 and 5.

15. The author has never witnessed such a recreation. See James M. McPherson, "The War that Never Goes Away," in *Drawn with the Sword: Reflections on the American Civil War* for an essay on the continuing and amazing popularity of the Civil War.

Earl J. Hess's *The Union Soldier in Battle* incisively describes how Union men behaved in combat yet almost completely avoids the mental effects of war, even in a chapter named "The Psychology of Battle." While Hess does reflect briefly on killing and conscience in his "Holding On" chapter, he addresses it principally as a moral and religious dilemma. *That* it certainly was, but he does not discuss the consequences of deviating from that moral code.[16]

Dr. R. Gregory Lande tackles the subject in the self-descriptively titled *Madness, Malingering and Malfeasance: The Transformation of Psychiatry and the Law in the Civil War Era* but with little in the way of medical case study. George Worthington Adams's 1952 dissertation-turned-standard reference, *Doctors in Blue*, allows just one sentence for "shell shock" and one more for "nostalgia." C. Keith Wilbur's *Civil War Medicine, 1861–1865* ignores mental illness, and Frank Freemon's *Gangrene and Glory* begins and ends with a definition of nostalgia that does not admit its relationship to depression. Even Bell Irvin Wiley, whose research into the common soldier perhaps has put his name in more footnotes than any other Civil War historian, avoids the topic in his seminal works *The Life of Johnny Reb* and *The Life of Billy Yank*.[17]

James M. McPherson uses a number of primary accounts to describe mental anguish in *For Cause and Comrades* and gives us one of the reasons that the subject remains well hidden. Civil War combatants, lacking psychological terminology to understand mental stress, deemed psychological trauma "loss of courage." It was often difficult to distinguish the true psychological victim from those who were just scared or the malingerers faking insanity to escape battle. Moreover, many cases went unreported. Angelo Crapsey's medical records, for example, reflect physical, not psychological, problems. McPherson's wide-reaching subject matter in *For Cause and Comrades* allows only a few pages on this one topic, and many of his anecdotes could be as much statements of men's physical exhaustion as mental, related though the two are.[18]

Alfred Jay Bollet touches briefly on mental illness in *Civil War Medicine: Challenges and Triumphs*. He notes a Confederate soldier who

---

16. Hess, *The Union Soldier in Battle*.

17. Lande, *Madness, Malingering and Malfeasance*, 157–202. C. Keith Wilbur, Civil War Medicine, 1861–1865; Frank R. Freemon, *Gangrene and Glory: Medical Care During the American Civil War*; Wiley, *Life of Billy Yank*, chap. 11, 275–95; *The Life of Johnny Reb: The Common Soldier of the Confederacy*.

18. James McPherson, *For Cause and Comrades: Why Men Fought in the Civil War*, 165–66.

refused an arm amputation and died from the wound "complicated by nostalgia and despondency in an old man." He was describing the soldier's mental state, not his chronological age. Bollet relates how surgeons treated nostalgia by having patients drink alcoholic beverages, which we now know was the worse thing they could have prescribed. In all, Bollet shows that 903 Union soldiers received discharges for psychological problems, and the army institutionalized 2,603 more at Washington's Government Hospital for the Insane (aka St. Elizabeth). Given the size of the army, those were small numbers indeed.[19]

An occasional book on the stress of modern warfare may briefly touch on the Civil War. Penny Coleman's *Flashback: Posttraumatic Stress Disorder, Suicide, and the Lessons of War* reveals her personal struggle dealing with a Vietnam veteran husband whose PTSD-induced behavior forced their separation and ultimately pushed him to suicide. Unfortunately, Ms. Coleman willingly reveals her antiwar political beliefs, and that tends to bias her work. Furthermore, while her point of PTSD not being a new phenomenon is well taken (she goes back as far as Achilles), her knowledge of the Civil War barely skims the surface. Without evidence, she implies that PTSD was the principle cause for desertion and that death and a lonely burial was standard punishment for those caught and convicted. She also contends there were 145,000 reported cases of constipation. Her source is the best reference yet available, but sadly, she miscited it.[20]

That reference is Eric T. Dean's *Shook Over Hell: Post-Traumatic Stress, Vietnam, and the Civil War*. Using 291 case histories of Indiana veterans committed to an asylum, Dean paints a horrifying picture of these patients' individual journeys on their pathways to hell. He then goes a step further by comparing them to similar circumstances among Vietnam veterans whose situations were analyzed and treated by modern mental health professionals. Thankfully, Dean deals with the Vietnam subject free of political bias.

Angelo Crapsey's situation mirrors many of Dean's case histories, especially that of Rainey Johns, 101st Indiana. Like Angelo, Johns contracted a malarial disease that wasted away both body and mind. Also like Angelo, Johns later became so psychotic that it took several men to hold him down during flashbacks. Unlike Angelo, Johns sur-

19. Alfred Jay Bollet, *Civil War Medicine: Challenges and Triumphs*, 157, 232, 318.

20. Penny Coleman, *Flashback: Posttraumatic Stress Disorder, Suicide, and the Lessons of War*, 23–25.

vived the immediate aftermath of war only to have his symptoms reappear in more severe form ten years later.[21]

The names Crapsey, Flaharty, Johns, and countless others not mentioned here exemplify how Civil War soldiers no more gained instant peace of mind after Appomattox Court House than their Vietnam equivalents did after the last helicopter lifted from the American embassy in Saigon. Frank Kenfield, 17th Vermont, never found peace. The slaughter of black Federals he witnessed in the infamous battle of the crater at Petersburg, Virginia, forever put a "cold shudder" through him whenever he recalled "how those poor colored men were butchered in cold blood."[22] Many Civil War veterans had to put years behind them before the psychological anguish lessened and they could reunite on the battlefields of their youth. They had a chance to relish the glory then, glory they did not feel amid bursting shells and whizzing bullets, glory impossible while bedded down in a disease-ridden camp.

Before veterans of any conflict can face the horrors of their pasts, they have to move forward. Angelo Crapsey discovered that forward was a direction blocked by emotional and physical barriers too high for him to scale.[23]

21. Dean, *Shook Over Hell*, chap. 5, "For God's Sake Please Help Me: Post-Traumatic Stress," 104–5.

22. Burkhardt, *Confederate Rage, Yankee Wrath*, 170.

23. The first national military park at Chickamauga was not dedicated until 1895. Gettysburg followed shortly afterward. Thanks to the efforts of Clara Barton, Andersonville became a national shrine right after the war ended. See Oates, *A Woman of Valor*. Order Book of Co. K. The Bucktails first reunion occurred in 1887 in Williamsport, Pennsylvania.

Epilogue

To look backward for a while is to refresh the eye, to restore it, and to render it the more fit for its prime function of looking forward.

—Margaret Fairless

A<small>NGELO'S FRIENDS AND FAMILY DID NOT END THEIR MOURNING WITH</small> his burial. On September 18, 1864, they gathered in Liberty to honor his memory with a formal service. Charlie Robbins had survived his three-year hitch with the army and was able to attend. Laroy selected the minister, an Adventist, the first preacher of that faith to minister a funeral service in the area.[1]

In early 1865, John Crapsey sold his farm for a pittance and moved to Roulette. Folks there must have taken pity on the reverend because they made no effort to keep him out. That October he preached his final sermon in the town without apparent fuss, and he and his family shortly thereafter moved to Minnesota. Both Charles Robbins and Laroy's daughter Sybil, once each was married, would follow.[2]

Alas, trouble followed the Crapseys. In 1886, for reasons unknown, John pressed assault and battery charges against one Frank Gilbert and his son, but the jury acquitted. A year later, Lura Crapsey and her two youngest children arrived home to find that Gilbert had padlocked the door to their farm house, forcing them to break in. Gilbert

---

1. Diaries of Laroy Lyman; Pension of Angelo M. Crapsey, deposition of Charles H. Robbins, Jan. 18, 1893.

2. Pension of Angelo M. Crapsey, affidavit of Charles and Viola Robbins, Nov. 15, 1882. Charles and Viola remembered the Liberty (Port Allegany) land as being twenty acres in size, but other witnesses recalled it to be the seven or eight acres that John Crapsey claimed. Certificate of Property Assessments, McKean County commissioner's clerk, John R. Shoemaker, Oct. 14, 1884, shows "13 acres improved land and 92 acres unimproved." John Crapsey denied owning 92 acres of land, and the farm's sale price of $250.00 would seem to verify that. Laroy Lyman's diaries chronicle the Crapseys' move to Roulette.

179

arrived later with several Crapsey tenants shouting threats that included, according to Lura, a warning that they would "kill every G——d—— one of us and take out our hearts before Christmas." Gilbert and his companions began flinging stones at the house. While the children screamed in terror, Lura barred the door with a spear and announced bravely she would defend herself. The Crapsey-Gilbert war, as a local newspaper dubbed the ongoing feud, apparently ended with no serious casualties on either side.[3]

John became a well-known Pentecostal minister throughout the Midwest. Lura often joined her husband on the "inspirational speaker" circuit and became a sufragette. He became sufficiently famous that someone—probably John himself since the book mentions no author—thought his life and religious experiences interesting enough to put in booklet form. A. P. Miller held the copyright and receives tacit authorship here, but the information it contains could only have come from John Crapsey. Knowing him from other sources, the book reveals a man who avoided the truth whenever it failed to serve his reputation.[4]

John Crapsey waged a long battle to earn a pension from Angelo's army service. His first goal was to collect Angelo's bounty, essentially a signing bonus the army promised volunteers at enlistment. During the war's early stages, soldiers received their bounty upon discharge, or their families could claim it if they died. Although John was legally entitled to it, the process required eight years and the intervention of Minnesota's adjutant general to complete.[5]

John had made his first inquiry into obtaining a pension a year after Angelo's death but did not make formal application until 1882. Washington denied his pension claims twice, once for nondependence and a second time because Angelo's death was "not a result of his military service." John stayed persistent and finally succeeded in obtaining the monthly pension payment. He needed the money. In 1892, a pension investigator described him as "a feeble old man and lives in surroundings which are clearly indicative of poverty."[6] By being persistent, he left behind the details of a nineteenth-century horror story.

---

3. *Windom Reporter,* Sept. 15, 1887.

4. U.S. Census, 1880; Ephemera Web site, www.spirithistory.com/80relphl.html, Directory of the Religio-Philosphical Journal (Chicago: May 15, 1880).

5. Pension of Angelo M. Crapsey. John Crapsey to Commissioner of Pensions, Feb. 3, 1889.

6. Pension of Angelo M. Crapsey, Report of pension examiner E. R. Waite, Nov. 8, 1892. The Crapseys were then living in St. Paul, Minnesota.

John Crapsey's pension records also expose a man who lied easily and often as in his explanation as to why he failed to attend his son's funeral. He claimed, "I hurt myself unyoking oxen the day of the funeral." Immediately he changed his mind, saying, "No, the day of the suicide."[7] Was that a confused old man trying to recollect faded memories, or was he tripping over lies searching for a way out of an embarrassing experience? Whichever it was, neither makes sense. If he had not injured himself until the day of the funeral on August 6, 1864, why did Laroy have to force him to go to Roulette on August 5? If John had injured himself so badly on August 4 that he could not attend his son's funeral two days later, how could he have traveled to Roulette and back on August 5? If he had managed the trip on the 5th with a bad back, why not return the 6th as well? Better yet, why not stay overnight with the Lymans as he had on August 2 and many other occasions? Guilt and embarrassment most likely kept John Crapsey from Angelo's funeral, not a bad back. How could Crazy Crapsey return to the town he had so antagonized twelve years before and admit he had been unable to save his own son?[8]

A comparison of his 1888 autobiography to his pension records further reveals him a charlatan. In his first correspondence regarding a military pension in 1865, he gave an accurate, verifiable history of Angelo's service. In the same letter he also declared, "I am a poor man and have not a foot of land in this world," neatly omitting the fact that he had no land because he had just sold his farm in preparation for leaving Pennsylvania. Then, he claims in his autobiography that he used faith healing to cure Angelo of the near-fatal fever he contracted in 1852. His pension records tell a different story. "Angelo . . . had typhoid fever when he was about 9 years old," John told a pension examiner. "A Dr. Ellis at Allegany, New York attended him. He got entirely well."[9]

His autobiography asserts he also had faith-healed Angelo at Carver Hospital. As previously noted, John alleged that Angelo had requested him to use his faith-healing skills there, and that is plausible. But John then insists he performed his incantations so well that "the boy sprang out of bed and cried out, 'Why, Father! I am going to get well!'" John then supposedly took his son home completely

---

7. Pension of Angelo M. Crapsey, deposition of John Crapsey, Jan. 29, 1887.
8. Ibid.; Diaries of Laroy Lyman.
9. Pension of Angelo M. Crapsey, John Crapsey to E. B. French, Sept. 11, 1865, and deposition of John Crapsey, Jan. 29, 1887.

cured. Alas, Angelo had to return to the army to fight at Gettysburg and there suffered a fatal downfall only because John could not be present to heal his son one more time.[10]

All that is nonsense. It is a matter of record that Angelo entered Carver Hospital *after* Gettysburg and recorded in both Angelo's diary and John Crapsey's pension depositions that John had been in the hospitals in both Washington and Philadelphia with his son. John's motives are easy to deduce. By the time of his autobiography, it was not Roulette the faith-healing preacher had to fool but the entire Midwest. How could his public believe in his spiritual power of healing if he had failed to cure his son? John asserted Angelo's death occurred only because he had the bad luck of not being in the right place at the right time. He never explained why he had not cured Angelo in the ten months after his discharge and before his suicide. Senility did not cause John's lies. About the same time his autobiography came out, he was relating a different, verifiable story to pension examiners.[11]

After rejection by the pension office, John demonstrated he could contradict himself within one reporting venue, too. In 1887, he testified (probably truthfully) that Angelo had provided the family with little financial support after he went to work for Laroy. At most, he said, Angelo occasionally sent home supplies, which most likely came from Laroy. John claimed that Angelo never sent home money and, after he had moved to Cuba, no supplies whatever. John could only recall him sending home eight dollars and a pair of boots while in the army. When the pension examiner asked him if he were certain that Angelo had offered no support prior to the war, John replied, "No sir, he did not contribute to my support except what I have told you."

Fifteen months and a rejected pension application later, John insisted that Angelo virtually had been his *sole* support and that the pension examiner was guilty of misrepresentation. Suddenly, John recalled that Angelo had paid the family's taxes, supplied feed for the farm animals, and while in the army sent home fifteen dollars worth of lithographic pictures for John to sell and keep the proceeds. John accused the examiner of being "harsh, upbraiding, [and] overbearing" for refusing to allow his attorney to be present. John claimed to be stunned that the examiner "would understand me to say that I supported myself without the aid of my son Angelo."[12]

---

10. Miller, *Modern Pentecost*, 44.
11. Pension of Angelo M. Crapsey, deposition of John Crapsey, Jan. 29, 1887.
12. Ibid., Jan. 29, 1887, and Dec. 22, 1889.

John's previous capacity for physical labor also changed during those fifteen months. In 1887, he stated that at the time of Angelo's enlistment, "I was working on my farm of 7 or 8 acres" and "also went out with Laroy Lyman digging coal," which Laroy's diary at least once verifies. But in 1888, John's story became, "I was considered physically a weakly man . . . [and] I never worked in a coal bed."[13]

Lies followed John Crapsey even unto death. The headline for his 1903 obituary reads, "BORN MORE THAN A CENTURY AGO," and lists his birth date as December 28, 1799, exactly seventeen years too early. How like John Crapsey to reach even from the grave to create a sensational headline.[14]

◦✁◦

After the war, Laroy Lyman continued to expand his business enterprises and never stopped spending money almost as fast as he earned it. As age crept upon him, hunting slipped from profession to pastime. In the end, the animal kingdom got its revenge. A bull gored Laroy on December 31, 1885, and sent him down a long and painful road of recuperation. The following June, he was leading another bull into the barn when, perhaps, memories of the previous attack caused him to emit signals of fear. Without warning, the bull drove a horn into Laroy's thigh and snapped its head upward. The big man flew over the animal like a rag doll and thumped to the ground. He watched helplessly as the bull lowered its head and charged, driving its horns into Laroy's abdomen. Bystanders rushed to help, but it was too late. Laroy "came out more dead than alive."[15]

He lay near death for days before regaining his senses. Even then, he could "just crawl around" and was experiencing severe abdominal pain. He recovered somewhat, but medical science of the day could do little with injuries to vital soft tissues and the infections that often followed. His body began to fail. Knowing the end was near, he had his bed moved before the wall-sized fireplace where Angelo's body had lain at rest twenty-two years earlier.[16]

---

13. Ibid., Jan. 29, 1887, and Apr. 7, 1888.

14. *St. Paul Pioneer Press*, Sept. 19, 1903. For the headline to have been accurate, John had to have lied to every census taker and in his autobiography. Lura Crapsey preceded her husband in death, date unknown.

15. Laroy Lyman to "friend Kepler" of Lancaster, Pennsylvania, June 30, 1886, KLC.

16. Laroy Lyman to "friend Kepler," Aug. 12, 1886, KLC; Diaries of Laroy Lyman; *Potter County Journal*, Oct. 14, 1886. The Lyman family still has the killer bull's horns.

On October 8, 1886, Laroy Lyman, "The Great Nimrod" as one obituary dubbed him, passed into memory. He may have had enemies in life, but Coudersport had to commission a special train to carry his mourners to the funeral. He left behind a reputation so large that newspapers as far away as Harrisburg printed his obituary. Unfortunately, he also bequeathed debts that forced his family to liquidate many of their holdings. Thankful Lyman survived her husband by only a few years, but their son, Milo, continued a Roulette family tradition that remains to this day.[17]

Charles Robbins survived the war but had to spend seven months in hospitals recovering from his Gettysburg wounds. The original Bucktail Regiment ended its existence on May 31, 1864. Those with unfulfilled enlistments finished their service with the new 190th Pennsylvania Infantry. Charlie's early bout with measles had forced him to muster late, so he was among those transferring to the 190th. Although physically incapable of performing strenuous duty, he continued in service until completing his term August 12, 1864.[18]

On October 24, 1864, Rev. John Crapsey officiated at Charlie's marriage to Angelo's stepsister, Viola Girtrude Peck. Charlie and "Vi" Robbins moved to Hesperia, Michigan, and claimed to be the town's first residents. In 1872, they moved on to Minnesota to live with John and Lura Crapsey. Charlie showed that the Civil War had not blunted his fighting spirit when he joined a militia unit to fight Indians. He even dabbled in politics as a Republican. Eventually, the couple returned to Hesperia to live out their lives.[19]

If Charlie had bad memories of his army days, he did not display them later in life. At a family picnic held in a public park, the elderly veteran arrived dressed in a uniform bedecked with medals that no Civil War general had bestowed upon him. Climbing shakily onto a picnic table, he stood erect and shouted a demand for silence. The old soldiers wanted to hold a meeting, he announced, and they by God wanted respectful quiet for that to happen. The crowd gracefully complied. Charlie proudly carried the Union flag in every parade in

---

17. A. G. Kepler of Lancaster, Pennsylvania, to Thankful Lyman, Dec. 5, 1886, KLC; *Potter County Journal,* June 25 and Oct. 14, 1886. "The Great Nimrod" (hunter) was a description often used to describe Laroy.

18. CMSR of Charles H. Robbins, Co. I, 42nd Pa. Inf.

19. Pension of Charles H. Robbins; *Windom Reporter,* Oct. 1875.

which his Grand Army of the Republic post participated. By his eighty-seventh year, he had to admit Old Glory was getting a little too heavy to handle and passed that torch to a younger man. He died in Hesperia on January 20, 1934.[20]

❧

In 1873, Congress allotted funds to purchase headstones for honorably discharged deceased soldiers buried in public cemeteries and six years later extended funding to include private burial sites. With that, Laroy Lyman acted on John Crapsey's behalf to procure a headstone for Angelo. The D. W. Whitney Company installed the same style monument that ultimately adorned the graves of 166,000 other Union soldiers. The graves of Laroy and Thankful Lyman lie forty-five yards from Angelo's. As might be expected in a cemetery named Lyman, their monument is the tallest. Laroy would not have had it any other way.[21]

Four years after Angelo's death, Laroy was assisting John Crapsey in the retrieval of a federal bounty payment and received correspondence from someone who had known Angelo well during the war. The brief letter sums up the Angelo Crapsey we should all remember.

Jan 22, 1869

Laroy Lyman Esq
Dear sir

In returning the certificate signed as you request I would have you present my sincere respects to Angelo Crapsey's father. I loved no one of my men more than I did Angelo. He came up to my ideal of the youthful patriot, the heroic American soldier.

Thomas L. Kane[22]

---

20. Ibid.; Jean Frances Follett and Family Papers; Robbins interview. The nickname "Vi" comes from memorandum found in the Follett papers. In August 1998, Charles Robbins's descendant, Robert Robbins, an eyewitness to the picnic event, told the author that story in a phone conversation. Charlie belonged to John A. Dix Post Number Nine in Hesperia, Michigan.

21. Quartermaster General's Office, RG-92, Card Records of Headstone Contracts and U.S. Soldiers. The statement of relative heights of tombstones in the John Lyman Cemetery is as of mid-2004.

22. Thomas L. Kane to Laroy Lyman, KLC. This is a copy made by John Crapsey. The original was not found.

28. "These be three silent things: The Falling snow . . . the hour before dawn . . . the mouth of one just dead." Adelaide Crapsey.[23] Photo courtesy of Dan's Creative Portraiture, Coudersport, Pennsylvania.

---

23. Adelaide Crapsey, *Triad* (ellipses in original). Since their families both came from New York, it is possible that Adelaide and Angelo were distant cousins.

A Psychiatric Meditation:
Thoughts on Angelo Crapsey

Dr. Thomas P. Lowry, MD

P<small>SYCHOHISTORY, THE ART OF ANALYZING THE THOUGHT OF MEN AND</small> women long dead, is a dubious field, fraught with the possibility of error and, of necessity, shot through with speculation and theorizing. Yet, to have no opinion on important matters in the past would be an abdication of the brains with which we are blessed, a descent into mental laziness and cerebral sloth. The life of Angelo Crapsey has every shade of the existential spectrum from triumph to tragedy, and we can honor his memory by examining it seriously.

Every writer has a point of view. Mine is shaped by some or all of the following. I was raised in a California suburb, in an intact family. My father left for the war when I was ten and returned when I was twelve; he returned intact. Religion? A rarely invoked Episcopalianism. My own work paid for half of seven years of college. I graduated from medical school in 1957 and was board-certified in psychiatry in 1964. My training included two years of personal psychoanalysis, along with the usual general psychiatric training. In the forty years before my retirement, my work included a suburban private practice, three years on the staff at San Quentin Prison, two years in the U.S. Air Force medical corps, and directorship of a large state mental hospital. Now I write history books.

Our subject is the suffering of Angelo Crapsey. To my surprise, I found many connections between his life and my own.

We are all shaped on the anvil of heredity by the hammer of environment. We know little of Angelo's heredity other than that of his father, the Reverend John Crapsey Jr., a self-ordained preacher who could make a church shake and a congregation be swallowed up in fire and celestial music. His preaching was considered so disruptive that he was literally torn from the pulpit. With his preaching prohibited, he retreated into lifelong indolence, doing nothing to support his family.

During his glory days, the Reverend Crapsey had encounters with death. Typhoid struck his wife, his stepdaughter, and his son, Angelo. The preacher laid his hands on all three and invoked a divine healing. Although only Angelo survived, his father perceived this 33 percent cure rate as a sign that God had called him to be a healer, a conclusion suggesting major self-deception.

Bipolar disorder (once called manic depressive psychosis) is a disturbance in mood—irrational excitements, incapacitating depressions, or both. Although the genetics are unclear, there is a strong hereditary component. In the "up" phase, religious mania, grandiose ideas, and a conviction of superior power are common. In the depressed phase, energy, ambition, and self-confidence evaporate. This could well be the story of the Reverend Crapsey.

And yet—could religious frenzy be normal? The northeast United States in the early 1800s was a hotbed of new and schismatic religions. William Miller founded the Seventh Day Adventists. The revelations of Joseph Smith brought forth the Mormons. Alexander Campbell created the Disciples of Christ. My own great-grandfather was a Campbellite and paid his way through Bethany College by working as a printer for the *Millenial Harbinger*.[1]

Were the religious passions of the Reverend John Crapsey Jr. the chemical imbalances of bipolar disorder or a descent of the Holy Spirit? Hard questions.

A true-life parable may suggest an answer. In 1967, I was consulted by a woman whose husband had quit his job in order to stay home and receive dictation from Joan of Arc. His own mother had been hospitalized for decades with bipolar disorder. After a few weeks on lithium, my patient lost touch with Joan and returned to work.

So much for what can be known of the biological heritage and religious environment of Angelo Crapsey. Having entered this world, he was now worked upon by the pitiless hammer of events. Nearly from birth, his father preached visions of angels and hellfire to the young

---

1. The *Millennial Harbinger* was the official periodical of the Disciples of Christ, first published Jan. 4, 1830. Alexander Campbell was editor for many years and founder of Bethany College in what is now West Virginia. See National Historic Landmarks Program, National Park Service, Campbell Mansion, http://tps.cr.nps.gov/nhl/detail.cfm?ResourceId=989&ResourceType=District. See also Stephen D. Lane, Alexander Campbell, and Church Cooperation at http://www.truthmagazine.com/archives/volume2/TM002099.html

boy. When he was ten, his mother and half sister died, and his father left home to take his "gift of healing" on the road. When Angelo was twelve, his father was violently defrocked and, either through profound and sullen disillusionment or a deep depression, left the entire burden of the family on twelve-year-old Angelo.

Angelo came under the wing of Laroy Lyman, a famous hunter, crack shot with a rifle, and ardent pacifist. War broke out and nineteen-year-old Angelo enlisted, over the protestations of his antiwar mentor. Now Angelo was without a mother, without a functioning father, and in conflict with his hero, role model, and mentor.

Angelo's self-confidence as a rifleman and his devotion to the Union cause sustained him. However, he was soon surrounded by death in all its awful forms. The sights of battlefield mutilation were compounded by homesickness and diarrhea. By the battle of Cedar Mountain in August 1862, his nerves and optimism were wearing thin, and his rage at those back home who failed to enlist ate at him something fierce.

There was worse to come. At Antietam, the fighting was dreadful and his assigned work on a burial detail was, perhaps, even worse. Then came Fredericksburg. In this Union disaster, there was one bright shining moment. On the Union's far left, a hole opened in the Confederate lines and boys in blue rushed in. But the Union commanders failed to reinforce success and the spearhead soldiers were killed or ran for their lives. My great-great-uncle, Michael Lowry, 10th Pennsylvania Reserves, was there; his body was never found.

Angelo was there, too, but he surrendered. After staying three weeks in louse-infected Libby Prison, he was released and sent to Maryland's Camp Parole, where he languished, becoming increasingly strange. Back in his regiment, he seemed distant and preoccupied with imaginary insects. A few weeks later, the Angel of Death flew past his shoulder at Gettysburg's Little Round Top, but still Angelo lived. A few days later, fever and diarrhea so weakened him that he could not walk. At Washington, D.C.'s Carver Hospital, he was described as wasted and shriveled. Soon Angelo could no longer recognize even his own father. A discharge from the army and return to home did no good. The madness and anguish worsened. The only cure was the fatal musket shot.

Was this post-traumatic stress disorder? A good friend of mine was a tough-as-nails old soldier, his chest a wallpaper of medals. Bob was unable to speak of his nights in Korea, more than fifty years ago. His eyes would fill with tears, but no words would come. He could only shake his head. Is post-traumatic stress disorder real? The answer is "yes."

And Angelo Crapsey? What a vale of tears. His father a burned-out hellfire preacher and probable exhausted manic depressive, his mother dead, his army comrades mangled or rotting in distant fields. The unspeakable horrors of combat, the crushing debility of chronic diarrhea and malnutrition, and the shame of surrender all bore down on him. These terrible burdens may have rested upon the constitutional vulnerability inherited from his father.

In his twenty-two years, Angelo had lived centuries too long. Every factor in his life, even before his birth, played a role in the final wreck. Heredity or environment? The answer is, "Yes."

Selected Bibliography

Primary Sources

Adjutant General's Office of the State of New York. *Annual Report for the Year 1899, Registers 20th—25th Regiments of the Infantry*. Albany, N.Y.: James B. Lyon State Printer, 1900.

Alexander, Edwin Porter. *Fighting for the Confederacy*, edited by Gary Gallagher. Chapel Hill: University of North Carolina Press, 1989.

Bass, Major M. J. Vertical file 7-GA59. Library of the Gettysburg National Military Park, Gettysburg, Pa.

Battle of Fredericksburg [maps 1–5]. Historical research by Frank A. O'Reilly. Illustrated by John Dove. Produced by Steve Stanley. Fredericksburg, Va.: Fredericksburg National Military Park, 2001.

Bell, Frank J. Recollections. Library of the Gettysburg National Military Park, Gettysburg, Pa.

Blackford, William Willis. *War Years with Jeb Stuart*. Baton Rouge: Louisiana State University Press, 1993.

Brake, Robert L. Collection. U.S. Army Military History Institute, Carlisle, Pa.

Burlingame, Herman L. Manuscript collection. McKean County Historical Society, Smethport, Pa.

Certificate of Property Assessments. McKean County Commissioner's Clerk. John R. Shoemaker, Smethport, Pa.

Coffin, Charles Carleton. *The Boys of '61: Four Years of Fighting*. Boston: Estes and Lauriat, 1883.

Confederate Veteran. Nashville, Tenn.: Trustees of the Confederate Veteran.

Crawford, Samuel. Letters. Library of the Gettysburg National Military Park, Gettysburg, Pa.

Fluker, William Thomas, Jr. "A Graphic Account of the Battle of Little Round Top Hill at Gettysburg." Produced by Terri Lee Fluker. Vertical file 7-GA15, Library of the Gettysburg National Military Park, Gettysburg, Pa.

Follet, Jean Frances, and Family Papers, 1862–1989. Minnesota Historical Society, St. Paul, Minn.

Frassanito, William A. *Antietam: The Photographic Legacy of America's Bloodiest Day*. New York: Charles Scribner's Sons, 1978.

Gopsill's Harrisburg Directory, 1861–1881. Pennsylvania State Library, Harrisburg, Pa.

Graves, Kenneth. Private collection courtesy of Kenneth Graves.

Haley, John W. *The Rebel Yell and the Yankee Hurrah: The Civil War Journal of a Maine Volunteer.* Edited by Ruth L. Silliker. Camden, Maine: Down East Books, 1985.

Heiman, Michael. Recollections. *York Gazette,* July 9, 1891.

Hillyer, George. "Battle of Gettysburg." Vertical file 7-GA9. Library of the Gettysburg National Military Park.

Hobson, Charles F., and Arnold Shankman, eds. "Colonel of the Bucktails: Civil War Letters of Charles Frederick Taylor." *Pennsylvania Magazine of History and Biography,* vol. 97. Philadelphia: The Historical Society of Pennsylvania, 1973.

Journals of the Annual Meetings of the Franckean Evangelic Lutheran Synod, 1839 through 1852 (various publishers).

Kautz, August V. *The 1865 Customs of Service for Non-Commissioned Officers and Soldiers.* 2nd ed. Philadelphia: Lippincott, 1865; Mechanicsburg, Pa.: Stackpole Books, 2001.

Krista Lyman Collection. Letters of Angelo Crapsey; Diaries, Letters, and Personal Papers and Artifacts of Laroy and Thankful Lyman. Private collection courtesy of Krista Lyman. Roulette, Pa.

Lee, Robert E. *Wartime Papers of Robert E. Lee.* Edited by Clifford Dowdey and Louis H. Manarin. Boston: Little Brown, 1961, Da Capo paperback reprint.

Means, William W. *Corporal Brewer: A Bucktail Survivor.* Edmonton: Commonwealth Publications, 1996 (only the Wallace Brewer letters are used as a source).

Miller, A. P. *A Modern Pentecost: An Account of the Marvelous Ministry and Mediumship of the Rev. John Crapsey.* Worthingon, Minn.: Advance Book and Job Printing House, 1888.

Minutes of Anti-Draft Meeting November 29, 1864. Potter County Historical Society, Coudersport, Pa.

Moore, Wallace Mordecai. Recollections. Submitted by Rev. Richard Moore. Manuscript copy courtesy of Donald C. Pfanz, Fredericksburg National Military Park, Fredericksburg, Va.

Personal Sketches. Grand Army of the Republic Memorial Book. McKean Post No. 347, McKean County Historical Society, Smethport, Pa.

Presely, William. Letters. Harrisburg Civil War Round Table Collection, U.S. Army Military History Institute, Carlisle, Pa.

Proceedings of a Convention of Ministers and Delegates from Evangelical Lutheran Churches in the State of New York. West Sandlake, N.Y.: Herald Office, 1844.

Robbins, Charles H. Interview from an unknown Michigan newspaper published ca. 1930. Courtesy of the Robbins family.

Southern Historical Society Papers, vol. 32. Edited by R. A. Brock. Richmond, Va.: Southern Historical Society, 1904; Carmel, Ind.: Guild Press, CD-ROM, 1998.

U.S. Bureau of the Census. United States Census, 1850–1860. Washington, D.C.

U.S. Congress. *Joint Committee on the Conduct of the War.* Washington, D.C.: Government Printing Office, 1863.

U.S. Government. *Population of the United States Compiled from the Original Returns of the Eighth Census.* Washington, D.C.: Government Printing Office, 1864.

U.S. House of Representatives, Thirty-seventh Congress, 2nd session, 1861–1862, *The Executive Documents.* Washington, D.C.: U.S. Government Printing Office, 1862.

U.S. War Department. *War of the Rebellion: A Compilation of the Official Records of the Union and Confederate Armies.* Compiled by Lt. Col. Robert N. Scott. Washington, D.C.: Government Printing Office, 1880; Zionsville: Guild Press of Indiana, CD-ROM v.1.60, 2000.

RECORDS IN THE NATIONAL ARCHIVES

Department of the Interior. RG-15, Pension Application Files, Civil War and Later.

Preliminary Inventory of the Records of United States Army Continental Commands, 1821–1920. RG-393, Part 2, Entry 5804, Army of Virginia, Letters and Telegrams Sent, Endorsements, and Special Orders, 1862.

Quartermaster General's Office. Card Records of Headstones. Provided for Deceased Civil War Veterans, ca. 1879–1903. RG-92, M1845.

Records of the Adjutant General's Office. RG-94. Indexes of Philadelphia Hospitals, Entry 544.

———. RG-94. Carded Medical Records Volunteers, Mexican, and Civil Wars, 1846-1865, Entry 534.

———. RG-94. Civil War Muster Rolls and Papers, Thirteenth Infantry Pennsylvania Reserves, Box 4248.

———. RG-94. Muster Rolls of the First Pennsylvania Rifles.

———. RG-94. Compiled Military Service Records.

U.S. Army. RG-249, Record of Paroled Prisoners of War Received at Camp Parole, 1862 and 1863.

RECORDS IN THE PENNSYLVANIA STATE ARCHIVES

Beary, F. D. "Battle Flag History." Forty-second Regiment ("Bucktails"), P.V. Order Book of Company K, 1863-64. MG-234.

Curtin, Andrew G. RG-26. Message to the Pennsylvania Senate and House, January 12, 1863.

Executive Correspondence, January 1, 1860–February 27, 1862. RG-26. Department of State, Secretary of the Commonwealth.

McNeil, Hugh, Collection, 1855–1916. MG-87.

Taggart, John, Papers, 1861–1864. MG-124, Diary of Robert Taggert, 1862, reel 4021.

Third Annual Reunion-Regimental Association of the Bucktail or First Rifle Regiment. P.R.V.C, 1890. MG-7, folder 0278.

Newspapers

Adams (Pa.) Sentinel and General Advertiser,
   aka *The Adams Sentinel, Star and Sentinel.*
Cameron (Pa.) Citizen.
Gettysburg (Pa.) Compiler.
Gettysburg (Pa.) Star and Banner.
Grand Army Scout and Soldiers' Mail.
Harrisburg (Pa.) Patriot and Union.
Indiana (Pa.) Messenger.
Lancaster (Pa.) Daily Express.
McKean (Pa.) Miner.

National Tribune.
New York Herald.
Pennsylvania Daily Telegraph.
Philadelphia Weekly Press.
Potter County (Pa.) Journal.
St. Paul (Mn.) Pioneer Press.
Tioga County (Pa.) Agitator.
Windom (Mn.) Reporter
York (Pa.) Gazette.

Secondary Sources

Adams, George Worthington. *Doctors in Blue: The Medical History of the Union Army in the Civil War.* Baton Rouge: Louisiana State University Press, 1996.

Alexander, Franz G., and Sheldon T. Selesnick. *The History of Psychiatry: An Evaluation of Psychiatric Thought and Practice from Prehistoric Times to the Present.* New York: Harper & Row, 1966.

American Psychiatric Association. *Diagnostic and Statistical Manual of Mental Disorders.* 4th ed. Text Revision. Washington, D.C.: American Psychiatric Association, 2000.

Bard, John P. "Pennsylvania in the War: The 'Old Bucktails,' 42d Regt., P.V. at the Battle of Gettysburg," *Philadelphia Weekly Press,* April 1888.

Bates, Samuel Penniman. *History of Pennsylvania Volunteers.* Harrisburg, Pa.: State Printing Office, 1868.

Beebe, Victor L. *History of Potter County Pennsylvania.* Coudersport, Pa.: Potter County Historical Society, 1934.

Bliss, Sylvester. *Memoirs of William Miller: Generally Known as a Lecturer on the Prophecies, and the Second Coming of Christ.* Brooklyn, N.Y.: AMS Press, 1953.

Blustein, Bonnie Ellen. *Preserve Your Love of Science: Life of William A. Hammond, American Neurologist.* Cambridge: Cambridge University Press, 1991.

Bollet, Alfred Jay. *Civil War Medicine: Challenges and Triumphs.* Tucson, Ariz.: Galen Press, 2002.

Brende, Joel Osler, and Erwin Randolph Parson. *Vietnam Veterans: The Road to Recovery.* New York: Plenum Press, 1985.

Burkhardt, George S. *Confederate Rage, Yankee Wrath: No Quarter in the Civil War.* Carbondale: Southern Illinois University Press, 2007.

Catton, Bruce. *Bruce Catton's Civil War: Mr. Lincoln's Army.* New York: Fairfax Press, 1984.

Chandler, David G., and James Lawton Collins, Jr., eds. *D-Day Encyclopedia.* New York: Simon & Schuster, 1978.

Coleman, Penny. *Flashback: Posttraumatic Stress Disorder, Suicide, and the Lessons of War.* Boston: Beacon Press, 2006.

Cornish, Dudley Taylor. *The Sable Arm: Negro Troops in the Union Army, 1861–1865.* New York: W. W. Norton, 1966.

Cross, Whitney R. *The Burned-Over District: The Social and Intellectual History of Enthusiastic Religion in Western New York, 1800–1850.* New York: Harper & Row, 1950.

Davis, William C., ed. *The Image of War: 1861–1865.* 6 vols. New York: Doubleday, 1982.

Dean, Eric T., Jr. *Shook Over Hell: Post-Traumatic Stress, Vietnam, and the Civil War.* Cambridge, Mass.: Harvard University Press, 1997.

Donald, David Herbert. *Charles Sumner and the Coming of the Civil War.* Chicago: University of Chicago Press, 1960.

Dyer, Frederick. *A Compendium of the War of the Rebellion.* Des Moines, Iowa: Dyer, 1908; Carmel, Ind.: Guild Press, CD-ROM v.1.6.

Freemon, Frank R. *Gangrene and Glory: Medical Care During the Civil War.* Urbana: University of Illinois Press, 2001.

Hess, Earl J. *The Union Soldier in Battle: Enduring the Ordeal of Combat.* Lawrence: University Press of Kansas, 1997.

Gallagher, Gary W. "The Autumn of 1862: A Season of Opportunity." In *Antietam: Essays on the 1862 Maryland Campaign,* edited by Gary W. Gallagher. Kent, Ohio: Kent State University Press, 1989.

Garrison, Nancy Scripture. *With Courage and Delicacy: Civil War on the Peninsula; Women and the U.S. Sanitary Commission.* Mason City, Iowa: Savas, 1999.

Glover, Edwin A. *Bucktailed Wildcats.* New York: Thomas Yoseloff, 1960.

Goff, Richard D. *Confederate Supply.* Durham, N.C.: Duke University Press, 1969.

Grimsley, Mark. *The Hard Hand of War: Union Military Policy Toward Southern Civilians, 1861–1865.* New York: Cambridge University Press, 1995.

Hennessy, John J. *Return to Bull Run: The Campaign and Battle of Second Manassas.* New York: Touchstone Books, 1993.

History of Allegany County, N.Y. New York: F. W. Beers, 1879.

History of the Counties of McKean, Elk, Cameron, and Potter, Pennsylvania. Chicago: J. H. Beers, 1890.

Krick, Robert K. *Lee's Colonels.* 4th ed. rev. Dayton, Ohio: Morningside House, 1992.

Kross, Gary, "To Die Like Soldiers: The Retreat From Sickles' Front, July 2, 1863." *Blue and Gray* 15 (special issue).

Lande, R. Gregory. *Madness, Malingering and Malfeasance: The Transformation of Psychiatry and the Law in the Civil War Era.* Washington, D.C.: Brassey's, 2003.

Luvaas, Jay, and Harold W. Nelson. *The U.S. Army War College Guide to the Battles of Chancellorsville and Fredericksburg.* Carlisle: South Mountain Press, 1988.

Lyman, Robert R., Jr. *History of Roulet, Pa. and the Life of Burrel Lyman.* Coudersport, Pa.: Potter County Historical Society, 1967.

Marvel, William. *Burnside.* Chapel Hill: University of North Carolina Press, 1991.

McPherson, James M. *Battle Cry of Freedom: The Civil War Era.* New York: Oxford University Press, 1988.

———. *For Cause and Comrades: Why Men Fought in the Civil War.* New York: Oxford University Press, 1997.

———. "The War that Never Goes Away." In *Drawn by the Sword,* edited by James M. McPherson. New York: Oxford University Press, 1996.

Minard, John. *Civic History and Illustrated Progress of Cuba, NY.* Evansville, Ind.: Windmill Publications, 1991. Publication sponsored by the Cuba Historical Society.

Muckenhoupt, Margaret. *Dorothea Dix: Advocate for Mental Health Care.* Oxford: Oxford University Press, 2003.

Murfin, James V. *The Gleam of Bayonets: The Battle of Antietam and Robert E. Lee's Maryland Campaign, September 1862.* Baton Rouge: Louisiana State University Press, 1965.

Oates, Stephen B. *A Woman of Valor: Clara Barton and the Civil War.* New York: Free Press, 1994.

O'Reilly, Francis Augustín (Frank A.). *The Fredericksburg Campaign: Winter War on the Rappahannock.* Baton Rouge: Louisiana State University Press, 2006.

O'Reilly, Frank A. "Busted Up and Gone to Hell: The Assault of the Pennsylvania Reserves at Fredericksburg." *Civil War Regiments: A Journal of the American Civil War* 4, no. 4 ( ): 1–27.

———. *Stonewall Jackson at Fredericksburg: The Battle of Prospect Hill, December 13, 1862.* Lynchburg, Va.: H. E. Howard, 1993.

Parker, Sandra V. *Richmond Civil War Prisons.* Virginia Civil War Battles and Leaders Series. Lynchburg, Va.: H. E. Howard, 1990.

Pfanz, Harry W. *Gettysburg: Culp's Hill and Cemetery Hill.* Chapel Hill: University of North Carolina Press, 1993.

Priest, John Michael. *Before Antietam: The Battle for South Mountain.* Shippensburg, Pa.: White Mane, 1992.

Rand McNally Atlas. Skokie, Ill.: Rand-McNally, 1999.

Robertson, James I., Jr. *Stonewall Jackson: The Man, The Soldier, The Legend.* New York: Simon & Schuster Macmillan, 1997.

Sears, Stephen W. *George B. McClellan: The Young Napoleon.* New York: Ticknor & Fields, 1988.

———. *Landscape Turned Red: The Battle of Antietam.* New York: Ticknor & Fields, 1983.

Shephard, Ben. *A War of Nerves: Soldiers and Psychiatrists in the Twentieth Century.* Cambridge, Mass.: Harvard University Press, 2001.

Snell, Mark A. *From First to Last: The Life of Major General William B. Franklin.* New York: Fordham University Press, 2002.

Sypher, Justin R. *History of the Pennsylvania Reserve Corps.* Lancaster, Pa.: Elias Barr, 1865.

Taylor, Frank H. *Philadelphia in the Civil War.* Philadelphia: Dunlap Printing, 1913.

Thomas L. Kane Memorial Chapel. Bulletin. Kane, Pa.

Thomson, O[smund] R[hodes] Howard, and William H. Rauch. *History of the "Bucktails," Kane Rifle Regiment of the Pennsylvania Reserve Corps.* Dayton, Ohio: Morningside House, 1988.

Tillman, Barrett, ed. *Brassey's D-Day Encyclopedia: Normandy Invasion A–Z*. Dulles, Va.: Brassey's, 2004.

Warner, Ezra. *Generals in Blue: Lives of the Union Commanders*. Baton Rouge: Louisiana State University Press, 1964.

———. *Generals in Gray: Lives of the Confederate Commanders*. Baton Rouge: Louisiana State University Press, 1959.

Wilbur, C. Keith. *Civil War Medicine, 1861–1865*. Guilford, N.C.: The Globe Pequot Press, 1998.

Wiley, Bell Irvin. *The Life of Billy Yank: The Common Soldier of the Union*. Baton Rouge: Louisiana State University Press, 1952, revised 1971.

———. *The Life of Johnny Reb: The Common Soldier of the Confederacy*. Baton Rouge: Louisiana State University Press, 1943, 1994 printing.

Williams, T[homas] Harry. *Lincoln and the Radicals*. Madison: University of Wisconsin Press, 1941, 3rd printing, 1965.

PHOTOGRAPHS

Alex Chamberlain Collection. U.S. Army Military History Institute, Carlisle, Pa.

Bertha Robbins. Personal collection of Robbins family photos.

Dan's Creative Portraiture. Coudersport, Pa.

Krista Lyman Collection. Courtesy Krista Lyman, Roulette, Pa.

Library of Congress. Washington, D.C.

Mollus Collection. U.S. Army Military History Institute, Carlisle, Pa.

Potter County Historical Society, Coudersport, Pa.

Raymond Handy Collection. Winham, Mn.

Ronn Palm's Museum of Civil War Images, Gettysburg, Pa.

Index

Page nos. in italics refer to illustration pages.